Bilkent University Lecture Series

Bilkent University Lecture Series

Vol. 1: S. Ranka and S. Sahni: Hypercube Algorithms. With Applications to Image Processing and Pattern Recognition.

Vol. 2: I. Sahin: Regenerative Inventory Systems. Operating Characteristics and Optimization.

Vol. 3: C.J. Morrison: A Microeconomic Approach to the Measurement of Economic Performance. Productivity Growth, Capacity Utilization, and Related Performance Indicators.

Catherine J. Morrison

A Microeconomic Approach to the Measurement of Economic Performance

Productivity Growth, Capacity Utilization, and Related Performance Indicators

Springer-Verlag
New York Berlin Heidelberg London Paris
Tokyo Hong Kong Barcelona Budapest

Prof. CATHERINE J. MORRISON

Department of Economics
Tufts University
Medford, MA 02155
USA

With 6 figures.

Library of Congress Cataloging-in-Publication Data
Morrison, Catherine J.
A microeconomic approach to the measurement of economic performance: productivity growth, capacity utilization, and related performance indicators/Catherine J. Morrison.
p. cm. – (Bilkent University lecture series)
Includes bibliographical references.
ISBN-13:978-1-4613-9762-5
1. Efficiency, Industrial – Mathematical models. 2. Industrial productivity – Mathematical models. 3. Industrial capacity – Mathematical models. 4. Economic indicators. 5. Microeconomics.
I. Title. II. Series.
HC79.I52M67 1992
338′.06 – dc20 92-24787

Printed on acid-free paper.

Softcover reprint of the hardcover 1st edition 1993

Production managed by Francine Sikorski; manufacturing supervised by Vincent Scelta.
Camera-ready copy prepared by the author, using LaTeX.

9 8 7 6 5 4 3 2 1

ISBN-13:978-1-4613-9762-5 e-ISBN-13:978-1-4613-9760-1
DOI: 10.1007/978-1-4613-9760-1

To Ernie

Preface

This text is designed to provide a comprehensive guide to students, researchers, or consultants who wish to carry out and to interpret analyses of economic performance, with an emphasis on productivity growth. The text includes an overview of standard productivity growth measurement techniques and adaptations, and data construction procedures. It goes further, however, by expanding the traditional growth accounting (index number) framework to allow consideration of how different aspects of firm behavior underlying productivity growth are interrelated, how they can be measured consistently in a parametric model, and how they permit a well-defined decomposition of standard productivity growth measures. These ideas are developed by considering in detail a number of underlying theoretical results and econometric issues. The impacts of various production characteristics on productivity growth trends are also evaluated by overviewing selected methodological extensions and empirical evidence.

More specifically, in the methodological extensions, emphasis is placed on incorporation of cost and demand characteristics, such as fixity and adjustment costs, returns to scale, and the existence of market power, into analyses of productivity growth. These characteristics, generally disregarded in such analyses, can have very important impacts on production structure and firm behavior, and thus on economic performance. They also provide the conceptual basis for measures that are often used independently as indicators of economic performance, such as investment, capacity utilization, and profit measures. If the traditional restrictive assumptions made about these aspects of the production structure are invalid, imposing them will not only cause biases in productivity growth measures, but will also imply that measurement of the economic impacts of these characteristics is erroneous. To allow a more complete assessment of economic performance, therefore, the interrelationships of these characteristics and, thus, the linkages among the indicators are emphasized.

The text also devotes special attention to the treatment of capital formation, identified by many researchers as an important determinant of economic growth. Dealing effectively with capital requires consideration of constraints arising from short-run fixity of capital—and therefore capacity utilization—and their impacts on productivity growth. Pursuing the empirical implications emerging from the theoretical structure prompts elaboration of

(1) different components of the capital stock that might have disparate effects on production (R & D, capital required to satisfy regulatory constraints, and inventories);
(2) difficulties involved in capital data construction; and
(3) exogenous changes that might affect the "effectiveness" of a given capital stock (obsolescence from changes in energy prices or vintage structure).

The chapters are organized (1) to introduce the overall ideas involved in measurement of economic performance (Chapter 1); (2) to motivate the theoretical and conceptual structure underlying standard productivity growth and capacity utilization indexes (Chapters 2 and 3); (3) to indicate the relationships among and some potential extensions of these types of measures (Chapter 4); (4) to develop in more detail the underlying theoretical structure, the data construction procedures, and the econometric issues required for empirical implementation (Chapters 5 to 7); (5) to provide selected empirical evidence and to pursue interpretation issues (Chapter 8); (6) to discuss several important recent refinements of productivity growth analysis (Chapter 9); and, finally, (7) to tie up some loose ends, indicate omissions, and mention a number of current research areas (Chapter 10).

The treatment in this text is not meant to provide an exhaustive overview of contributions to the productivity literature and of methodologies underlying productivity and economic performance measurement. Instead, it is designed to feature the usefulness of a production-theoretical approach to the measurement of productivity and economic performance. Therefore, the text provides a foundation to facilitate understanding of the literature in this area, to generate and interpret empirical measures of productivity growth, and to carry out econometric estimation to identify and quantify important characteristics of production processes.

My understanding of and belief in the contributions possible from this type of analysis have to a large extent resulted from my associations with Professor W.E. Diewert of the University of British Columbia and Professor E.R. Berndt of the Massachusetts Institute of Technology. My interest in the areas of applied production theory and productivity analysis evolved from research started as a student of Erwin Diewert's and continued with both him and Ernie Berndt through joint work in this area. This work motivated me to attempt to provide an integrated foundation and synthesis of the extensive and important research in this area, since they did not seem readily available. I wish to acknowledge my great intellectual debt to both of these outstanding economists, researchers, people, and friends.

Catherine J. Morrison
Tufts University

Contents

Chapter 1

Introduction

The economic performance and efficiency of firms is a major concern of many individuals, including policy makers, consumers, economists, and managers of the firms themselves. Policy makers attempt to determine how economic growth, full employment and other indicators of economic performance can be enhanced, or at least not harmed, by policies that affect firm behavior. Consumers believe firms that produce more efficiently tend to produce at lower prices and higher production levels. Economists are interested in what causes fluctuations in production, costs, and associated economic performance measures, and how decisions of firms are linked to realizations of these indicators. Firms' desires to provide quality product at the lowest cost in order to maximize revenues for any given cost structure are facilitated by efficient production. All of these economic agents, therefore, need interpretable measures of economic performance and efficiency to use to motivate their analyses and actions.

This chapter introduces the concepts underlying some of the most often-used measures of economic performance, especially productivity growth and capacity utilization measures. The first section (Section 1.1) provides an overview of the notion of productivity growth. The efficiency connotations of capacity utilization are also outlined, with a view toward linking these performance characteristics. Several issues about the construction of appropriate measures to represent these aspects of economic efficiency and their interactions are then explored. The dependence of these performance indicators on firm behavior is noted, and this motivates the initial development of these ideas in terms of basic production theory in Section 1.2. In this section more formal definitions of productivity growth and capacity utilization are presented, and the theoretical relationship between these concepts, and other production components, is established. Section 1.3 then presents the essentials of standard approaches to measurement of productivity and capacity utilization, building on the concepts and definitions from Section 1.2. The framework sketched in these introductory sections begins to provide a basis for evaluating and measuring linkages among economic performance indicators representing different aspects of the production structure. Finally, in Section 1.4, these linkages are motivated in an alternative but related context, in terms of the literature on business cycle indicators.

The following chapters pursue the issues and ideas raised in this introductory chapter in more detail, by exploring different approaches to measurement of these interrelated performance measures, and by elaborating the theoretical background underlying methodological and empirical extensions of such approaches. This allows detailed consideration of issues about measurement and interpretation of performance indicators encountered by those who construct and use such measures.

1.1 Concepts Underlying Productivity Growth and Capacity Utilization Measures

Some of the most common measures used to determine the status of economic performance are productivity growth and capacity utilization indexes. These measures reflect other information that might also provide the basis for economic performance indicators, such as growth in GNP (gross national product or output) and investment. However, they embody more information than this; both measures may be thought of as indicators of how efficiently production is accomplished.

Ideally, if more output is possible from a given amount of inputs, or, equivalently, production of a given output level is accomplished at a lower cost, productivity growth measures will reflect this augmentation of efficiency. This is generally interpreted as an improvement in welfare. If fewer usable capital and labor inputs are left idle, capacity utilization indexes will capture this enhanced input effectiveness. If either of these measures declines, economic performance may be thought to have worsened, and thus welfare has deteriorated, in the sense that less product is possible given resource constraints.

Indexes of productivity growth and capacity utilization, published by various private and public agencies for selected industries, have therefore become important indicators of fluctuations in the economic "health" of a nation, industry or firm. They are often used as "red flags" for various purposes; stock market and other industrial measures of valuation of the economy tend to be sensitive to whether these cyclical indicators predict upturns or downturns, and policy is often based on analysis of their movements. In addition, these indicators are regularly used in economic analyses to help explain movements in costs, investment, employment and prices.

Again, the ultimate focus is on determining overall welfare, and in some cases on isolating the effects on different components of the economy. Unfortunately, however, defining indicators that appropriately measure these aspects of efficiency or performance is not as straightforward as it might initially seem. Welfare is a combination of a number of elements, only some of which are incorporated in measures used to evaluate economic performance. The underlying question is how a useful measure may therefore be developed and interpreted; care must be taken to recognize the diverse changes embodied in such measures.

Productivity growth measures summarize a number of these changes in the economic climate since they depend on all movements in output and input quantities and prices, which are crucial pieces of the economic performance puzzle. Examination of these different pieces helps to determine how appropriate measurement, interpretation and application of the indicators might proceed.

Assessing the contribution of GNP (output) increases, for example, first requires isolating the physical increase in output from the inflation that is included in the value measure. The resulting "constant dollar" (or other monetary unit) measure of the economy's production may be thought of as an indicator of "growth" and therefore "welfare" in the economy. However, some of an observed change in GNP likely results from variations in scarce labor used for production. Therefore, the only part of output growth affecting overall welfare will be that arising from factors other than expansion in labor use. Removing this impact requires measuring the effects of the change in effective labor input, which requires identifying any wage or quality changes that might have occurred separately from the pure quantity change.

When this has been accomplished, an indicator of enhanced output stemming from more "efficient" or "productive" labor – usually presented as a change in output per hour – is found. This labor productivity measure appears more appropriately to measure an increase in welfare from growth than does a measure of pure GNP increases. However, other questions remain, such as, how much of this might be due to an increase in capital per worker? This capital deepening captures the role in the perceived boost in labor efficiency due purely to input substitution. An increase in the capital-labor ratio represents a shift in production processes but not necessarily improved performance, although it is a determinant of the labor productivity measure. Since capital is scarce, increasing labor productivity arising from an expanded capital stock has a very different implication for overall welfare than if the increase had occurred without incurring additional capital costs.

This suggests further ambiguities for measurement and interpretation of welfare. Once capital is included in the analysis one must recognize that the "effective" contribution of this input may change due to, say, capacity utilization changes, the imposition of regulatory constraints or obsolescence. These must also be identified in order to refine assessments of economic performance, yet this is tricky to accomplish.

Considering this sequence of difficulties a productivity analyst must face – which is indicative but clearly not a complete list – highlights the types of serious questions often ignored when constructing and using economic performance measures. Although various types of performance and productivity measures might be valid for different purposes, to facilitate interpretation and application of the numbers the measures must be defined carefully and the issues well understood.

One important matter this overview raises is that of capacity utilization, since this is a crucial determinant of the "effectiveness" of capital (and possibly other input stocks firms hold). Dealing with this issue is not simple; the concept of capacity utilization must first be clarified and then its impact on other economic performance indicators must be delineated. In particular, inherent interpretation problems with the concept of capacity utilization arise because the idea of "capacity" itself is not easily defined. For example, the output possible from working a machine at its maximum rate (such as 24 hours per day) might be considered capacity output – full capacity utilization exists at this output level – if "capacity" denotes "maximum". However this range of capital use has no economic significance if it requires paying prohibitive labor or maintenance costs.

One would think a more useful economic definition of full capacity utilization might be when the firm is producing the most "economical" level of output (the steady state level) given the current level of the capital stock. In this case the firm would not choose to move from the current level of output production given its available capital, because costs would increase too substantially. Underutilization (overutilization) would occur if the capital level were too high (low) to attain the lowest possible costs of producing the currently demanded output, given input supply patterns faced by the firm. Thus, capital availability must be constrained in the short run for utilization to be an issue, or the firm would simply sell (buy) it and reach the minimum cost point. Utilization therefore has a close connection to input fixity, and therefore costs of production and productivity.

In addition, utilization of labor and other stocks available to the firm might be of interest to incorporate in a definition of capacity, as contrasted to capital, utilization. In this case utilization becomes a multi-dimensional problem. For example, if salaried employees are sitting semi-idle at their desks, it may be feasible to induce additional production without an additional outlay in terms of wage bill, implying that labor inputs may currently be underutilized. This requires some fixity of labor due to, say, hiring, firing and training costs, which is often summarized in the general expression "labor hoarding". Again, this implies some association of utilization with costs and thus productivity.

The linkage between productivity growth and capacity utilization may be one of the most important facets of the interpretation complexities involved in productivity analysis, since it critically affects representation of the notions of performance and efficiency. If more production occurs because of greater use (utilization) of already existing capital, this may reflect some aspect of increased efficiency, but it does not have the same technical change connotations one mighnt think of as representing "increased efficiency of production" or productivity. Although these two types of efficiency determinants have very different implications, both of these impacts are captured in observed economic data. Therefore they should be untangled theoretically and empirically to determine exactly what is happening to economic performance.

The interactions between capacity utilization and productivity growth were highlighted in the Bureau of Labor Statistics (BLS) publication *Trends in Multifactor Productivity, 1948-81*, where it was stated that:

> "Short-term fluctuations in aggregate demand result in cyclical changes in the utilization of capital and labor, and these too are reflected in the BLS measures of multifactor productivity. ... To the extent that labor is a quasi-fixed factor and there is labor hoarding, firms tend to underutilize (overutilize) the work force during periods of recession (expansion), and this is reflected in the BLS measures of multifactor productivity. ... In the case of capital, firms mainly adjust their inputs to meet changes in their short-run production needs by changing the utilization of existing stocks. The magnitude of the adjustments for the

utilization of capital inputs is therefore likely to be larger than that for labor." (pp.27-28)

Although this quotation emphasizes that standard productivity growth measures reflect some combination of returns to these two different characteristics of the production process, BLS then proceeds to say that a justifiable method for isolating the independent impacts of utilization and productivity may not exist. BLS attempts a first approximation to this decomposition by calculating growth rates between cyclical peaks, implying that the remaining fluctuations arise from changes in utilization. This approach, although quite common in the past, is *ad hoc*, since it is not at all clear whether these different peaks are comparable, or even whether the capacity utilization definition underlying their measurement has any economic basis. It therefore does not effectively capture the concept of utilization presented above.

Recognition of the important relationship between productivity growth and capacity utilization has also prompted other *ad hoc* methods of decomposition. For example, these measures are sometimes used as "explanations" for each other. This is based on the idea that an observed output change may be a combination of growth in output production from investing in capital to move closer to an optimal utilization level, and an output increase supported by a change in technology itself. Some of the observed output change attributed to productivity is therefore "explained" by utilization fluctuations. Identifying the independent impact of capacity utilization on productivity growth trends is thus often carried out just by appending a measure of capacity utilization to regressions of productivity growth on its possible determinants. However, there are negligible, if any, theoretical "underpinnings" to support such a simplistic procedure.

It is clearly more desirable to attempt to formalize the relationship between productivity growth and capacity utilization within a justifiable theoretical structure, based on the conceptual development outlined above. This is possible by considering theoretically exactly what the definitions of productivity growth, technical change and capacity utilization imply for measurement, interpretation and implementation. Since the implied theoretical structure is, however, somewhat complex, empirically isolating these different aspects of the production structure is difficult. Measurement and application of these concepts requires construction of an empirically implementable econometric model. Data manipulation and *ad hoc* methods are simply insufficient for such a purpose because too much must be untangled from the data.

More specifically, productivity growth measures are designed to reflect enhanced possibilities for output production from a given input vector as technology progresses over time. This concept can be defined in terms of the firms' potential increased output, holding the input levels fixed, or the diminution of input costs possible, holding output fixed. Theoretically, these ideas are represented by a shift inward of the isoquant map representing the production function facing firms, or a downward shift in the unit cost function. These shifts reflect a pure technical change or true productivity effect.

Capacity utilization refers to the amount of output produced compared to some optimum potential given the inputs available. As suggested above, an economic theory-oriented capacity output notion is the "best" or equilibrium output level given available input stocks. This is defined according to an isoquant map (if only capital is a fixed input) as the output corresponding to the isoquant for which the existing capital stock is the minimum cost capital level. Representing the utilization of this capacity, and the cost consequences of this utilization level, depends on comparing this capacity output to actual output production.

The relationship between capacity utilization and productivity growth, therefore, and the interaction of these and other economic performance indicators, have an important theoretical basis. They can all be motivated within a formal model of firm decisions and technology, which in turn can be used as a basis of measurement and analysis of economic performance. Outlining a theoretical structure that can be used to isolate the technical change and utilization contributions to fluctuations in overall "productivity", and ultimately to distinguish the impacts of other characteristics of the production process causing changing patterns of input use, is the primary purpose of this text.

1.2 The Theoretical Relationship Between Productivity and Capacity Utilization

To develop the structure necessary to model, evaluate and measure economic performance and its determinants, let us start by defining formally the most important concepts. In general, these concepts and their relationships have as their basis the theory of the firm and the production function.

The idea underlying the production function is that it summarizes the state of technology – the maximum production of a particular output technically possible given a certain amount of inputs. As alluded to above, "true" productivity growth or technical change arises from a change or shift in the production function, so that more production is technically possible from the available amount of inputs. Increases in capacity utilization, by contrast, occur when approaching a cost minimizing combination of inputs from a technically efficient but not cost effective situation, where the existing level of capital was not the minimum cost level consistent with current output production. This does not imply a change in the production function. Although, as stated, these effects are difficult to untangle empirically, it is fairly straightforward to identify them formally and theoretically.

More specifically, we can formalize the notion of the production function mathematically as $Y = f(v,t) = f(K,L,t)$, where Y is output, t is the state of technology or time, and v is a vector of inputs, for the moment assumed to be capital, K, and labor, L. This may be thought of as a "value added" production function since no other inputs are recognized. This functional relationship in a sense represents the "blueprints" outlining the technical features of the production process. This association between output and the two inputs the firm uses for production can alternatively be summarized graphically using an isoquant map, where each isoquant is a "level surface" of the production function. Each isoquant, therefore, represents the different combinations of K and L that could potentially be used to produce a given amount of Y given the current technology. Increases in the technology are in this case expressed by inward shifts in isoquants; to produce a given output level less capital and/or labor are necessary.

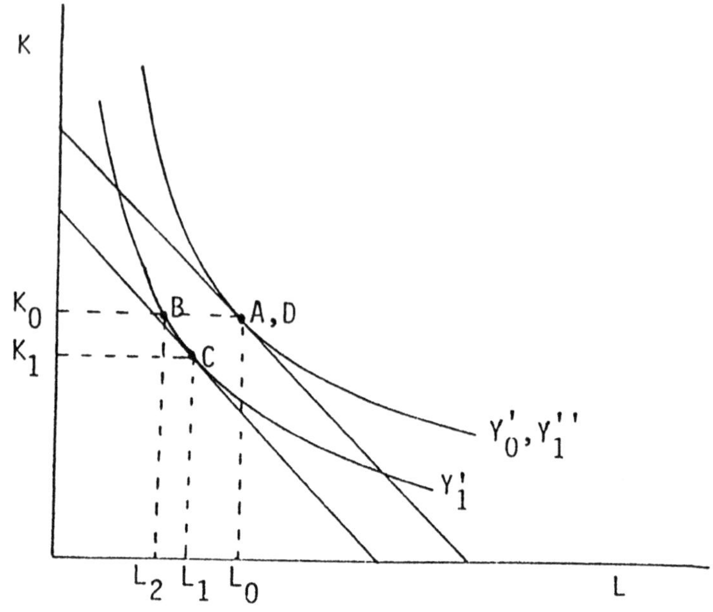

Fig.1.1. Productivity growth displayed as shifts of isoquants

This phenomenon can be diagrammed as in Figure 1.1. Say the firm wishes to produce the given level of output Y' in period 0; denote this Y'_0. Productivity growth may be thought of as a change in the isoquant map so the Y' isoquant shifts toward the origin in period 1. After the shift, therefore, capital and labor are more "productive" since the same output, $Y'_1 = Y'_0$ may be produced using less inputs. Alternatively, the original isoquant may be renamed Y''_1 where $Y'' > Y'$ and thus $Y''_1 > Y'_1 = Y'_0$; using the same amount of inputs more output may be produced in period 1 than in period 0.

It is straightforward to add cost minimization to this to incorporate the cost consequences of such a technological shift. To produce the level of output Y' in period 0, the cost minimizing firm chooses its optimal capital and labor input levels at the point where an isocost line is tangent to the Y'_0 isoquant (where the isocost line represents the set of combinations of K and L that cost a certain amount, say C_0, given current input prices p_K and p_L). This initial steady state equilibrium (in the sense that as long as Y' is the desired production level and technology and input prices are constant the firm is at its optimum long run input demand levels) is at point A, where K_0 units of capital and L_0 units of labor are demanded.[1] In reverse, Y' may be considered "capacity" output given (K_0, L_0) in the sense that it is a steady state output level given this input use; we will call this capacity level $Y^*(K_0, L_0)$.

The process of cost minimization implies a set of tangencies (a scale expansion path) between isoquants representing different potential output levels and their corresponding tangent isocost lines, thereby identifying the minimum cost of producing any output level given current input prices p (a vector of the input prices p_L and p_K) and state of the technology. This relationship is generally formalized as the cost function $C(p, Y, t)$, where both the technology and the firm's behavior are incorporated. This function is called "dual" to the production function since it equivalently represents the technology, but does so in terms of cost rather than output levels.

When a technological change occurs, so the Y' isoquant shifts toward the origin to become Y_1', the corresponding equilibrium input demands become K_1 and L_1 (implying a total cost of $C_1 = p_L L_1 + p_K K_1$). Now capital and labor are more "productive" since the same output may be produced using less inputs and therefore at less cost $(C_1(Y', p, t_1) < C_0(Y', p, t_0))$.

The effect of technological change can therefore be measured as the difference between cost of producing Y' before and after the change – C_0 and C_1. Alternatively, the focus may be placed on the isoquant going through the point (K_0, L_0), renamed Y_1'' in period 1. Since this reflects a higher level of production given available inputs than was possible in period 0, comparison of the Y_0' and Y_1'' levels generates a measure of the implied technical change. This latter output comparison is generally referred to as reflecting "primal" productivity growth, whereas the cost-based measure is called "dual" to this, since the functions they are based on are dual to each other.[2]

[1] These optimal demands can more rigorously be represented as functions of the demanded output level and the technology as $K_0 = K^*(Y', L_0), L_0 = L^*(Y', K_0)$, where the asterisk denotes a steady state.

Although this fundamental theory of productivity change is reasonably straightforward to motivate, measurement of the implied concepts may not be so easy. Numerous examples may be used to highlight this difficulty. One already alluded to is the possibly difficult task of appropriately measuring the inputs and output. Also, since both inputs and output will have changed between two data points, it is necessary to impute what output (costs) would have been if inputs (output) had remained the same to generate the primal (dual) measure. This again might not be straightforward to carry out in practice. In addition, other inputs and outputs might exist, causing complexities due to substitution patterns. This shift in the production function might also not be parallel – it may "twist" – and it may be difficult empirically to distinguish a movement along from a shift or twist in the isoquant. Many complications therefore arise when implementation of these ideas is attempted.

Capacity utilization is an example of these complications, and one of the most important to take into account. As already mentioned, the "true" productivity change may be difficult to identify independently of capacity utilization if one of these inputs (such as capital) is fixed (or quasi-fixed).[3] In this case, movement from one equilibrium to another will not be instantaneous; technical change will cause both productivity and capacity utilization to change in the short run. If capital is fixed, for example, at K_0, or at least cannot be changed to K_1 instantaneously, observed productivity growth will not reflect the full shift from K_0 to K_1 and L_0 to L_1, and production will not be carried out at an optimal (long run equilibrium) point in period one. This implies short run misutilization of the fixed input,[4] rep-

[2] Duality notions are elaborated in detail in Chapter 2.

[3] Quasi-fixed might mean that even in the short run the capital stock can be adjusted, but it will not be adjusted all the way to the equilibrium level because of constraints such as adjustment costs.

[4] It should also be recognized that short run optimization in terms of profit maximization might, for example, exist here (as well as cost minimization), even though the full long run equilibrium point is not reached due to fixity constraints. Note also that this concept of utilization may include other inputs such as labor. However, in our two input diagram cost minimization is meaningless if both inputs are fixed. In this case, if it is true that only Y_1^0 output is desired, even if the

resented by a deviation between produced and capacity output, and thus mismeasurement of productivity growth if this is ignored.

Figures 1.1 and 1.2 together can be used to illustrate this. Define economic capacity utilization to be equal to one when full equilibrium exists at point A for period 0 in Figures 1.1 and 1.2. By definition this equilibrium is associated with a tangency of the isoquant and isocost lines and also of the short and long run cost curves.[5] Only at this point is the given capital stock K_0 consistent with minimum long run cost. Since at point A the steady state output corresponding to the given capital stock K_0 (the capacity output $Y_0^* = Y^*(K_0)$) and the demanded level of $Y(Y_0' = Y')$ coincide by construction, capacity utilization, defined as $Y_0'/Y_0^* = Y/Y^*$, is equal to one, as required.

In time period 1, after the technology has changed, production of the output level Y' requires less capital than before (K_1 instead of K_0) but reduction in the capital stock cannot be accomplished instantaneously. Assuming capital is completely fixed, in the short run too much capital (K_0) is used and too little labor (L_2). In Figure 1.1 the input change associated with the change in technology is represented by shifting the Y' isoquant in from Y_0' to Y_1' but not changing the capital stock from K_0, so a higher cost level is maintained (at point B) than would be the case with full cost minimization (at point C in period 1 given output demand Y').

In Figure 1.2 this sequence of events is reflected by a shift in the short run and long run average cost curves in period 0 ($SRAC_0$ and $LRAC_0$) to $SRAC_1$ and $LRAC_1$ in period 1. After this shift Y_1' no longer corresponds to a tangency of the short and long run average cost curves $SRAC_1(K_0)$ and $LRAC_1$. Thus, with the capital level fixed at K_0, the full decline in inputs and therefore costs permitted for a particular level of output by the change in technology (A to C) is not represented correctly by the data; observed costs corresponding to point B exceed those for point C. This arises because in time

technological shift occurs the firm keeps paying for K_0 and L_0 inputs. For labor to be fixed and cost minimization to occur, therefore, at least one other "variable" input must be available to use to respond to technical change fluctuations or other changes in the economic climate facing the firm.

[5]These ideas are developed more extensively in Chapter 3.

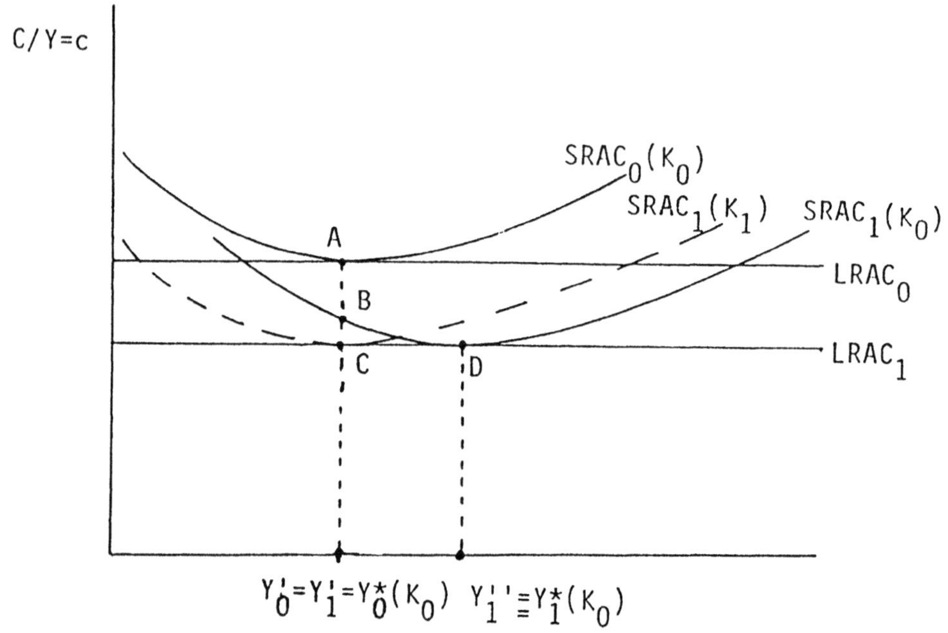

Fig.1.2. Short run and long run average cost

period one $Y_1' < Y_1^*$ where $Y_0^* = Y_1'$ is the capacity output given K_1 (by definition of full equilibrium and the construction of K_1) and Y_1^* is capacity output given K_0.[6] Note that $Y_1' < Y_1^*$ implies both that $K_1 < K_0$ and $Y/Y^* < 1$; underutilization of the given capital stock exists because the actual level of K is too high for full equilibrium given output production Y'.

Note that if capital is quasi-fixed so it adjusts, but only partially, cost minimization would be more closely approximated. Thus capacity utilization would be closer to one, because the new capital level would be between K_0 and K_1. However, this still would not reflect a steady state characterized by full utilization of capacity. Quasi-fixity of factors therefore still causes capacity utilization to differ from one in the short run. In the long run given a constant output demand capital will adjust to K_1 where Y' is again produced at minimum cost, the full productivity change (in terms of decreased costs of producing Y') will be observed, and capacity and produced output will again coincide.[7]

It is clear from this limited but representative exposition that economic measures of productivity growth and capacity utilization are directly related. This implies that independent measures of these indexes may not be consistent with each other, or with the economic principles underlying construction of the indicators. This in turn suggests that using productivity growth or capacity utilization as explanatory variables for each other or for other economic indicators

[6] A similar argument can be made in the context of profit maximization. In this case output is not fixed after a change in the technology, but the short run profit maximization point will not in general correspond to the tangency of the short and long run average cost curves. Again, therefore, capacity output differs from that produced and capacity utilization deviates from unity. In fact, when produced output differs between the two periods in question for this or for any other reason (such as a change in demand), the analysis becomes somewhat more complicated, and difficult to motivate in a two-dimensional diagram, but the essential points remain valid. These extensions will be elaborated later in this text.

[7] Clearly, when considering "real world" data, output demands, input prices and other economic factors affecting firm decisions will also be varying over time. The simplifications about fixed exogenous factors used in this analysis are therefore useful for exposition of the ideas but must be accommodated for estimation, as will be seen below.

does not provide a particularly interpretable framework for empirical or theoretical analyses. Assuming all capacity utilization "peaks" are similar and assessing productivity growth between these points will also generally not be appropriate. Thus, studies of productivity growth should take capacity utilization explicitly into account unless an assumption of instantaneous adjustment is valid; productivity growth measures assuming no impact of capacity utilization, or based on *ad hoc* adjustments, will almost certainly be biased.

Later in this text we will provide an implementable theoretical framework in which this, and similar adjustments of standard productivity growth measures, can be accomplished. For now, we will proceed to an initial overview of standard techniques for measurement of the individual productivity growth and capacity utilization concepts identified in these diagrams.

1.3 Measurement of Performance Indexes in an Economic Framework

To construct indexes of productivity growth in the primal, or output sense, we need to develop an implementable structure to measure the difference between Y_0' and Y_1'' – the potential production levels associated with the different technologies available in periods 0 and 1, using period 0 input levels K_0 and L_0. Indexes representing comparisons of these output levels are typically specified in terms of rates of growth of output between two time periods. This generally takes the form of measuring $d\ln Y/dt$, where dt denotes a change in technology or time, $t_1 - t_0$ and $d\ln Y$ is $\ln Y_1'' - \ln Y_0'$, and where the logarithmic difference by definition reflects a rate of growth.[8]

However, we have seen that it is not the pure observed output change between two periods that is of interest when considering productivity

[8]Note that this (and the following) treatment ignores the distinction between discrete and continuous measures. In most cases the theoretical framework is specified in terms of continuous time but application to the data requires, of course, the use of discrete numbers. The potential biases from this, mentioned in Chapter 5, are small if fluctuations in the data are not substantial.

growth, but the change corresponding to a given vector of inputs. Since observed data do not hold inputs fixed, the measure must be adapted to capture the output change independently of input growth during this time period (or possibly other changes in the production structure implicitly assumed fixed in the analysis).

More formally, if productivity is thought of as an output per input ratio Y/V (where V is a measure of aggregated inputs), then productivity growth is actually represented by the change in this ratio over time, $(\ln Y_1 - \ln Y_0) - (\ln V_1 - \ln V_0)$, rather than just the rate of growth of output. This is represented by the logarithmic derivative

$$\partial \ln Y/\partial t = \%\Delta Y/\Delta t - \%\Delta V/\Delta t = d\ln Y/dt - d\ln V/dt$$

(where the distinction between continuous and discrete time is overlooked for now).[9] This expression removes the impacts of changing input use, and of substitution among inputs if V is not a single input, from the implied measure of efficiency change. It is therefore consistent with the graphical development of the concept of productivity growth above, and provides the basis for the traditional growth accounting productivity growth measure developed in Chapter 2.[10]

Similarly (and, as we will see in Chapter 2, equivalently), a dual cost measure of productivity growth can be specified as $\ln C_1 - \ln C_0 = d\ln C/dt$, where C_0 is the minimum cost associated with Y' at time 0. Y_0' and C_1 corresponds to the cost level on the new isocost line tangent to the Y' isoquant in period 1, Y_1', as above. Again this cost change reflecting productivity growth should correspond only to the impact of technological change with all other exogenous factors constant; it must be independent of observed changes in output and the prices of inputs. Therefore, in practice, these changes must be purged from the observed change in total cost similarly to the adaptation of the output

[9]The theoretical basis for this expression, as well as that for the corresponding dual measure below, is developed in detail in Chapter 2.

[10]Note that productivity growth measures grounded more formally on index number theory tend to exponentiate the usual measure ($\ln(Y_1''/Y_0') = \ln Y_1'' - \ln Y_0' = d\ln Y/dt$) to obtain Y_1''/Y_0'. This avoids some approximation problems and thus is more precise than the usual logarithmic measure, as well as being conceptually more similar to capacity utilization indicators. See Diewert and Morrison [1989] for further discussion.

change measure above. This results in a cost diminution expression like

$$\begin{aligned} \partial \ln C/\partial t &= \%\Delta C/\Delta t - \%\Delta Y/\Delta t - \%\Delta P/\Delta t \\ &= d\ln C/dt - d\ln Y/dt - d\ln P/dt, \end{aligned}$$

where P is a measure of aggregated input prices and $d\ln P/dt$ represents a weighted average of input price changes.[11]

Productivity growth measures are thus expressed in the form of the residual of output growth or cost decline less the impacts of exogenous changes that should not be included as efficiency determinants. This residual ideally reflects only changes in technology, but, as developed so far, does not incorporate any changes in the structure of the production process except input level and price changes and thus input substitution. Therefore, the resulting measures include the effects of changes in any other factors which affect firm behavior but were ignored in the simple graphical analysis above. This is why the productivity growth residual has been called a "measure of our ignorance", and why much current research on productivity is devoted to decomposing this residual measure further to purge the technical change measure of other identifiable changes in the market or production structure.

For example, in addition to input changes, other production characteristics such as capacity utilization (as developed here and in Chapter 4) and scale economies (discussed in Chapter 4) should also be purged from this measure. If this is accomplished, the resulting measure more closely approximates true productivity change – it ideally captures technical change independent of input substitution, utilization changes and scale economies. Incorporating production characteristics other than substitution takes a form analogous to that for

[11] This expression is more formally developed later; the treatment here provides only a motivation for the idea and does not deal with the differences between derivatives and differentials, or continuous and discrete time, in a mathematically rigorous manner. In addition, the cost expression is often written without the $d\ln Y/dt$ component; this generally occurs because the cost change is expressed in terms of unit rather than total costs and constant returns is assumed. The idea of adjusting for observed changes that are held constant in the theory is the main point here. These more technical distinctions will be dealt with more carefully in Chapter 2.

input changes, and will be dealt with in terms of "adjustments" to the traditional measure.

As an initial – and primary – example of this, the framework developed in this chapter can be used to introduce the idea of adjusting productivity growth measures to identfy the impact of capacity utilization.[12] Essentially the observed output change is not only a combination of output growth and input growth (recognized in productivity growth measures), but also the intensity of input usage (utilization). We must therefore determine how much to allocate to these different determinants, and remove the utilization impact to reproduce just the technical change impact. More specifically, observed output growth will be a combination of the difference between Y_0' and Y_1'' (productivity growth) and the difference between observed output, Y', and Y^*, and the latter should not be attributed to technical change.

Similarly to the measurement of productivity growth, to accommodate capacity utilization into the measurement procedure we require a way to identify and compare different levels of output – in this case Y' and Y^* instead of Y' and Y''. However, one of these levels is in this case imputed as a steady state value. I.e., to measure capacity utilization we wish to construct ratios of Y and Y^* to indicate the difference between actual and potential equilibrium output, given all available input stocks. This involves finding a way to measure the output at the tangency between the short and long run average cost curves to compare to the observed output level. On the dual cost side, taking account of capacity utilization similarly requires assessing the costs corresponding to these output levels. It is therefore difficult to construct a justifiable economic measure of capacity utilization without an empirically implementable structural model of firm behavior in which to determine the shapes of short and long run cost functions, and to find Y^*.

The productivity growth and capacity utilization indexes computed as outlined here have clear interpretations in terms of the associated conceptual notions developed above. The $d\ln Y/dt - d\ln V/dt$ mea-

[12]This is further developed in Chapter 4.

sure, for example, states the percentage output growth that would have been possible this period given the level of input use experienced in the last time period; a measure of .02 means output could have increased 2 % with no input increase. A measure of $d\ln C/dt - d\ln Y/dt - d\ln P/dt$ has an analogous interpretation; costs could have declined by 2 % with no change in input prices or output production. The Y/Y^* ratio indicates how much proportionately the actual value of output exceeds or falls short of that which would be economically optimal. If this is 0.9, for example, it says about 10 % more output could be produced in full equilibrium without putting pressure on the existing inputs, in the sense of causing increases in unit costs. The cost-side counterpart can be interpreted similarly as the percentage cost change (at a given output level) permitted by a relaxation of fixity constraints.

1.4 Relationships Among These and Other Indicators of Economic Performance

Productivity growth and capacity utilization not only are closely interrelated, but are in turn associated with many other economic factors due to their dependence on firm behavior. Since many of these factors are the basis for construction of standard economic performance indicators, the indicators themselves are also closely related. These measures include those which are directly based on firm decisions, such as inventory to sales ratios, profits and levels of investment, and those which appear to be more macro-oriented, like price indexes and unemployment (or employment) rates. All of these indicators, like the productivity growth and capacity utilization measures, tend to fluctuate in systematic ways over business cycles.

Observed similarities in the fluctuations of these indexes have motivated many types of studies. Two typical types of analyses based on economic performance indicators and their linkages are: (i) attempted "explanations" of one indicator as a function of the other; and (ii) evaluations of business cycles in terms of leading as compared to lagging indicators.

The former type generally take the form of regression analyses similar to that mentioned for productivity growth and capacity utilization; since the indicators are expected to be closely related, regressions of one on the other are simply carried out with an implicit "causality" implication. As noted earlier, however, the true explanatory power of this sort of exercise is questionable because of the lack of economic theory underlying the statistical investigation.

The other type of analysis – evaluating leading and lagged indicators directly – is quite widely used, and often provides the basis for policy decisions. It is useful therefore to pursue a bit further how these types of analyses might be related to our theoretical models of firm behavior, and thus ultimately to an integrated theoretical structure linking economic performance indicators.

Studies of business cycles link different indicators on the basis of when they begin to rise or fall during the cycle. Analysis of the systematic relationships among indicators and the regularity of their cyclical behavior has suggested that most of these indicators have some leading and some lagging components. For example, for fixed capital investment, new investment commitments and formation of business enterprises have been identified as leading indicators. Backlogs of investment commitments are "roughly coincident" and investment expenditures are lagging. Similarly, in terms of prices and costs, stock prices, profits, profit margins and cash flows are considered leading indicators, the wholesale price index for industrial commodities is roughly coincident, and labor cost per unit of output is lagging. Total production, income and sales are by definition "roughly coincident", as they in fact form the basis for the definition of the cycles.

Although business cycle analyses focusing on these patterns tend to be strictly data-based rather than founded on economic theory,[13] movements of these indicators do have an important theoretical footing. Various theories have been proposed to "explain" cycles. Some are based on analyses of the supply of money and credit or government spending and tax policies. Others focus on fluctuations in capital investment (and inventories) driven by final demand. Still others

[13]See the often-cited piece by T. Koopmans [1947] on "Measurement Without Theory" for one discussion of problems arising from these types of practices.

identify relationships among prices, costs and profits as the motivating force behind the cyclical behavior of indicators.[14] The first of these approaches stems strictly from a macroeconomic perspective. However, the others are intimately connected to firm decisions; even the consumer price index ultimately depends on the pricing behavior of firms. This suggests that production theory can provide a useful structural framework for consideration of the relationships among indicators, particularly when slow adjustment that may drive cyclical swings is explicitly recognized.

For example, production theory informs us that new investment commitments and creation of new businesses will occur when output demand becomes high enough to make such investments profitable. This simple implication is consistent with the sequence of leading and lagging indicator responses outlined above. As output demand expands, an increase in capacity utilization will occur, since firms will be attempting to produce more output using their given capital stock, which will result in pressure to increase the stock. The marginal product (and thus the shadow value on the margin) of the capital stock will rise, which will tend to show up as increased stock prices and profits. Production will increase, and may eventually overshoot demand (resulting in inventory expansion) if expectations of future demand and recognition of adjustments made by other firms in the industry are not correct.

Note that a critical part of this analysis is slow adjustment by firms. If firms could respond instantaneously to market conditions, this sequence of events would not occur over the duration of a business cycle, but instead would take place immediately. This also helps to explain why certain indicators such as investment might appear somewhat perverse. For example, since the accumulation of capital goods proceeds slowly, it is likely that many investment expenditures will become evident in the data when the "boom" is winding down. It is therefore necessary to distinguish short and long run behavior in theoretical models of economic performance and cyclical responses used for analyses of these trends.

[14]See Moore [1980] for further elaboration and for additional information on lagging as compared to leading indicators.

This overview of firm responses and the corresponding patterns of leading and lagging indicators also has implications for productivity growth; productivity as generally measured will likely increase (and then possibly decrease) over the cycle. This will result not only from technological change that may be stimulated by expansionary economic conditions, but also from changes in inventory use (inventories being drawn down implies more potential sales from available inputs); variations in profitability (increased demand may result in a higher value of output given costs); adjustments in utilization of input stocks (increased use of variable inputs given capacity); changes in cost per unit due to volume production (decreasing average cost from scale economies), and other phenomena. Indicators that reflects some of these characteristics of the economy, such as sales to inventory ratios, investment levels and profit margins as well as capacity utilization, thus are all closely related to productivity growth, since their movements and effect on observed "productivity" can be predicted using the theory of the firm.

One might think that measures of true productivity growth should not include all of these impacts, since they do not imply increases in the state of technology, or often even changes in efficiency. Even if it is the case that efficiency is affected, such as with scale economies, this effect should be independently distinguished from "true" productivity change for clear interpretation and application of the measure. However, standard measures include all this information and the components are not identifiable using only data analysis. Providing a more complete theoretical structure for analysis of economic performance allows not only assessment of the many forces underlying fluctuations in performance indicators, but also empirical measurement of these independent effects. In later chapters we will explore further the use of production theory models for measuring and analyzing not only productivity growth and capacity utilization, but also other market and technical characteristics that affect economic performance, provide the basis for indicators of performance, and should be identified independently of productivity growth.

Developing a theoretical foundation for analysis and interpretation of these economic indicators is particularly important since the measures are used as a basis for important and wide-ranging policy decisions. As mentioned earlier, cyclical indicators are often used to provide a foundation for attempted "fine tuning" of the economy in terms of monetary and fiscal policy. Economic indicators also provide a crucial basis for determining the distribution of federal funds for creation of jobs, public works, etc., based on the economic performance of different regions. These types of policy responses can have an enormous impact on the economy, so they should be based on as solid a foundation as possible. Both the distributional effect and the overall policy impact are also intensifying over time as people other than those in academia increasingly use these indicators.

This increased usage of economic performance measures has been emphasized by Shiskin [1977], who wrote:

> "This is a new world for both producers and users of economic indicators. We are just becoming aware of these new problems and have not yet thought through all their implications. Although we may be years away from optimal solutions, we find ourselves in the middle of the arena because somewhere in the neighborhood of $30 billion a year, or about 1.5 % of GNP, is being transferred among U.S. businesses and individuals on the basis of movements of these key indicators."

In sum, it is clear that providing economic "underpinning" for the analysis of such indicators as productivity growth and capacity utilization is an important objective. The goal of this text is to outline a methodology for formalizing the relationships among these and other characteristics of the production technology, and thus to provide a framework in which corresponding economic performance indicators can be measured and interpreted as usefully as possible.

* * * * *

This chapter has provided an overview of the concepts involved in modeling and measuring economic performance. We will now start from the beginning to develop an integrated framework in which to assess the trends in, and relationships among, indicators of economic performance such as productivity growth and capacity utilization. We will first elaborate the traditional methodology for measurement of productivity growth and capacity utilization, to determine to what extent this framework facilitates interpretation of the measures and analyses of the theoretical linkages among these and other indicators. Then we will discuss restrictions embodied in the traditional approaches, methods of adapting these procedures to more appropriately deal with these issues, and the theoretical and empirical impacts of these adjustments. As we proceed, we will explore how a structural model of firm behavior can provide a framework in which consistent measures of these indicators and their determinants can be obtained.

Chapter 2

The Traditional Measurement of Productivity Growth: Theoretical Issues

The word "productivity" has widely varying connotations for different people because the word is used so extensively and loosely. Although it is generally understood that increased productivity is somehow advantageous, most people would find it difficult to define clearly the notion of productivity.

The general concept of productivity stems from the amount of output that can be produced from a given amount of input. Productivity growth, therefore, can arise from an increase in the output that can be produced for a given level of input, or a decrease in input (and therefore costs) necessary to produce a given amount of output, as outlined in Chapter 1. In this sense productivity growth is desirable since the efficiency of production has increased; society can obtain more goods given available scarce resources. This straighforward idea, however, is not as easy to formalize and use as it is to express, since there are so many determinants of observed changes in output production and input use.

In this chapter we look at traditional methods of productivity growth measurement and their theoretical basis, to see what is really being represented by these measures. We consider what interpretation is possible from these measures and what limitations are implied, to provide a basis for an extension of the traditional methods and linkages with other performance indicators discussed in subsequent chapters.

In the first section we outline the earliest and most easily computable measures of productivity growth – single factor measures. The simplicity of these measures, however, generates interpretation problems. One of these problems stems from ignoring substitution among factors of production. The extension to include substitution, resulting in multifactor productivity growth measures, is elaborated in Section 2.2. Extensions to this index number or "accounting" basis of productivity growth measurement are then outlined in Section 2.3. The final two sections then discuss in more detail the theory underlying these indexes, focusing on the interpretation of productivity growth measures as measures of "technical change", and on the relationship between cost- and output-based measures of productivity growth, respectively.

2.1 Single Factor Measures of Productivity Growth

One of the difficulties that is immediately obvious when measurement of productivity is attempted is finding relevant definitions of "output" and "input". Often a firm produces only one type of output. Even in this case, however, "goods" or "bads" that could potentially be termed "output" may be produced using the hired inputs. For example, pollution may be produced, causing society to be worse off. For a full accounting of the "production" of a firm, therefore, this ideally should be taken into account. On the other side, firms may purchase equipment that does not produce output for sale, but does reduce the pollution produced, to satisfy legal regulations, or otherwise to provide a contribution that is not explicitly linked to the production of goods and services. These contributions will not show up in measures of output, but are assets for society that perhaps should be taken into account when considering the "productivity" of the firm's inputs. Dealing with these issues is not, however, straightforward.

Many firms also produce multiple outputs using the same inputs. In this case it is difficult to measure output effectively because changes in the composition of output may affect input use independently of true productivity growth. The standard method of dealing with this problem is to aggregate the various outputs into a single output quantity index, which is sometimes justifiable but becomes increasingly questionable over periods of substantial relative price and quality changes. The problem is further aggravated when productivity must be measured for a large sector of the economy, so outputs must be aggregated over a large number of firms or even industries.[1]

A primary issue that arises when defining the relevant input base for productivity analysis is what inputs should be taken into account for a firm. To avoid double counting, productivity accounting is often based on value added output, which is defined as the contribution of capital and labor inputs. By construction, therefore, capital and labor become the only inputs under consideration. Many times researchers expand this base to encompass the concept of gross output, which includes intermediate materials as part of the input measure. Often the inputs assumed to exist for this gross output measure are capital, labor, energy and non-energy intermediate materials.

One problem with both of these input specifications, particularly when considering a single firm, is that under usual accounting practices capital is not measured as part of input expenditure. Special measures of the rental value of capital must therefore be imputed. The gross output-based measure also is not as complete as it appears, since it typically ignores some inputs such as purchased services, advertising and research and development which appear on the balance sheets and income statements of most firms and therefore might also be included.[2] Aggregation of the components of these input indexes

[1]Issues of aggregation and measurement are dealt with in further detail in Chapter 6 and touched on in Chapter 10.

[2]The Bureau of Labor Statistics in the U.S. now includes a category for purchased services in the data of inputs and outputs used for productivity growth computations.

also suggests a number of difficulties, since different types of capital and labor inputs could alternatively be identified separately for analysis.

For measurement of productivity growth, many definitional difficulties such as these arise. One of the most fundamental and critical issues both conceptually and empirically, however, is to determine which inputs should provide the basis for comparing output and input growth. Single factor productivity growth measures focus on the productivity of a single input, ignoring substitution of this input and others in response to relative price changes. More complete multifactor measures, which include assessment of the changes in other inputs, provide a more clearly interpretable measure of overall productivity, but are more complex to motivate and construct.

Often the choice of input for measurement of single-factor productivity growth is determined by the application the productivity measure is designed to address. For example, if wage negotations are being held, the productivity of labor might be important. Since labor is the focus of the negotiations, implicitly the scarcity of that input and its resulting level of compensation is the primary consideration. In this case, even though more generally an "overall" input measure may be more appropriate for formalizing the notion of efficiency and productivity outlined above, single-factor measures may be relevant.

These measures are used in many cases, however, where their application is more questionable. It is crucial to recognize the distinctions between these simpler types of measures and more comprehensive measures in order not to make inappropriate conclusions. For example, in most cases one would not want to interpret increases in labor productivity as representing an overall increase in welfare.

One of the first applications of single factor productivity measurement was in agriculture, where productivity was taken to mean the yield per acre – the output possible from a given amount of land.[3] This single factor measure is constructed by measuring the quantity of output as Y and acres of land as A and computing the index Y/A

[3]See Rutten [1954, 1956] for an early example of this.

as a measure of the level of productivity. Productivity therefore is said to have increased when this ratio rises, which implies a positive value for $d \ln Y/dt - d \ln A/dt$ (where t denotes time). This (average) productivity growth measure (often designated the *residual* that remains when the impact of changes in A on output growth is removed) appears easily interpretable since it expresses growth in terms of percentage changes between time periods.[4] It summarizes, however, many different market and technological changes that may have occurred between two time periods and are imputed simply to "productivity".

More specifically, in terms of substitution of inputs, this single factor measure focuses on land as "the" scarce input. In other words, this easily computable measure ignores changes in everything other than acreage as causes of the full output growth (or decline) observed between time periods. Thus, increases in the use of labor, fertilizer, capital machinery or any other input are not recognized, and will instead be picked up as an unidentified cause of the output increase – part of the residual. These changes are, however, due to a well defined change in the production process; additional use of other scarce inputs. Therefore, even if yield per acre increases, it is not possible to say whether productivity as a whole has increased. The yield per acre measure is a limited productivity measure focusing only on the scarcity of land.

Similar problems exist with respect to the later energy productivity emphasis of followers of the technocracy movement in the U.S. and Canada in the 1920s and 1930s,[5] and net energy analysts in the 1970s and 1980s. The focus of these groups was to determine the efficiency of energy use, which required constructing measures of the

---

[4]This can be motivated quite simply by noting that the (discrete) change in the Y/A ratio can be written $\Delta(Y/A) = \Delta Y/\Delta A$, where $\Delta Y = Y_1 - Y_0$ between time periods 0 and 1, and $\Delta A = A_1 - A_0$. This change, however, depends on the units in which Y and A are measured. To create a scale-free measure, therefore, the proportionate change $(\Delta Y/Y)/(\Delta A/A)$ is used. This is generally restated in terms of logarithms as $\Delta \ln(Y/A)$, or $\Delta \ln Y - \Delta \ln A$, which translates to $\%\Delta Y - \%\Delta A$, since taking logarithms simply causes absolute changes to be transformed into relative, or proportionate, changes. This discrete change can, of course, be written in terms of continuous changes using calculus notation as $d \ln Y/dt - d \ln A/dt$.

[5]See Berndt [1985] for an interesting analysis of this group.

output to energy (E) ratio Y/E. Productivity or efficiency growth in this context can be said to have increased if $d \ln Y/dt - d \ln E/dt$ is positive.

Again, although this concept is useful for some types of analysis, it does not reflect a full accounting of productivity changes because it focuses solely on the scarcity of energy. It does not recognize the substitution of other types of scarce resources for energy by the firms, which causes this increase in Y/E. Therefore, no matter how expensive it is in terms of use of other inputs, any small saving in energy use is considered an improvement in performance. Clearly, this is a limited economic performance indicator.

Labor productivity measures are also single-factor productivity measures, although they are still sometimes interpreted as more general productivity indicators. In this case, productivity growth is defined as an increase in output per labor hour or laborer (L). Formally productivity is defined as Y/L and productivity growth is therefore $d \ln Y/dt - d \ln L/dt$. Although for some applications such as wage negotiations output per hour is justifiably emphasized, again this measure does not take into account the fact that part of an increase in Y/L could be a result of, for example, moving toward more capital intensive production or increasing the use of energy, neither of which necessarily is consistent with better economic performance.

In fact, since the interpretation of such issues is difficult, conflicting interpretations may be consistent with increasing productivity measured in this context. For example, increases in wages relative to the price of capital or energy might cause substitution away from labor. The resulting higher labor productivity might be interpreted by some as an indicator that additional wage increases are justified, but it instead results in this circumstance from a compositional change induced by increases in wages above labor's initial marginal product. It is unclear, therefore, whether labor benefits from increasing productivity in this case, since it is not an exogenous indicator of efficiency change but is instead an indicator of changes in exogenous economic factors and subsequent (endogenous) substitution decisions. The marginal person is simply more productive because employment is reduced and diminishing returns exists. Therefore, the standard reasoning that labor productivity calculations measure the "fruitfulness" of labor, so people are by definition better off when labor productivity increases (implying less work is necessary to obtain the same amount of goods and services), may not be entirely legitimate.[6]

Finally, a single factor measure of output per unit of capital, although not generally touted as an efficiency measure, has been used as a basis of capacity utilization-type indexes. The idea underlying construction of these measures is that if output per unit of capital increases, the firm is utilizing capital more heavily and therefore approaching its maximum potential. Peaks in this measure can therefore be thought of as points where capacity output is reached given the available capital stock. This type of single factor measure is generally motivated more in the context of capital or capacity utilization than productivity, but the measure clearly has productivity growth connotations, in this case in terms of capital productivity.

Although these indexes (and other related measures which may be defined when other inputs are considered[7]) are limited in their individual interpretative power, in total they provide a basis for decomposition of output growth into the different forces causing that growth. That is the focus of some of the recent literature from the U.S. Bureau of Labor Statistics, where single factor productivity growth measures for all recognized inputs are specified in order to provide a more overall picture of changes in production processes.[8] These indexes, for example, might show that although labor productivity declined in the mid-1970's, this was at least partly because of a push toward saving energy use and a resulting increase in the productivity of energy. Whether this reflects an increase or decrease in overall productiv-

---

[6] Note that not only productivity analysts but also labor economists have recognized the interpretation problems with single factor productivity measures. This is evident, for example, from Rees [1980] and Griliches [1980].

[7] For example, the productivity of materials (M) or purchased services (S) may be measured.

[8] Harper and Gullickson [1989] use an extended version of the growth accounting methods outlined below, based on share weights from a parametric translog estimation process, to assess the contribution to multifactor productivity growth of capital, labor, energy, materials and purchased services. See also U.S. Department of Labor [1983] for an assessment of the contributions of different inputs to productivity growth.

ity requires a method of evaluating the total contribution of inputs, which is the purpose of the development of multifactor productivity measures.

2.2 Accounting Measures of Multifactor Productivity

None of the single factor measures of productivity growth is particularly illuminating as a measure of overall productivity change; the measured productivity growth residual is a combination of technological changes and other market responses that we might want to isolate independently. Measured productivity could, for example, include changes in scale economies or capacity utilization as well as technical change. Market changes might involve changes in pricing policy, inventory behavior or substitution among inputs. Although ultimately it will be useful to identify the contribution to the residual of various technological and market factors, the most obvious interpretation difficulty involving productivity growth measures arises from input substitution, which most clearly should not be considered a change in efficiency.

To eliminate the portion of the productivity residual that can be explained by substitution, the contributions of different inputs are generally combined by weighting growth rates of inputs by their revenue shares. This results in the overall measure of productivity growth:[9]

$$\epsilon_{Yt} = \frac{\partial \ln Y}{\partial t} = \frac{d \ln Y}{dt} - \sum_j S_j \frac{d \ln v_j}{dt}, \tag{2.1}$$

where v_j is the quantity of input j, S_j is the share of input j in the value of output, $p_j v_j / p_Y Y, p_j$ is the price of v_j, and p_Y is the price of Y. This residual measure, designed to represent what one might mean by an overall increase in productivity given scarce inputs, has alternatively been denoted an index of growth in total factor produc-

[9]Theoretically this should be in terms of cost shares, but generally revenue shares are used, which is rationalized by the assumption of perfect competition.

tivity or multifactor productivity. I will use the latter terminology, which is also used by the U.S. Bureau of Labor Statistics.[10]

Note that with some rewriting (2.1) becomes:

$$\epsilon_{Yt} = \sum_j S_j \left[\frac{d \ln Y}{dt} - \frac{d \ln v_j}{dt} \right], \tag{2.2}$$

as long as the shares sum to one. Since the $[\cdot]$ terms represent the rate of growth of single factor productivity, this makes it clear that multifactor productivity is a weighted average of individual single factor productivity growth measures. Therefore, if all single factor productivity measures grow at the same rate, there is a common rate of productivity growth.[11] Otherwise, inputs with a smaller cost share have a smaller impact on the overall productivity growth measure.

Some further manipulation facilitates elaboration of why a single factor measure embodies both technical change and input substitution. Since $d \ln Y/dt = \epsilon_{Yt} + \Sigma_j S_j \, d \ln v_j/dt$ from (2.1), for example, if $d \ln L/dt$ is subtracted from the left hand side of this expression, and $\Sigma_j S_j \, d \ln L/dt$ (where $\Sigma_j S_j = 1$) is subtracted from the right hand side, (2.1) becomes

$$\frac{d \ln Y}{dt} - \frac{d \ln L}{dt} = \epsilon_{Yt} + \sum_j S_j \left[\frac{d \ln v_j}{dt} - \frac{d \ln L}{dt} \right]. \tag{2.3}$$

This explicitly shows that single factor productivity measures (here for labor) include both the effects of overall technical progress (ϵ_{Yt}) and input substitution, represented by the change in the v_j to L ratio. Labor productivity growth could, therefore, be caused not only by technical change, but by increased investment in capital plant and equipment (or increased use of any other input) relative to labor.

---

[10]Note that the single factor productivity measures cannot be interpreted directly as a decomposition of the multifactor measure since the single-factor measures do not share-weight the input growth. The substitution implications implied by the share-weighting are necessary to include to decompose the full change in output. This slight inconsistency between the single factor and multifactor procedures has the potential to generate some confusion.

[11]This could result from the existence of Hicks neutral technical change, so isoquants do not "twist" when they change over time. Further discussion of neutrality and biases is given in Chapter 4.

The multifactor productivity index ϵ_{Yt} is often termed an accounting measure of productivity growth because no econometric estimation is required to compute the necessary components of the index; straightforward accounting methods can be used to construct measures of the prices and quantities of inputs and output and then they can simply be added. These measures are sometimes based on a value-added type of approach, which identifies only capital and labor as potential inputs, avoiding consideration of substitution between these and intermediate inputs. In this case, of course, the measure of output must be consistent with this – it must be a value-added output measure. More often, however, multifactor measures are based on a broader definition of inputs, in order to include as many of the firm's costs and substitution possibilities as possible, and thus facilitate interpretation.

Differences between the value of costs reflected by the inputs considered and the revenues generated may cause the revenue shares not to add to one. This could suggest the importance of a number of issues not taken into consideration with this measure. For example, deviations between revenue and costs could imply that not all costs are taken into account; advertising, land acquisitions, inventory holdings and other costly choices made by the firm may be ignored. In addition, if price is not equal to marginal revenue (market power exists), revenue might exceed costs even if all inputs are represented. Scale economies that are exploited could also allow economic profits to exist because marginal and average costs would differ.

The problem of a deviation between revenue and cost shares is sometimes dealt with simply by constructing the capital measure as a residual; any costs not reflected in other inputs are therefore assumed to be a result of required payments to some component of the capital stock. Although this is somewhat justifiable for accommodating problems related to excluding inputs such as land and inventories, theoretically it imputes any returns to other market or technological characteristics, such as market power and scale economies, to the capital stock. This is not justifiable since if these characteristics exist economic profits might well be non-zero, and this should be recognized.

When the issue is not resolved by data construction, it is generally bypassed by working simply with cost rather than revenue shares. If total costs are defined as the sum of the payments to all the factors under consideration, the sum of these shares will then equal one by construction. The problem with this is that the measure then is implicitly based on a cost-side measure of productivity growth rather than an output-based measure, the latter of which is the conceptual motivation underlying single-factor productivity measures and the usual simple extension to multifactor techniques. An additional problem is that the measure is not, strictly speaking, correct in this case, because for the cost motivation to be theoretically valid, the $d \ln Y/dt$ term should be weighted by the ratio of revenue and cost. This point will be developed further when the distinction between cost (dual) and output (primal) measures is presented in Section 2.5.

The residual implied by the accounting measure of multifactor productivity growth ϵ_{Yt} (sometimes called a "measure of our ignorance", as mentioned in the Introduction), therefore includes the impacts of many economic phenomena, even though substitution effects are recognized. The production structure assumptions underlying the multifactor measure implicitly incorporate a number of restrictions, and suggest many important issues that should be clarified.

This is true even more for the multifactor measure than its single factor counterparts because the productivity growth rate no longer is based on a simple increase in a ratio. As we have seen, the motivation of the productivity growth measure as the growth rate of a ratio implies the residual is a conglomeration of all impacts other than a simple growth of one input. For the multifactor measure, however, since substitution possibilities are embodied in the index, technological and market characteristics facing the firm become important to represent correctly. This will become clearer when the theoretical background of the measure is developed in Section 2.4.

Untangling the impact of various restrictions implied by standard multifactor productivity growth measurement techniques is difficult. Since these simple accounting-type measures are based only on data manipulation, and thus only on the information available from the raw data, numerous factors potentially affecting productivity are not directly observable. In particular, relaxing the implicit assumptions of instantaneous adjustment, constant returns to scale and perfect competition, which are embodied in most accounting measures, requires either heroic assumptions or a parametric framework. Adapting for other phenomena, such as the impacts of changes in regulation, has been accomplished more effectively in the accounting framework, although again a more complete structural model is generally useful to facilitate interpretation. We will now turn to a brief overview of attempts to deal with these issues within the confines of the nonparametric approach.

2.3 Adaptations to the Traditional Accounting Framework

Numerous economic factors which affect firms' behavior and productivity growth, and thus should be taken into consideration for productivity measurement, have been mentioned in the literature. Perhaps the most complete studies focusing on these issues in a nonparametric framework, in terms of spanning most topics in the literature, have been carried out by Edward Denison [1979, 1985]. In this section we briefly overview adaptations to the standard measures, designed to identify the impacts of these factors, which have been suggested by him and others.

The general framework Denison developed and used for a number of studies has been termed "growth accounting". This methodology is designed to decompose the total growth in output in the economy into its different potential factors. These components "explain" evidence of output increases in the economy, and whatever is left may be called technical change. This is based on the same productivity growth concept we have been developing. We have said $d \ln Y/dt$ is the change in output over time, and if we subtract from this increases in inputs, the contribution of input growth is purged from the measure. If in addition we identify other factors that affect production, and therefore in truth should be included in the production function, we can also eliminate the impacts of these components of growth that should not be attributed to technology from the residual, eventually leaving only pure "technical change".

Early researchers in this area attempted to adjust productivity growth measurements by recognizing the impact of these factors directly on the factor inputs, and adjusting the data accordingly. This was the basis for dissension among a number of researchers in the 1950's when the large productivity growth residual found by Solow [1958] was "explained" by some researchers by direct adjustments of capital measures.[12]. In most cases, unfortunately, these adjustments tend to be based on rather *ad-hoc* arguments. Therefore it has been fairly easy for researchers in this area to dispute the work of other productivity growth analysts.

Denison tried to work within the nonparametric growth accounting framework to identify factors both directly and indirectly affecting inputs which one might postulate would influence growth independently of technical change. He thus built on the earlier work on adjusting inputs in the sense that he first adapted the measures of labor and capital inputs for such characteristics as the composition of the labor force,[13] and then computed a residual called the "semi-residual", based on the "effective" input measures. He subsequently, however, identified more than twenty additional factors that could affect productivity growth, and he proceeded to use to adjust this semi-residual to obtain a final measure of "advances in knowledge".

Unfortunately, a multitude of different factors could be thought of as affecting input effectiveness and firm behavior (and therefore measured output) independently of technical change, and these are extremely difficult to isolate reliably from the raw data. Some measures of these factors can be obtained directly from published statistics such as national income accounts, but these may not directly be based on relevant economic reasoning. In addition, returns to scale, the con-

[12]For example, see Jorgenson and Griliches [1967].

[13]Some of this can be thought of as an attempt to adjust for "quality" of the inputs. This is a measurement issue that has sometimes been dealt with using hedonic methods, similar to those outlined later for embodied technical change or capital obsolescence. A large literature has recently been developing, however, focusing directly on measurement issues and the construction of index numbers; this is referred to in Chapter 10 but is not a focus of this text.

tribution of education to labor input, obsolescence of capital, and numerous other factors cannot be directly measured and must thus be imputed using available data and judgement.

Problems therefore arise with the methodology used because the theoretical basis of many of the adjustments is weak. This is especially true since these problems are confounded by the difficulty of generating not only theoretically justifiable but also consistent estimates of production characteristics from the raw data; a number of these characteristics are closely interrelated. The validity of many of the measures is therefore subject to question, although Denison carries out as careful an analysis as can be accomplished without a structural model of the production process.

Denison's procedures for output growth measurement are based on first identifying the observed growth in real national income (net national product at factor cost). One distinction he makes about this growth rate is that between potential and measured output growth; potential output growth may increase faster than measured if unemployment is high. Measured growth is then allocated to various factors. For example, under the heading of total factor input, three factors of production are identified; labor, capital, and land. These in turn are divided into different characteristics. Labor is sub-divided into the contributions of employment, hours (average hours, efficiency offset, intergroup shift offset), age-sex composition, and education. Capital components include inventories separately from nonresidential structures and equipment.

Other contributions that are identified are improved resource allocation (farm and nonfarm), legal and human environment (pollution abatement, worker safety and health, and dishonesty and crime), economies of scale, and irregular factors (weather in farming, labor disputes, intensity of demand). Clearly the magnitudes of the impact of many of these factors are problematic to assess effectively, although whether the impact is positive or negative might be relatively easy to determine.

Denison's procedures attempt to eliminate double counting, but because he does not directly base his adjustments on an integrated structural (neoclassical) framework, he sometimes appears not to accomplish this. For example, as Norsworthy [1984] points out, his adjustments for cyclical effects appear incomplete since the residual retains a strong cyclical pattern after the adjustments, and his treatment of capital and depreciation "makes his framework unsuitable for analyzing the impact of capital on economic growth or on labor productivity growth". This problem is primarily due to Denison's national accounts perspective, whereby the economy is viewed as producing income rather than output and therefore the costs of capital depreciation are excluded.

The questionable treatment of capital is a serious problem since capital's role in productivity changes – in terms of the impact of capital accumulation, restrictions on adjustment and capacity utilization (which are all related) – is critical for assessing economic performance. The interactions among such factors as cyclical effects, utilization and investment also cannot be identified in such a framework, causing potentially serious difficulties of maintaining consistency.

A related consistency problem has to do with returns to scale; inputs are measured as if constant returns to scale exists, and then a scale adjustment is made based on an assumed level of returns to scale and the implied cost change associated only with output increases. This is unreliable since "scale effects" can appear from either short or long run responses to output changes; differentiating short run effects (which have to do with fixed inputs such as capital), and long run or true scale effects, is difficult to do without a structural framework.

Another researcher who questioned this particular aspect of the Denison procedure but on a somewhat different basis is Usher [1975]. Usher argues that technical change embodied in the capital (and labor) stocks are not correctly identified, and that Denison's scale economies measure of about 12% per year is suspect for an entire economy, which will bias the estimated contribution of technical change or "advances in knowledge". He therefore rejects the results of Denison's study, while agreeing that the concepts it is based on are useful for generating information crucial for an understanding of economic performance and for motivating policy.[14]

[14]In particular, he states that "The problem is of considerable importance be-

Kendrick [1979] and Kendrick and Grossman [1980] have carried out similar procedures to Denison's, and therefore retain some of the problems inherent in the growth accounting approach. However, some differences facilitate interpretation and comparison. For example, Denison's treatment is at the national level, with a focus on the level of national income, whereas Kendrick's analyses are based on industry level data and therefore on output production. In addition, Kendrick and Grossman use unadjusted capital and labor inputs as the basis for analysis and then use changes in the effective capital and labor stocks, such as changes in labor force composition and quality of capital, directly as part of the explanation of growth. As Norsworthy [1984] points out, however, since the conceptual basis for analysis is the same for Denison, "there is probably considerable double counting among the quantitative effects he assigns to various causes".

In sum, these researchers have included numerous factors that one might think affect productivity growth, and have attempted to assess their impacts, which is critical for interpretation of overall productivity change. However, due to the lack of a structural framework for analysis, the adjustments have little theoretical basis and likely involve serious consistency problems.

The importance of a structural model has been emphasized in much of the work of Dale Jorgenson. In Jorgenson [1988], for example, it is stated that: "the decline in economic growth would be left unexplained without an econometric model to determine the rate of productivity growth ...". To deal with this, Jorgenson allows the rate of productivity growth to be an endogenous variable and incorporates consideration of the determinants of firm demand for various inputs. This emphasis on the structural framework is consistent with Norsworthy's somewhat stronger conclusion that

---

cause our prescriptions for generating economic growth from now on are likely to be conditioned by our understanding of the causes of the growth we have already enjoyed. We are more likely to promote education and scientific activity as means for fostering continued economic growth if we believe that observed growth has been due for the most part to technical change than if we believe that it has been due to capital formation or other changes which can be thought of as movements along a given production function".

> "The neoclassical framework is, in reality, the only basis for aggregating the various factors of production into a measure of multifactor input... Consequently, insofar as these investigators depart from the neoclassical framework, they may be accused of using *ad-hoc* procedures that will necessarily render their measurements inconsistent and incomparable with measurements using that framework."

Some of the adaptations identified by Denison, Kendrick and others have been provided with a more complete neoclassical theoretical basis by other researchers, even though the adjustments of the productivity growth indexes themselves tend to be simple and based primarily on accounting methods or straightforward index number manipulations. For example, the differential impacts of investment in research and development (R & D) from other types of capital have been summarized by Griliches [1988], and considered by a number of other researchers within a structural model of firm decision making.[15] These studies essentially recognize that R&D and other categories of productive capital have different price trends, time paths of investment and depreciation, and other characteristics. Therefore the two types of capital must be considered separately in models of firm behavior. Some of this can be accomplished simply by including R&D as another type of capital. Strictly speaking, however, these distinctions can only be assessed effectively within a model which allows explicit consideration of investment behavior.

Similarly, the distinction between pollution abatement capital (or other regulatory capital such as that required by safety standards) and capital purchased to produce measured output has been considered by Gray [1984], Norsworthy, Harper and Kunze [1979] and Conrad and Morrison [1989], among others.[16] The Conrad and Morrison study recognizes that pollution abatement capital is not "productive" in the same sense as is usually thought of for the capital stock; instead of producing output it produces a cleaner environment. Since this "output" is not represented in measured output,

[15]This extension will be briefly elaborated in Chapter 10.

[16]These studies will be discussed in more depth in Chapter 9.

a bias in traditional measures results. A model is useful here not only to motivate how the adjustment for regulatory requirements on capital should proceed, but also to identify the interactions among responses to such regulation and other types of firm decisions, such as the different relationships between this capital and other inputs.

Clearly these few examples provide a very limited view of attempts made to provide a more complete theoretical or data basis for adjustments of productivity computations. However, they do indicate the importance of using a structural model as a basis for providing consistent and justifiable productivity measures, as well as for motivating adaptations for characteristics of the production process other than technical change which are possible to identify and measure. Much of the remainder of this text will be devoted to how the development and use of such structural models might be accomplished.

2.4 The Linkage Between Technical Change and Productivity Growth Measures

We began this chapter by defining productivity growth as the difference between the growth rates of output production and input use, or a change in the output to input ratio. The idea behind this is that this difference reflects a change in technology that allows more output to be produced from a given amount of inputs. Developing the theoretical linkage between technical change and productivity growth involves formalizing this concept of productivity using a production function as a representation of the production technology, and considering its implications for the definition of technical change, as we will do in this section. Further elaboration of this idea will provide the basis for construction of a theoretical model of the production structure in later chapters.

Solow [1958] was one of the first researchers to motivate the use of a production function for measuring productivity growth.[17] This development is based on a production function of the form $Y = f(v,t)$,

[17] This is often jointly attributed to Tinbergen [1942].

where t represents technology, generally proxied by a time counter, and v is a vector of J inputs with elements v_j, as in Chapter 1. Using this function, we can express the change in output with a change in time, dY/dt, as

$$\frac{dY}{dt} = \sum_j \frac{\partial f}{\partial v_j}\frac{dv_j}{dt} + \frac{\partial f}{\partial t}. \tag{2.4}$$

Rewriting this expression in terms of Y instead of f, dividing by Y to put it in proportionate terms, recognizing that $\partial f/\partial v_j$ is by definition equal to MP_j (the marginal product of input j), and rearranging, results in

$$\begin{aligned} \frac{\partial Y/\partial t}{Y} &= \frac{\partial \ln Y}{\partial t} = \frac{dY/dt}{Y} - \sum_j \frac{MP_j v_j}{Y}\frac{dv_j/dt}{v_j} \\ &= \frac{\dot{Y}}{Y} - \sum_j \frac{MP_j v_j}{Y}\frac{\dot{v}_j}{v_j} = \epsilon_{Yt} \end{aligned} \tag{2.5}$$

where the time derivative is represented by "$\cdot$", and ϵ_{Yt} represents the technological or technical change – the output change not accounted for by changes in inputs and the input mix.

Substituting further requires recognizing that in profit maximizing equilibrium MP_j equals p_j/p_Y.[18] This can be motivated by minimizing costs ($C = \Sigma_j p_j v_j$) subject to an output constraint ($Y - f(X) = 0$) to generate the first order conditions $p_j = \lambda \cdot (\partial f/\partial v_j)$; recognizing that the Lagrange multiplier λ represents the change in the objective function given a relaxation of the constraint, or marginal cost (MC); and then using the profit maximization result that $MC = p_Y$ in equilibrium to complete the equilibrium condition. Alternatively, direct maximization of profits specified in terms of inputs ($\pi = p_Y \cdot f(v) - \Sigma_j p_j v_j$) results in the first order conditions $p_Y \cdot (\partial f/\partial v_j) = p_j$.

[18] Notice the dependence of this derivation on instantaneous adjustment since the market price reflects the marginal product, which implies full capacity utilization. This assumption will need to be relaxed once we consider the impact of fixity and therefore non-optimal capacity utilization. This also depends on perfect competition because we are relying on the equality of the value of the marginal product, $MP_j p_Y$, and p_j.

Given a profit maximization model of firm behavior with perfect competition and instantaneous adjustment, therefore, (2.5) becomes

$$\begin{aligned} \frac{\partial Y/\partial t}{Y} &= \frac{\partial \ln Y}{\partial t} = \frac{dY/dt}{Y} - \sum_j \frac{p_j v_j}{p_Y Y} \frac{dv_j/dt}{v_j} \\ &= \frac{\dot{Y}}{Y} - \sum_j \frac{p_j v_j}{p_Y Y} \frac{\dot{v}_j}{v_j} = \frac{\dot{Y}}{Y} - \Sigma_j S_j \frac{\dot{v}_j}{v_j} = \epsilon_{Yt}. \qquad (2.6) \end{aligned}$$

Since $d \ln v_j/dt = (d\dot{v}_j/dt)/v_j$, it is clear that this measure is identical to the productivity growth expression we have been working with so far. Technical change can therefore be given a formal definition that coincides with our conceptual idea of productivity growth, given certain assumptions.

An even more simple and specific derivation of this equivalence of the productivity residual and a measure of technical change may be developed if the production process can be represented by a Cobb-Douglas production function. This simplicity arises due to a restrictive substitution assumption; by construction price and demand changes exactly offset each other to keep the shares constant when a Cobb-Douglas function is assumed. This is a straightforward result obtainable by specifying the production function as

$$Y = A \cdot \Pi_j v_j^{\lambda_j}, \qquad (2.7)$$

so that

$$S_j = (\partial f/\partial v_j) \cdot v_j/Y = \lambda_j \cdot A \cdot \sum_j v_j^{\lambda_j}/Y = \lambda_j,$$

where A represents technical change, as in Solow [1958], and Π_j represents a product over all the j values. In this case the production function can be written as:

$$Y = A \cdot \Pi_j v_j^{S_j}, \quad \text{so} \quad \ln Y = \ln A + \sum_j S_j \ln v_j. \qquad (2.8)$$

Taking derivatives, this implies that

$$d \ln Y/dt = \partial \ln A/\partial t + \sum_j S_j d \ln v_j/dt,$$

so

$$\partial \ln A/\partial t = d\ln Y/dt - \sum_j S_j d\ln v_j/dt = d\ln Y/dt - \sum_j \lambda_j d\ln v_j/dt.$$

$\partial \ln A/\partial t$ therefore captures the technical change component earlier denoted ϵ_{Yt} – the percent output shift in the production function due to technical progress from (2.6), with constant shares determined only by the λ_j parameters.

More general parameterized productivity growth specifications are obtainable by assuming a more "flexible" functional form for the production function which allows further unconstrained representation of substitution among inputs. The transcendental logarithmic (translog) function developed by Christensen, Jorgenson and Lau [1973], for example, places an *a priori* restriction on substitution elasticities and can be interpreted as a second order Taylor series approximation (in logarithms) to an arbitrary production function.

It turns out that specifying a translog function (which is a second order extension of the Cobb-Douglas), implies a Divisia indexing procedure; the share weight is variable rather than constant since the shares are a more complex combination of parameters and data.[19] The "exact" or "superlative" correspondence between the translog function and the Divisia (or Törnqvist when discrete) index was recognized by Diewert [1976]. We will return to a more complete discussion of duality theory and different functional forms, and their implications for productivity measurement and index number construction, in subsequent chapters.

[19] The Törnqvist index simply looks like a share weighted sum of growth rates, like the aggregate input measure in (2.6), where the share weights are generally measured as the sample mean between two successive data points (see Chapter 6 for elaboration of this measure). Direct use of the translog function, however, identifies the determinants of the shares in terms of exogenous variables facing the firm since the shares depend on the marginal products and the marginal products depend on all arguments of the production function.

2.5 The Relationship Between Primal and Dual Measures of Productivity Growth

A further extension to productivity growth measurement, formally motivated by developments in duality theory, is to a cost-side rather than production- or primal-side measure. The concept of a cost-side productivity growth measure was implied by the initial definition of productivity growth presented above. The idea is that if a given output may be produced using less inputs once productivity growth has occurred, that output may by definition be produced at lower cost; cost diminution for a given output level is "dual" to output augmentation for a given set of inputs. Using this notion, and the representation of productivity growth based on the production function already developed, we can easily develop the dual productivity growth concept from the cost function.

The formalization of a cost diminution measure of productivity change is based on the definition of a cost function $C(p, Y, t)$ as the lowest production cost possible given Y, t and the vector of input prices p. It therefore reflects the information contained in the production function (this will be formally developed further in Chapter 5). The change in costs with a change in t (between two periods) holding Y and p fixed, which is how we have motivated the cost-side productivity growth measure in words, can be written as $\partial C/\partial t$, or, in proportional terms, $\partial \ln C/\partial t$. Using the cost function, we write this as

$$\begin{aligned} \frac{\partial C/\partial t}{C} &= \frac{\partial \ln C}{\partial t} = \frac{dC/dt}{C} - \frac{dY/dt}{Y} - \sum_j \frac{p_j v_j}{C} \frac{dp_j/dt}{p_j} \\ &= \frac{\dot{c}}{c} - \sum_j \frac{p_j v_j}{C} \frac{\dot{p}_j}{p_j} = \epsilon_{Ct}, \end{aligned} \tag{2.9}$$

where as before $c = C/Y$. Similarly to the development of the primal-side measure above, this is based on taking the total derivative

$$\frac{dC}{dt} = \sum_j \frac{\partial C}{\partial p_j} \frac{dp_j}{dt} + \frac{\partial C}{\partial Y} \frac{dY}{dt} + \frac{\partial C}{\partial t} \tag{2.10}$$

and substituting.

Specifically, since constant returns to scale are traditionally assumed (we will generalize this later), the cost function can be written as $C(p,Y,t) = Y \cdot c(p,t)$, where $c = C/Y$ is unit costs. This implies that

$$d\ln C/dt - d\ln Y/dt = d\ln(C/Y)/dt = d\ln c/dt,$$

which is used to obtain the last expression in (2.9). Constant returns to scale also implies that $\epsilon_{CY} = \partial C/\partial Y(Y/C) = 1$, which causes the cost elasticity that otherwise would multiply the $d\ln Y/dt$ term to drop out.[20] Finally, a duality theory result known as Shephard's lemma says that for a cost function satisfying standard regularity properties, $\partial C/\partial p_j = v_j$ = the cost minimizing demand for v_j, which allows the substitution for the $\partial C/\partial p_j$ terms.

It turns out that, with constant returns to scale, this dual concept of productivity growth is equivalent to the original primal specification of productivity growth. This can be illustrated as in Figure 2.1.

Consider a firm producing according to a constant returns to scale technology but with some inputs fixed in the short run. The firm in equilibrium may be thought of as producing at the point where the given short run average cost curve ($SRAC_0$) is tangent to the long run curve ($LRAC_0$), at output level Y_0.[21]

When technical change occurs between two periods, the cost of producing any given output level drops. This is represented by a downward shift in the long run average cost function. Given the available capital stock (for whatever fixed inputs distinguish the short run from the long run), therefore, more output can be produced. This output level, Y_1, is reflected by the tangency between the new short run

[20] Note again the importance of constant returns to scale for these derivations. Ohta [1975] outlined the adjustment to these measures when constant returns to scale does not exist. This was extended by Morrison [1985a, 1986a]. These extensions to the traditional framework will be taken into account later in the text.

[21] Recall that the long run equilibrium is not defined here for a perfectly competitive profit maximizing firm that has a constant returns technology. Some hand waving must therefore be done to motivate the reasoning behind long run behavior of the firm, unless we allow for one of these three restrictions to be relaxed. This is often accomplished by assuming the firm is a cost minimizer, producing output level Y_0 at the lowest cost possible.

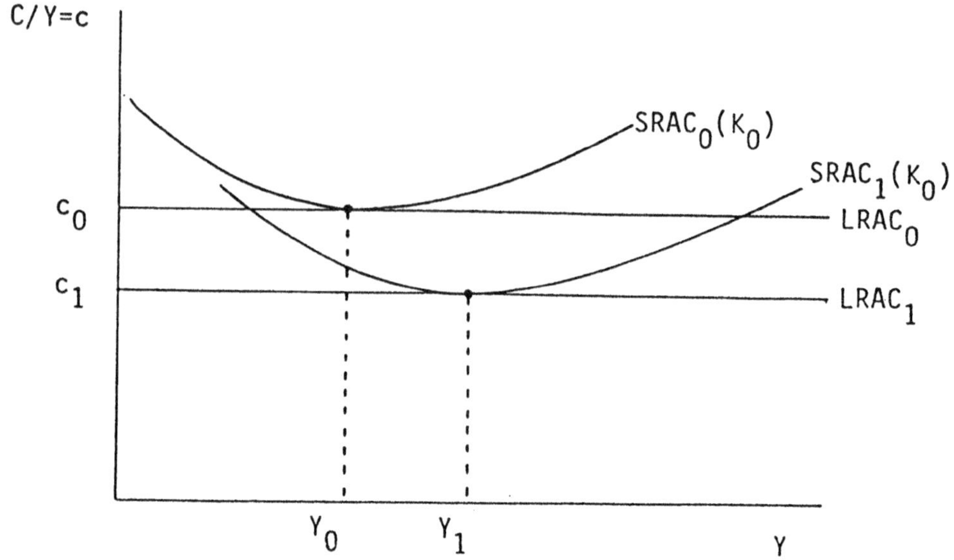

Fig.2.1. Dual Concept of productivity growth

average cost curve ($SRAC_1$) and the corresponding long run curve ($LRAC_1$). In this case the potential total cost decrease (in proportional terms), represented by the difference between c_0 and c_1 at any given output level is exactly equivalent to the possible proportional increase in output from Y_0 to Y_1. This captures the duality of the two notions of productivity growth.

Ohta demonstrated this result analytically using the expressions for primal and dual cost productivity growth (2.6) and (2.9). To outline his argument, first note that if cost is defined as

$$C = \sum_j p_j v_j,$$

$(dC/dt)/C$ can be written as

$$\left(\sum_j v_j dp_j/dt + \sum_j p_j dv_j/dt \right) /C,$$

or

$$\frac{dC/dt}{C} = \sum_j \frac{p_j v_j}{C} \frac{dp_j/dt}{p_j} + \sum_j \frac{p_j v_j}{C} \frac{dv_j/dt}{v_j}. \tag{2.11}$$

Substituting this into (2.9) yields:

$$-\frac{\partial \ln C}{\partial t} = -\epsilon_{Ct} = \frac{dY/dt}{Y} - \sum_j \frac{p_j v_j}{C}\frac{dv_j/dt}{v_j} = \epsilon_{Yt}, \qquad (2.12)$$

recognizing that $p_Y Y = C$ with perfect competition, constant returns to scale and full equilibrium, which for the moment are maintained hypotheses.

These primal and dual productivity growth measure expressions have provided the basis for measurement of productivity growth using both accounting and parametric approaches, since the accounting practices can be theoretically justified by empirically estimable production and cost functions. The theoretical basis has also provided a stepping stone toward extension of the measures to relax some of the assumptions that the simple formulations maintain, including instantaneous adjustment (full capacity utilization).

* * * * *

We will return to overview some of these empirical and theoretical developments and extensions in later chapters. In the next chapter, however, we first consider the traditional and theoretical measurement issues surrounding another performance indicator which we have seen has close linkages with productivity growth – capacity utilization. Once we have an integrated theoretical framework in which to consider both these measures, we can then develop a consistent approach for measurement of the different economic performance indexes and assessment of their interactions.

Chapter 3

The Measurement and Interpretation of Capacity Utilization

Recognition of scarcity or fixity of resources is the key to development of the concepts of capacity and capacity utilization. The degree of scarcity, in fact, uniquely determines the amount of available capacity because "capacity" refers to the amount of resources – say fixed capital and/or labor and energy resources – one has available to "utilize" for production of output. If "not enough" (somehow defined) output is being produced, we say that capacity is underutilized. People could potentially obtain more goods and services at lower cost given the available inputs and technology.

This motivation implies that the concepts of capacity and capacity utilization have an economic basis because they can be expressed in terms of the optimization of firms given these available inputs – full utilization suggests the "best" use of a given amount of scarce factors. In this sense variations in capacity utilization also have connotations about efficiency and welfare, similarly to changes in productivity growth.

An economic basis for definition of capacity utilization is not only important for purposes of its measurement and interpretation, and for comparing its movements to other indicators which depend on firm behavior, but also for motivating its use. Capacity utilization variation has been used as an explanation of many types of economic phenomena, including not only productivity changes but also investment and inflation. The fundamental economic nature of these connections is clear when we consider what type of "capacity" situation would stimulate these economic phenomena. Investment does not take place after the existing capital reaches its "maximum" 24 hour production level, but before this – when the firm feels it is "utilizing" the given stock too heavily to be economic. Similarly, inflationary pressure does not start when inputs are utilized at their "maximum" levels – like three shifts a day and a full employment level for labor – but before this. Recognition of the economic foundations of phenomena such as investment and inflation implies that an economic basis for understanding their determinants, such as capacity utilization, is crucial.

Measures of capacity and capacity utilization have long been produced, but the traditional measures ignore their inherent economic foundations. In this chapter we consider the traditional motivation and measurement of capacity utilization, and how this relates to a more economic notion of utilization. This provides the foundation for recognizing the linkages between productivity and capacity utilization, in their joint determination of the overall efficient usage of scarce inputs, in subsequent chapters. It also motivates application of capacity utilization measures to analysis of production processes of firms, and corresponding decisions such as investment.

In the first Section (3.1) of this chapter standard measures of capacity utilization are outlined, and the "mechanical" nature of their construction are highlighted, as are the resulting interpretational problems that cause difficulties with application of the measures to economic issues. In Section 3.2 the economic nature of the idea of capacity utilization is discussed in detail, and a model within which capacity and capacity utilization may be measured is introduced. This model provides the initial theoretical structure necessary to separately identify the utilization and productivity components of overall

measures of growth. Section 3.3 outlines some extensions of these short run models that can be important for modeling investment behavior and capacity utilization. The final Section 3.4 then shows how the usual output-side notion of capacity utilization may be related to a cost-oriented concept and measure.

3.1 An Overview of Standard Measures of Capacity Utilization

The level of capacity available to a firm is determined by technology and the resources available for production in the short run. In other words, output is constrained by available levels of given inputs, which may be fixed because of overall scarcity or due to short run constraints on adjustment. If all factors of production are completely variable the problem of capacity, as such, does not exist; available inputs will be utilized in terms of their most effective long run equilibrium mixes given their supply functions and therefore costs, and a given "capacity" is simply not defined. Full utilization – in an economic sense – of available inputs will be the norm. Therefore, to determine capacity and capacity utilization one must identify the input fixities which result in non-optimal capacity utilization, the levels of the fixed inputs, and the magnitude of the constraints these fixities impose on production.

Most approaches to capacity utilization measurement are based on developing a measure of capacity output, Y^*, and comparing this to actual output, Y, by forming the ratio Y/Y^* to generate a capacity utilization index. The differences between the alternative traditional measures, and between these and more economic theory-based measures, depend on the methods used to measure Y^*. The Y^* implied by economic analysis of fixity is the "best" output level given available fixed inputs or "capacity". However, although they vary widely, the methods used to compute the traditional measures tend to be mechanical. They typically ignore the fact that capacity is ultimately based on an economic concept of optimality because of its dependence on firms' behavior and constraints. Instead traditional methods are generally based on some physical notion of "maximum" output.

The mechanical aspect of the traditional measurement procedures can be demonstrated by considering the notions underlying physical measures of capacity and capacity utilization. In this context the idea of "slack capacity" is generally motivated in terms of wasting "potential" production from existing capital. Capacity output Y^* should thus represent the *maximum* level of production the capital stock is technically capable of generating. This engineering notion of capacity is, however, not very interpretable due to its lack of an economic basis. This is evident from a number of limitations of this idea of a physical maximum.

One problem is that the potential or maximum capacity is generally defined only in terms of a given amount of capital, rather than more generally in terms of a combination of inputs.[1] In fact some studies develop the idea of capacity in the context of *capital utilization* rather than capacity utilization, directly implying that capital is the only important fixed input.[2] However, since capacity utilization reflects overall firm behavior, it really depends on all fixed factors facing firms.

This problem is similar to those that arise for single factor productivity measurement. For example, as noted in Chapter 2, labor and energy have each implicitly been considered the only important input when they have been the focus of single-factor productivity measures. Using these measures to evaluate economic performance suggests that maximum output per unit of labor (energy) input is the primary goal. As stated in our discussion of single factor productivity measures, however, scarcity has to do with all inputs, not just one. Similarly, capacity utilization measurement should take into account all scarce inputs. For a firm this means recognizing fixities in addition to constraints on adjustment of capital, such as the limited stock of skilled labor available to the firm in the short run.

In addition, sometimes capacity utilization measures are based on

[1] This distinction must be made as long as more inputs exhibit fixity than just capital, so capacity depends on all the fixed inputs.

[2] Betancourt and Clague [1981], for example, focus primarily on capital utilization.

the use of only one variable input. Foss [1963], for example, used the ratio of actual electricity consumption to the maximum possible electricity consumption, where the latter is obtained using the rated horsepower capacity of electric machinery to construct a measure of capital utilization. (Variable) labor use per unit of capital is also important, however, to determine utilization of capital; the combination of capital over stock is "utilized".

More fundamentally, the idea of physical maximization is often simply not well defined. For example, is the capacity of a machine determined by its production if it were run 24 hours a day? A full shift? Two? Running a machine at full speed all the time may not be a sustainable situation because of down time for repair and maintenance. Should this be allowed for? Problems also arise if there are insufficient amounts of other scarce resources, such as labor and energy, to reach "maximum" capacity.

Similar questions arise if fixity of labor and thus the "maximum" physical contribution of labor is taken into consideration. For example, to determine this maximum the relevant measure of labor input is unclear. If we try to include all unemployed laborers past the "natural" rate, we need to determine what this rate is; it could be argued that "maximum" implies it is zero. We might even want to take into account other potential laborers who do not show up in the unemployment statistics. The question of work week suggests that the maximum contribution might be considered to be more than a 40 hour work week – but how much more?

In addition to problems determining which inputs to take into account for capacity utilization measurement, therefore, difficulties arise simply defining the maximum. Together these problems imply that the physical idea of capacity may not provide a very comprehensible and applicable measure. Unfortunately, however, standard published capacity utilization indexes generally have some kind of mechanical measurement orientation, and thus are characterized by these types of interpretation difficulties.[3]

Survey methods are often used to measure capacity utilization; in

[3]See Schnader [1984] for further discussion of these measures.

the U.S. the index that has been published by the Bureau of the Census is representative of this type of measure. Others include the McGraw-Hill and the Bureau of Economic Analysis measures. These measures are based on survey questions which sometimes make a distinction between "preferred" and "maximum" levels of capacity. The first is an economics-oriented question and responses suggest that this "preferred" measure of capacity often results in a capacity utilization ratio of greater than one; firms say they would be better off if they contracted their current output levels, implying that they are considering the cost impact of fixed input constraints. The responses to this question are, however, generally ignored due to perceived ambiguity of the responses. Thus the focus is on the latter, which involves the idea of maximum capacity. More generally, a pervasive problem with survey data is that different firms may apply disparate interpretations to the survey questions, especially when the criteria the question is based on are somewhat nebulous. This can cause difficulties interpreting the resulting numbers.

One of the most common measures of capacity utilization in the U.S. is the Federal Reserve Board (FRB) measure. This is an eclectic measure taking many things into account, including survey information. Construction of the FRB measure of capacity utilization is based on FRB industrial production data, McGraw-Hill survey data and capital stock and expenditure data. Survey data by industry is used to generate a series of "long term trends" in capacity, which are then correlated with industrial capacity measures generated using estimates of gross capital stock and survey data on capacity expansion, and then aggregated. This measure, therefore, does not completely rely on a physical or engineering notion of capacity but it is not clear what it does rely on. It is based on a mechanical rather than economic evaluation of the maximum use of available capital, and on data analysis – both statistical and judgmental – rather than on economic theory.

The construction of the Wharton capacity utilization index poses other types of problems. This measure is a "trend through peaks" approach. Basically, it is a maximum output (Y) per unit of capital (K) measure linking the maximum Y/K point to determine the potential between peaks. After the last peak the numbers are extrap-

olated. This measure has definitional problems because the maximum output to capital ratio may vary with changing economic factors, so the peak level may shift. Underlying this problem is the issue that other factors are important and not taken into account; this is a single factor measure that ignores scarcity of other factors. Because the measure is not based on analysis of the production structure in general, the numbers are difficult to interpret because the peaks are not equal and there is no explanation of why they differ, yet all are called "1.0".[4]

Another type of capacity utilization measure sometimes constructed depends on the notion that the full employment level determines the possible or potential Y^*.[5] This idea can be based simply on the "maximum" possible level of labor input, although it has often also included other inputs which are assumed to be important to employ "fully". When only one input is considered, problems similar to those discussed for the one-factor Wharton measure arise. Also, even if more inputs are taken into account, a definitional problem arises concerning what "full" or maximum labor (or other factor) employment actually is.

A number of problems therefore exist with standard mechanical capacity utilization measures that cause interpretational difficulties. The overall problem is that the "maximization" problem is not well defined. Since economic theory is based on the notion of optimization (subject to constraints), however, this theory provides a potentially important basis for formalizing how the idea of capacity utilization might more effectively be developed and applied.

---

[4]The aggregate Wharton measure, however, never reaches 1.0 because it is a summation of indexes constructed for each industry separately and at least some of these will fall short of one.

[5]See, for example, Okun [1962] and Fromm, Klein, Ripley and Crawford [1979].

3.2 Incorporating Economics into Capacity Utilization Measurement

The short run responses of firms to constraints such as a quasi-fixed capital or labor stock depends on economic factors. These responses take the form of temporary or subequilibrium pricing and input demand decisions that differ from those in the long run when full adjustment, and therefore a steady state, is attainable. This behavior is well defined by economic theory; it involves economic signals such as the shadow values of quasi-fixed inputs. The deviations of these implicit values from their corresponding market prices indicate the magnitude of the existing disequilibrium, and therefore provide information on the constraints imposed by fixity. The consequence of this disequilibrium for the firm is to stimulate investment or disinvestment as well as to establish the short run variable input demand response that determines utilization of the fixed inputs – of existing capacity. Nonoptimal utilization of capacity is therefore a short run notion.

Constructing economic measures of capacity utilization involves representing fixity of factors and determining what production level would "optimally" be supported by these factors. If the demanded output level differs from this level, utilization of the fixed factors will not be optimal; full capacity utilization will not prevail. The optimal production level given short run constraints on adjustment is determined by what output would be produced in the steady state given the current levels of fixed factors (the level of "capacity"). This economic capacity level of production may be denoted Y^* as in Chapter 1, so capacity utilization Y/Y^* equals one when capacity is fully utilized – when the observed and optimal production levels coincide. Y^* is not, however, a "maximum" output, in the sense that the capacity utilization ratio can exceed, as well as fall short of, one; capacity can be over- as well as under-utilized in the economic sense.

The steady state output level Y^* is the production level where the fixities the firm faces are not binding, or where short run costs incurred are also minimum long run costs. At this output level the firm would not wish to change the current level of capacity, so it is

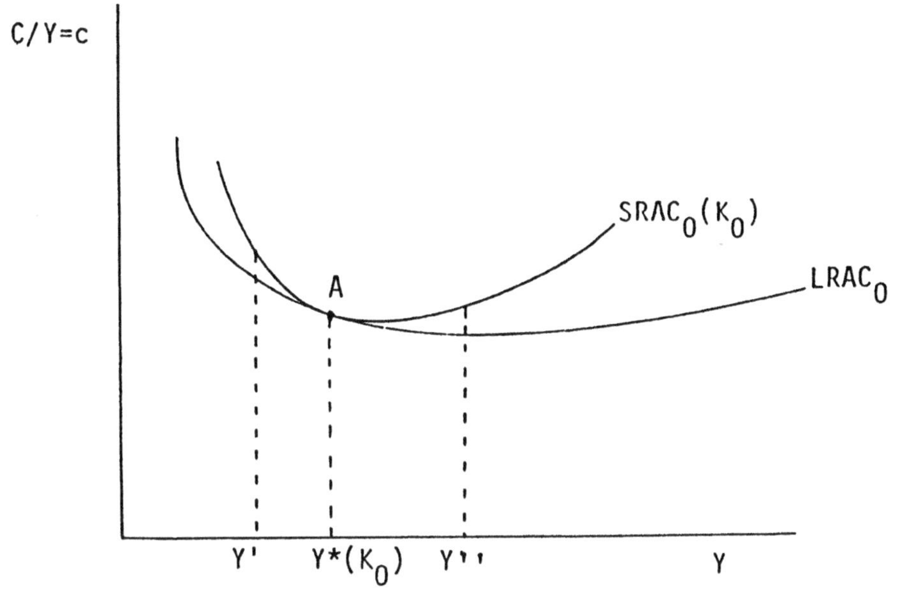

Fig.3.1. Nonconstant returns to scale

the economically "correct" production given existing capacity. With constant returns to scale this output is represented by the minimum point of the short run average cost (SRAC) curve which is tangent, by definition, to the flat long run average cost (LRAC) curve. If nonconstant returns to scale exist, the tangency of the SRAC and LRAC curves remains the relevant point determining Y^*, as shown in Figure 3.1; at this output the firm is in a steady state, even though the tangency does not reflect minimum possible unit costs.

The idea of measuring this tangency point as the "target" capacity output point was motivated by Klein [1960] and Hickman [1964], following Cassels [1937] who first noted that the minimum point on the cost function (long run in his treatment) was an important indicator of capacity.[6] The justification given by these authors was quite

[6] See Berndt, Morrison and Wood [1983] for further historical background and discussion of empirical work in this area, and Morrison [1987b] for one type of application of these ideas. Also see Gordon Winston [1977] for an outline of an integrated micro and macro analysis that focuses on this notion of microeconomic capacity, and Perloff and Wachter [1979] for a related treatment.

straightforward; if one wishes to determine how capacity utilization would affect other economic characteristics like investment behavior or prices, the steady state notion makes more sense than does a mechanical physical concept. Actual measurement of this point was not as straightforward at that time, however. To accomplish this the short run cost curves as well as the long run envelope must be estimated, which requires relatively sophisticated economic theory and econometric methods.

Recent developments in the theory of cost and production have provided a useful basis for measurement of these curves in the form of restricted or variable cost functions. These functions explicitly represent fixities and therefore are short run functions. Specifically, if a total cost function $C(p, Y, t)$ is specified, this implies that costs depend only on the prices of inputs, including any input that might potentially be thought of as fixed. This is not true in the short run, however. If, for example, capital (K) is fixed, then variable input demand and thus costs in the short run do not depend on the price but on the level of capital; if the price of capital changes no adjustment in capital is possible and therefore the other factors will not be affected. Thus, if fixities exist a restricted cost function of the form $G(p, t, Y, K)$ is relevant to represent short run costs, where $G(\cdot)$ captures variable costs, $p_K K$ are fixed costs, and short run total costs are defined as $C = G(\cdot) + p_K K$, which establishes the short run cost curves.

Using these functions and the relevant duality theory outlined in Chapter 5, we can define $-\partial G/\partial K = Z_K$ as the shadow value of capital – the value to the firm of having an extra unit of capital in terms of the reduction in variable inputs used to produce the given output. The corresponding "shadow cost function" is $C^* = G(\cdot) + Z_K K$. In a steady state, these two functions will coincide because capital will be demanded until its market price is equal to its shadow value to the firm, i.e., $p_K = Z_K$. However, in the short run this will not happen; if full equilibrium is unattainable the constraints resulting from the fixity will be reflected by the difference between Z_K and p_K.

Setting these two functions equal in this simple model with only one fixed input is equivalent to setting p_K and Z_K equal. If this were done and a corresponding value of K were solved for, this value would be the long run or steady state level of capital (K^*) given the output level and input prices faced by the firm. Substituting this into the expression for total costs identifies the long run cost curves.

Conversely, if the equality between p_K and Z_K were used to solve for a value of Y, then this value would be the steady state level of output (Y^*) given the capital level and input prices or the tangency between the given SRAC curve defined for the existing capital level and the LRAC curve. This therefore would be the "capacity" output.[7]

An alternative motivation for this steady state equality more clearly imposes the tangency between the SRAC and LRAC curves in terms of the definitions of the curves themselves. Briefly, when the SRAC and LRAC curves are tangent, short run marginal cost (SRMC) must equal long run marginal cost (LRMC) because the slopes of the two curves are equal at this output level. This can be formalized using the definitions

$$SRMC = \left.\frac{dC}{dY}\right|_{\Delta K=0} = \frac{\partial G}{\partial Y}, \tag{3.1}$$

and

$$LRMC = \frac{dC}{dY} = \frac{\partial G}{\partial Y} + \frac{\partial G}{\partial K}\frac{dK}{dY} + p_K\frac{dK}{dY}, \tag{3.2}$$

given the definition of total cost as $C = C(p,Y,K,t)$ where p_K is part of the p vector. Equating SRMC and LRMC and using the definition $Z_K \equiv -\partial G/\partial K$ thus results in the same steady state condition as before, namely, $Z_K = p_K$.

Thus, the information necessary to determine the tangency point of the short and long run average cost curves, reflecting the economic notion of capacity output, is captured by the variable cost function. This implies that once a functional form for $G(p,t,Y,K)$ and thus $Z_K(p,t,Y,K)$ is specified and estimated, $Y^*(p,t,Y,K)$ may be computed using parametric methods, even though Y^* cannot be identified

[7]It is important to recognize here that "capacity" in this example depends only on the fixed level of capital. However, other inputs might also be fixed, such as labor or other capital inputs. This will be further developed later.

directly from the data. In turn, the corresponding economic capacity utilization measure becomes $CU_y = Y/Y^*(p,t,Y,K)$.[8]

If demand is less than the output corresponding to the tangency of SRAC and LRAC, the measure reflects the existence of excess capital; $CU_y < 1$. However, as mentioned above, if demand is greater than that supported in the steady state by the existing stock of capital, this measure exceeds one, contrary to the mechanical measures which always fall short of one. This is the sense in which it represents optimal rather than maximal use of the given stock. In addition, the determinants of utilization are explicitly represented since Y^* is a function of all arguments of $G(\cdot)$.

The difference between the case where $CU_y < 1$ and $CU_y > 1$ was illustrated in Figure 3.1. If K_0 is the given level of capital, perhaps left over from a year before when the firm was in equilibrium with output demand at a different level, the corresponding short run average cost curve is $SRAC_0$. The long run curve which allows variation in all inputs is represented by $LRAC_0$. Since the only point where K_0 is an optimal (steady state or long run) level of capital is at point A, where $Y_0 = Y = Y^*$, this level of output is capacity output. If demand becomes larger than this ($Y'' > Y^*$) and capital cannot immediately adjust, then capital is overutilized; costs are higher than necessary in the long run to produce that output because too many variable inputs must be added to the now-scarce capital input ($Z_K > p_K$). If demand falls below Y^* ($Y' < Y^*$), then there is excess capacity; too much capital (and therefore fixed costs) is currently in place to produce at the lowest possible cost given the level of output Y' ($p_K > Z_K$).

It should be emphasized here that inputs other than capital can be considered fixed in this framework, and a corresponding value of CU_y defined. If, for example, labor is quasi-fixed due to short-term contracts, the shadow value of labor ($-\partial G/\partial L = Z_L$) will also differ from its market price (p_L), and the firm's capacity will depend on the given stock level of L as well as that for K. L rather than p_L will therefore

[8] Y can either be given to the firm, which is assumed in the cost function framework, or can be the optimal short run profit maximizing value of output the firm chooses. This short run profit maximizing value, Y', will not be equal to the capacity output level except in unusual circumstances.

appear as an argument of the variable cost function, which in this case reflects non-labor as well as non-capital costs. Thus the position of the $SRAC_0$ curve depends on both inputs. Y^* is then defined when both $Z_L = p_L$ and $Z_K = p_K$; Morrison [1982] has shown this can be computed by setting total costs $C = G(p, L, K, Y, t) + p_K K + p_L L$ equal to shadow costs $C^* = G(p, L, K, Y, t) + Z_K K + Z_L L$.[9]

More generally, with multiple fixed inputs C may be defined as $G(p, x, Y, t) + \Sigma_k p_k x_k$ and C^* as $G(p, x, Y, t) + \Sigma_k Z_k x_k$, where x is a vector of K fixed inputs x_k, p_k is the market price of x_k, and $Z_k = -\partial G/\partial x_k$. CU_y is of course still defined as the output level satisfying the equality $C^* = C$, although clearly the more quasi-fixed variables are taken into account the more possible combinations of their values could potentially satisfy this equality, as shown by Berndt and Fuss [1989].

Capacity and capital utilization therefore are distinguishable in this situation, whereas when only capital is fixed they coincide. This should be kept in mind throughout this text, although often the developments will be motivated in a fixed-capital-only context.[10] This is done only for simplicity of exposition; all the results carry over to more complete specifications.

It should also be noted that an explicit short-run long-run model has implications for capital investment modeling because if $Z_K > p_K$ the value of capital on the margin is greater than its market price, stimulating firms to purchase additional capital. This idea underlies construction of the measure known as Tobin's q, which compares the implicit or shadow value of a firm (measured by its stock market value in most cases) to its market replacement value (the book value of the firm). This comparison is carried out by generating a ratio of the two values, which will be larger than one when the shadow value

---

[9]Berndt and Fuss [1989] have discussed in detail the problems arising when trying to compute capacity utilization measures with multiple inputs and multiple outputs. Since total and shadow costs can be the same when shadow and market prices of each individual input deviate, for example, as long as they counteract each other, a unique measure of Y^* may not exist in this context.

[10]This less complete capacity utilization idea is more appropriately correctly called capital utilization. This distinction has been made, for example, in investment and capital utilization studies such as Bernstein and Nadiri [1988b].

of the firm exceeds its market price; clearly this is closely related to the economic concept of capacity utilization.

Although this highlights the similar foundations of investment indicators such as Tobin's q and our CU_y and Z_K measures, a number of differences exist between Tobin's q measures and the equivalent measure implied by our discussion of shadow values, Z_K/p_K. First, Hayashi [1982] has shown that average and marginal Tobin's q will coincide only when constant returns to scale exist, and standard Tobin's q computations are based on average values. Since Tobin's q compares total values, however, it can be thought of as a ratio of the average shadow and market prices of capital rather than marginal, the latter of which is implied by the comparison of Z_K and p_K.

Additional differences between the standard measures of Tobin's q and Z_K/p_K arise with respect to the computation of both the numerator and denominator. Most studies based on the determination of the shadow value Z_K depend not on a stock market rate but instead on an *ex-post* or residual computation of the price of capital[11] (with the implicit assumption that only capital is fixed) or a parametrically computed shadow value using the definition $-\partial G/\partial K = Z_K$. Computing the denominator as the firm's book value is also often questioned, since book value depends on accounting rather than economic principles. Instead, economists computing Z_K/p_K ratios tend to compute the market price as an *ex-ante* measure of capital price, as outlined in Chapter 6.[12]

Since investment and stock market values are generally thought of as important indicators of economic performance, substantial interest and literature has been generated about the theory of investment. Unfortunately most investment theories, including Tobin's q, have not had very much success at tracking or predicting trends in investment.[13] The idea of the deviation between Z_K and p_K being

[11]This is the basis of *ex-post* measures of capital in general, where the value of capital services is defined as $p_Y Y - G$, where p_Y is the price of Y, which reflects the "profits" of the firm after variable costs are paid. This idea is further developed in Chapter 6.

[12]A useful discussion of the measurement of both the *ex-ante* and *ex-post* price of capital is in Hulten [1986].

[13]See Berndt [1990] Chapter 6 for a detailed discussion of different investment theories and their empirical implementation.

an investment indicator has much promise, however, and suggests substantial interpretative power for CU_y indexes. If the interrelated determinants of changes in capacity utilization and investment can be identified, this suggests economic performance cannot only be mapped but also analyzed directly and affected by policy. This is highlighted by the strong relationship between high investment and productivity generally found in productivity growth studies.

3.3 Extensions to the Framework for Capacity Utilization Measurement

A framework that allows computation of shadow values and explicit determination of the arguments of the shadow value function is thus an important structure for analysis of investment and capacity utilization, and ultimately of the relationship between capacity utilization and productivity. The variable cost function framework, which includes fixed inputs as arguments of the cost function, and which we will be developing further in this text, provides such a structure. This type of framework is an extension of the traditional approach to investment modeling generally termed the "neoclassical" approach, into which short run fixities are explicitly incorporated. Other conceptually important adaptations that further facilitate interpretation, including consideration of dynamics, expectations formation and returns to scale, are also possible to incorporate to facilitate modeling and assessment of capacity utilization.

The problem of dynamic adjustment arises when one asks *why* fixity might occur, and how adjustment takes place if levels of quasi-fixed inputs deviate from their steady state values. In the current literature fixity is generally attributed to adjustment costs. The idea of adjustment costs is that some inputs require slow adjustment because the faster you attempt to adjust the more expensive it becomes. This is, in a sense, a formalization of the old adage "haste makes waste"; costs are incurred when investment takes place, and costs increase at the margin (the function is convex). These adjustment costs may occur for most inputs, and may be internal or external.

Many reasons for the existence of adjustment costs for capital may be postulated. For example, they may arise due to expenses from ordering or bolting down machinery; variable inputs may be necessary to use to put capital in place rather than to produce output. A second type of adjustment cost might stem from increased outlays to other firms; in response to increased demand for their product firms producing and supplying the machinery may have to increase overtime and therefore charge more for their product, or they may have to have more field people available to install or maintain the machinery. The first type of adjustment costs are generally called internal since they affect the internal workings of the firm. The second are called external since they imply a rising supply curve for capital due to the market configuration.

These internal and external adjustment costs could, of course, also arise for inputs other than capital. For labor, for example, hiring, firing and training costs can be considered as internal costs; funds that otherwise could be used to pay labor for production are instead used for hiring – to set up a personnel or training department. A rising supply curve for labor could also be generated (and therefore external costs incurred) if, for example, it takes longer to train more marginal recruits or is increasingly more expensive to transport them to the area in which the firm is located.

Incorporating adjustment costs in a model not only makes the model more complete, but also provides motivation for an investment equation that determines how much adjustment will take place in each period. It also implies that inputs are not completely fixed in the short run (except the "very" short run) but instead partially adjust. This changes our short run analysis slightly, and complicates defining and interpreting capacity utilization somewhat. Current adjustment must be taken into account because "fixed" input stocks are moving toward an equilibrium. Thus investment must be included as an argument of the shadow value of the (quasi-)fixed inputs.

Adjustment costs cause additional complexities for the modeling of firm behavior because expectations of the future become important when current behavior depends on anticipated values of exogenous variables. This must be the case when slow adjustment takes place because the firm's manager knows that next period he/she will be stuck with the decisions made now. Therefore if a change in exogenous variables is experienced that the firm manager perceives as temporary, very little adjustment might be expected to take place. However, if the change is permanent, movement toward a new long run level of the stock based on this same exogenous change may be more justified.

Although this extension is important, little work on capacity utilization has dealt with it. Morrison [1985b], however, has shown that, as might be expected, the present-valued and current-valued optimal levels of capacity utilization will not coincide when future expectations are important. For example, if the firm expects increased demand over time and wishes to begin to expand the scale of operations in anticipation of this, in terms of current numbers the firm may be thought to be operating with excess capacity ($CU_y < 1$) but in terms of a present value computation of future profits it could be at an optimal level.[14]

One other adaptation that is useful to consider briefly here is for components of the capital stock that might not be "productive" in the sense of producing observed output, such as pollution abatement capital that is regulated to be in place and produces a cleaner environment rather than measured product. Since the firm does not have a choice about this input, measured capacity utilization could differ depending on how much of the capital stock is not a choice variable.

Morrison [1988b], for example, has shown how capacity utilization will change due to changes in "regulatory capital" (R) by taking elasticities of capacity utilization with respect to the level of R.[15] The results imply, as would be expected, that regulation has a negative impact on capacity utilization. Given a constant output level,

[14]See Morrison [1985b] for a further formalization of this problem and empirical results for U.S. manufacturing.

[15]This type of elasticity, of course, can be taken with respect to any variable which determines Y^*, which, in turn, is any argument which enters the variable cost and therefore shadow value function.

increasing R implies more capacity to utilize but no growth in output demand to raise utilization. Thus the valuation of R on the margin drops, as does capacity utilization. This extension is further developed in Chapter 9.

A final point to highlight about the methodologies used to deal with the issue of utilization is how one alternative approach is related to our treatment of capacity utilization. In particular, Jorgenson and Griliches [1967] presented an important contribution to the literature on productivity and capital utilization which atttempted to "internalize" utilization of capital by measuring capital in the production function as utilized capital, or "true" capital services, rather than just assuming capital services were proportional to the stock. This was accomplished using the Foss [1963] estimates mentioned above; Jorgenson and Griliches multiplied the estimated capital stock by Foss's electric motor utilization index (U) for manufacturing to generate a measure of capital, K', that can be written as $K' = K \cdot U$ or $\ln K' = \ln K + \ln U$. K' was then assumed to be the relevant, effective or quality-adjusted capital stock for the production function, which can be written as $Y = f(K', L, t)$.

This K' expression can be written in a slightly more general form as $\ln K' = \ln K + b \ln U$, which is a simple hedonic expression for capital with the b parameter determining the impact of utilization on capital. It might well be thought that $b < 1$ rather than being equal to one, since the electricity-based index might vary more than an aggregate measure utilization of capital. If so, the Griliches-Jorgenson procedure is too restrictive and can be extended using hedonic methods to estimate b.[16]

In fact, this approach can be further extended to consider the effect on "quality-adjusted" capital of other factors. Berndt [1983] and Berndt and Wood [1984, 1987], for example, evaluated the impact

[16]It should be noted here that this can be thought of as recognizing a type of "embodied" as contrasted to "disembodied" technical change; compositional and other changes in the capital stock could result in extra-efficiency of capital independently of an overall isoquant shift. This distinction has been the basis of some controversy in a number of studies. For a useful overview of the literature and recent empirical application distinguishing between these two different factors affecting efficiency, see Berndt and Kolstad [1987].

of changes in the price of energy on the use of capital services; they interpreted this in terms of obsolescence. Morrison and Nelson [1989] have also considered the effect of the vintage structure on effective capital services in a similar framework.

In these studies, however, utilization was not an argument of the quality of capital and therefore was not in the hedonic function. Instead, if capacity utilization is to be assessed in the framework we have been developing above, the computation of Z_K should be based on the quality-adjusted or effective level of the capital stock rather than the measured level but utilization is not an argument of this effective level. In other words, K' will be an argument of Z_K since it is an argument of the production function and therefore the restricted cost function, but if CU_y is also a determinant of K' double counting occurs.[17] In this sense capacity utilization is endogenous rather than being an exogenous argument of the quality of capital function.

This underscores some important differences between the ideas of capital and capacity utilization, and among utilization and other determinants of effective capital services such as obsolescence. The Griliches-Jorgenson framework assumed that only capital determined capacity; it is based on a capital utilization rather than a capacity utilization concept. They also employed a rather questionable mechanical measure of utilization and implicitly a restricted hedonic equation. Finally, Griliches-Jorgenson did not recognize the importance of fixity for establishing the value of capital (or other fixed inputs), but instead attempted directly to adjust the quantity of capital for utilization.

Although it is not valid to both do this adjustment and construct the utilization measure Y/Y^*, the hedonic approach may be useful to incorporate other determinants of capital (or other input) effectiveness into the analysis; the hedonic approach can be used to augment the production theory-based model which incorporates a more general concept of utilization. It can be used to identify and include aspects of the production structure that otherwise would be difficult to untangle because they directly affect certain inputs – the effect is "embodied".

---

[17] This is developed in more detail in Chapter 9.

In sum, the computation of capacity utilization therefore requires a short run-long run model, but can include a number of different determinants if it appears they are important for the firm or industry in question. Clearly, additional extensions that have not been referred to here can be made along the lines of those mentioned. Once it is recognized that capacity is dependent on fixity, and that capacity utilization depends on the relationship between the fixities and the output produced, extensions are reasonably straightforward and result in increased interpretability of the estimated indexes. They do, however, also add to the complexity of the model for empirical implementation.

Other difficulties with the economic measure also clearly exist. For example, some important questions were raised by Klein in 1960 regarding whether economic measures of capacity output suffer from aggregation problems. I.e., capacity outputs for firms might all be increasing, and yet industry capacity output may not be consistent with the sum of the firm's individual capacity outputs because of, say, downward sloping industry demand, or upward sloping supply curves for inputs. This implies a problem with empirical implementation of the framework for constructing aggregate economic capacity utilization measures.

Although this is a problem, it is true for most applied economic research using aggregate data, and it is not at all clear what is best to do about it.[18] If we address the issue of the aggregation level at which a production or cost function is estimated econometrically, this implies that estimation should be carried out with very micro data. However, noise in the data, difficulty classifying firms by industry, and important systematic problems like materials bottlenecks and other supply constraints for the industry may plague these data, suggesting that aggregated data that is "cleaner" and has less "noise" may be preferable.[19] Therefore, it is not obvious which approach is prefer-

[18]This is dealt with in more detail in Chapter 10.

[19]This has been pointed out, for example, by de Leeuw [1962]. The interaction between micro capacity issues and their aggregate macroeconomic counterpart has been explored by Winston [1977].

able to pursue, although many economists in this line of research are attempting to construct and analyze more micro data sets.

3.4 Cost-Side or Dual Measures of Capacity Utilization

Since the output-side or primal capacity utilization measure is based on the comparison of shadow and market values, it might well be asked what the cost consequences are of being away from capacity output, rather than just what output deviation is experienced. This was the focus of the discussion about the investment determination ratio Z_K/p_K. The concept of the dual cost capacity utilization measure is also based on this question.

One of the important implications of this dual concept is that if short run average cost curves are rather flat, a primal capacity utilization measure may differ considerably from unity, but this might imply a relatively small increase in unit costs. This may provide insights about how critical deviations from full capacity utilization are to firms. In addition, since it is not necessary to solve an equality to estimate a level such as Y^*, cost measures may be more straightforward to calculate. They may even be computable using data such as those providing the basis for Tobin's q measures, although as mentioned earlier there are some economic problems with these measures.

The dual cost capacity utilization index, like the primal measure, is based on the deviation between shadow and market prices for the fixed factors. If the shadow value for an input exceeds its market price the input in question is being overutilized, and if this is true for all fixed inputs a general case of overutilization exists. This suggests that a dual capacity utilization measure can be constructed simply as $C^*/C = CU_c$, where, as before, C^* is shadow costs and C is total costs.

This measure indicates the overall deviation of shadow values from market prices and therefore represents the extent of adjustment pressure toward equilibrium for the firm. It also will always deviate from one in the same direction as the primal measure, given satisfaction of curvature properties for the variable cost function. If $C^* > C$, for example, the shadow value of capital (with capital the only fixed input) is greater than the market price, so not enough capital exists to produce the demanded output in the steady state and $Y > Y^*$. However, it is generally the case that the cost measure is less volatile than the output measure, as might be expected if average cost curves do not slope up dramatically.

Morrison [1985a] has shown that constructing this index is equivalent to computing the elasticity of costs with respect to capital, similarly to defining the cost-side measure of productivity growth as the elasticity with respect to t. With one quasi-fixed input, for example,

$$C = G(\cdot) + p_K K,$$

so

$$\epsilon_{CK} = \partial \ln C / \partial \ln K = (K/C) \cdot \partial(G + p_K K)/\partial K.$$

The equivalence of this with CU_c can be easily derived given the definition $Z_K \equiv -\partial G/\partial K$ from above as

$$\begin{aligned} CU_c &= \frac{C^*}{C} = \frac{G + Z_K K}{G + p_K K} = \frac{C - K(p_K - Z_K)}{C} \\ &= 1 - \frac{K(p_K + \partial G/\partial K)}{C} = 1 - \epsilon_{CK}, \end{aligned} \tag{3.3}$$

with only capital fixed. With multiple quasi-fixed inputs this is adjusted only slightly to read:

$$CU_c = 1 - \sum_k \epsilon_{Ck},$$

where k enumerates the K quasi-fixed factors x_k.

This definition of the dual cost capacity utilization index can be used to highlight the relationship between ϵ_{CK} or ϵ_{Ck} and the elasticity of costs with respect to output, $\epsilon_{CY} = \partial \ln C/\partial \ln Y$. This will be important for adjusting productivity growth measures for the impact of subequilibrium, where subequilibrium is the short run equilibrium that differs from full (steady state) equilibrium due to constraints from quasi-fixed inputs. This relationship is motivated by constructing an expression for the long run elasticity of costs with respect to output with only K fixed:

$$\begin{aligned} \epsilon_{CY}^{LR} \equiv \frac{d\ln C}{d\ln Y} &= \frac{\partial \ln C}{\partial \ln Y} + \frac{\partial \ln C}{\partial \ln K} = \epsilon_{CY} + \epsilon_{CK} = 1, \\ \text{so } \epsilon_{CY} &= 1 - \epsilon_{CK} = CU_c, \end{aligned} \tag{3.4}$$

where ϵ_{CY}^{LR} is the long run scale effect (the inverse of the returns to scale measure), and constant returns is assumed so

$$\epsilon_{CY}^{LR} = (dK/dY)Y/K = 1$$

and thus $dK/dY = K/Y$. This expression, derived by taking the total differential and substituting, can easily be extended with multiple quasi-fixed inputs to read $\epsilon_{CY} = 1 - \Sigma_k \epsilon_{Ck} = CU_c$. Thus, the short run cost elasticity with respect to output exactly determines capacity utilization when constant returns exists.[20] Capacity utilization can therefore be thought of as a short run scale effect; when capacity is overutilized costs in the short run increase more than proportionately with output, although they increase proportionately in the long run.

The equality of the ϵ_{CY} and CU_c measures is not maintained, however, when nonconstant returns exist. In this case, call the long run cost elasticity with respect to output η. With homotheticity, η will also reflect the elasticity of any input with respect to output in the long run; specifically $(dK/dY)Y/K = \eta$ with full adjustment to the long run. In this case manipulations equivalent to those in (3.4) result in $\epsilon_{CY} = \eta(1 - \epsilon_{CK})(= \eta(1 - \Sigma_k \epsilon_{Ck}))$ so the cost elasticity with respect to output includes both returns to scale and capacity utilization and the two must be untangled to identify their independent impacts.

This becomes even more complex when nonhomotheticity exists, since in this case $\partial C/\partial K(\partial K/\partial Y)(Y/C)$ cannot be written as $(\partial C/\partial K)K/C = \partial \ln C/\partial \ln K$ because $\partial K/\partial Y \neq K/Y \neq \eta K/Y$. In

[20] It is worth noting here that this value also reflects the ratio between marginal and average costs at this point, since $MC/AC = (\partial C/\partial Y)/(C/Y) = (Y/C)(\partial C/\partial Y)$.

particular, when this simplification is disallowed, (3.4) becomes:

$$\begin{aligned} \epsilon_{CY}^{LR} &\equiv \frac{d\ln C}{d\ln Y} = \frac{\partial C}{\partial Y}\frac{Y}{C} + \frac{\partial C}{\partial K}\frac{\partial K}{\partial Y}\frac{Y}{C} = \epsilon_{CY} + \epsilon_{CK}\epsilon_{KY} = \eta, \text{ or,} \\ \epsilon_{CY} &= \eta - \epsilon_{CK}\epsilon_{KY} = \eta\left(1 - \frac{\epsilon_{KY}}{\eta}\epsilon_{CK}\right) \end{aligned} \quad (3.5)$$

which makes it very difficult to untangle the differential scale effects, as well as complicates the computation of CU_c since it now becomes a combination of the scale effects; $CU_c = (1 - [\epsilon_{KY}/\eta]\epsilon_{CK})$.[21] An analogous result can easily be developed when fixed inputs other than capital exist.

Overall, these cost capacity utilization indicators, although sometimes somewhat complex to compute, provide useful interpretation for analysis of short run as compared to long run behavior, and for the interactions between scale and capacity utilization. Also, since they are directly dependent on the derivatives of the cost function rather than being solved for as with Y^*, the cost-based indexes facilitate computation of utilization biases (discussed in Chapter 4) and elasticities (computed as $\partial \ln CU_c/\partial \ln \phi$, where ϕ is any exogenous variable), further adding to the richness of the analysis that can be carried out in this framework.

In addition, any adjustments to the overall model that were discussed in the context of the primal capacity utilization measure can also be incorporated here. Shadow values with respect to pollution abatement capital, adaptation of the capital stock to be "quality-adjusted", and dynamic adjustment can, for example, be encompassed within the model.

Problems that were mentioned, however, like those with respect to complexity of the empirical model (and therefore limitations of data sets) and aggregation issues, also remain. The latter is particularly the case when returns to scale are incorporated because unless all firms are producing with respect to a constant returns to scale technology, it is not clear how to aggregate firms and obtain an interpretable measure of returns to scale. Even if interpretation is not

[21] See Morrison [1985a, 1988d] for further details of these computations and an empirical implementation.

transparent, however, it can be determined whether scale characteristics are important for representing the data.

A final point to emphasize is that assessment of the relationships between capacity utilization measures and other economic indicators are facilitated dramatically with the economic framework for capacity utilization from either the cost (dual) or output (primal) perspective. This is evident from the fact that either of these capacity utilization measures can exceed or fall short of unity, and this deviation from one has particular consequences.

For example, if the capacity utilization measure exceeds one investment will be positive because the stock constraint is binding – the shadow value of the fixed input(s) is greater than its market value. Similarly, other responses like increases in the price of output will likely occur because of inflationary pressures, and productivity (in particular with respect to the fixed input) will appear higher than it actually is because of overutilization of fixed inputs. This will occur only when $CU_c > 1$ and $CU_y > 1$, not when the capacity utilization ratio somehow "gets too close" to one, as is sometimes suggested with traditional measures. The linkages are therefore well defined within the economic theoretical model.

* * * * *

The development of the concept of capacity utilization in this chapter highlights the economic nature of this idea, and the resulting potential to formalize the notion of capacity utilization within a standard economic theory structure. The same type of structure was utilized, however, for motivating productivity growth measures in the last chapter. This suggests it can also be used to further explore the interrelationships between such economic performance indicators. In the next chapter we will pursue this to see how standard productivity growth measures can be corrected for fixity and adapted to identify the independent impacts of fixity (capacity utilization) and technical change.

Chapter 4

Interactions Among Measures of Productivity Growth, Returns to Scale and Capacity Utilization

So far we have considered traditional methodologies for productivity growth (technical change) and capacity utilization measurement. We have also touched briefly on the idea of scale economies and their relationship to capacity utilization measures. Although the standard theoretical motivations and measurement techniques for these different characteristics of the production process vary, it is clear they are closely related. In fact, erroneous measures may be generated if interactions among technical change, capacity utilization and scale are not explicitly recognized. As already mentioned a number of times, this suggests that traditional productivity growth measures should be adjusted to identify the impacts of fixity and returns to scale independently of technical change.

This adjustment process can be motivated conceptually as an attempt to untangle movements along, movements between and shifts in isoquants. Theoretically, this requires formalization of the fact that costs and output levels do not change proportionately with a technological shift when short run fixities or scale economies exist. To take this into account in the characterization of technical change requires two steps: a correction must be made to the standard productivity growth expressions, and a decomposition of the primal-side productivity growth measure may be undertaken to identify its separate components.

An additional refinement of standard productivity growth or technical change analysis involves determining the disparate impacts of technical change on different inputs; this implies "twists" in isoquants as the isoquant map is transformed due to technical changes. These differential impacts are generally expressed in terms of biases. Biases with respect to utilization and scale as well as technical change can be developed and used to analyze more fully the pattern of responses to exogenous changes that cause economic performance to vary.

This chapter outlines these diverse but related adaptations and extensions to productivity growth analysis, and begins to discuss how measures of these indicators and their interactions might be constructed empirically. In the first section the theoretical framework is developed for correcting and decomposing overall "productivity" growth measures for different determinants of efficiency change. This development is based on assessing the total cost consequences of different impacts on firms such as fixities and scale economies. The next three sections then outline the theoretical foundations for construction and interpretation of bias measures, which reflect the input-specific impacts. Section 4.2 summarizes the literature on technical change biases; Section 4.3 discusses extensions to these ideas and related concepts; and Section 4.4 establishes the theoretical similarities of these and other useful bias measures such as those for scale and utilization.

4.1 An Analytical Framework for Decomposing Productivity Growth Measures

It is very difficult to untangle movements of isoquants, between isoquants and around isoquants unless a full structural model is specified. These different effects, however, have distinct theoretical attributes and implications for interpretation of resulting changes in demand and supply patterns of firms. Therefore constructing a model that allows them to be identified separately is critically important for analyzing economic performance.

One might think that the main determinant of productivity growth to isolate from other aspects of productive efficiency is technical change. Technical change has a precise definition; it can be thought of as a shift in the isoquant map so that any output level may be produced with a smaller amount of inputs (and therefore costs). When an isoquant shifts, in addition, it may twist if technical change is not neutral. This can cause differential proportional impacts among inputs, which are generally termed technical change biases.

Scale economies arise when movement between isoquants causes a less than proportional increase in inputs and therefore costs, independently of any change in the isoquant map itself. When output production expands, this will result in lower unit costs of production due to currently available technological capabilities that differ according to plant size. This is a second component of overall efficiency or "productivity growth", which should be independently represented if the technical change aspect is to be correctly identified. Again, biases may occur if scale changes affect inputs differently, therefore saving on some more than others. This will arise when production is non-homothetic.

Changes in input use (and thus costs) can also occur in response to input price changes or other changes in the economic conditions facing the firm. The resulting alterations in the composition of input demand (and thus costs) do not imply any change in technology or scale, or have any necessary linkage with increasing efficiency. They simply reflect cost minimizing responses to economic forces that are exogenous to the firm's behavior. This reasoning provided the motivation in Chapter 2 for dividing out the impacts of substitution from single factor measures of technical efficiency to generate a more interpretable measure of true productivity growth – multifactor productivity.

Fixity of inputs, however, may cause this movement to be smaller than would be the case if full movement to a new equilibrium were to take place instantaneously. This in turn will result in a possibly inefficient (in terms of minimum costs) method of production in the short run, even though in the long run there is potential to reduce costs further given the current technology. Less than optimal capacity utilization therefore can cause elevated production costs even when the most optimal short run behavior possible is being carried out. The extent and pattern of these higher costs across inputs have to do with substitution and complementary relationships with the fixed factor(s), which result in biases.

In sum, these interactions imply that observed changes in costs can arise due to various changes in the production process, including technical change, scale economies, substitution and fixity.[1] If any of these facets of the production structure is ignored, the resulting estimates of technical change are likely to be erroneous, or at least not very interpretable.

To motivate the theoretical linkages between productivity growth, scale economies and capacity utilization formally, we will use two results developed in the previous two chapters. First, we will base our analysis of productivity change on the cost-side specification of productivity growth presented in equation (2.8), reproduced here in less detail as (4.1):

$$\frac{\partial \ln C}{\partial t} = \frac{dC/dt}{C} - \frac{dY/dt}{Y} - \sum_j \frac{p_j v_j}{C} \frac{dp_j/dt}{p_j} = \epsilon_{Ct}. \tag{4.1}$$

[1]Other impacts can also, of course, be important. Market power, for example, will affect the valuation of output, and therefore have an effect on measured productivity growth. Other choices a firm might make which are overlooked here, such as inventory or advertising changes, might also affect costs. These types of extensions will be considered later, in Chapters 9 and 10.

Secondly, we will use the idea that the cost elasticity with respect to output, $\epsilon_{CY} = \partial \ln C/\partial \ln Y$, is a combination of the impacts of long run returns to scale and capacity utilization. This relationship can be formalized as in Chapter 3 as

$$\epsilon_{CY} = \eta(1 - \epsilon_{CK}) = \epsilon_{CY}^{LR} \cdot CU_c = \frac{MC \cdot Y}{C^*}\frac{C^*}{C}, \tag{4.2}$$

where $\eta = \epsilon_{CY}^{LR} = (MC \cdot Y)/C^*$ is the inverse of returns to scale, $(1 - \epsilon_{CK}) = CU_c = C^*/C$ is the cost side measure of capacity utilization with only one quasi-fixed input, capital (K), and the second equality is from Morrison [1989b].[2]

The importance of this representation of the cost elasticity ϵ_{CY} is that if $\epsilon_{CY} \neq 1$ due to either scale economies or fixity, (4.1) is an invalid measure of technical change. It is, in fact, based on an erroneous assumption that causes it to have an error bias. As mentioned in Chapter 2, (4.1) is based on the assumption that the cost function can be represented by $C = Yc(p,t)$ so $\epsilon_{CY} = 1$ and

$$d\ln c/dt = d\ln(C/Y)/dt = d\ln C/dt - d\ln Y/dt,$$

but if $\epsilon_{CY} \neq 1$, this becomes $d\ln C/dt - \epsilon_{CY}(d\ln Y/dt)$.

More formally, to correct for $\epsilon_{CY} \neq 1$ if this occurs because of scale economies, the residual ϵ_{Ct} must be adjusted to

$$\begin{aligned} \epsilon_{Ct}^R = \frac{\dot{C}}{C} - \epsilon_{CY}\frac{\dot{Y}}{Y} - \sum_j \frac{p_j v_j}{C}\frac{\dot{p}_j}{p_j} &= -\epsilon_{CY}\frac{\dot{Y}}{Y} + \sum_j \frac{p_j v_j}{C}\frac{\dot{v}_j}{v_j} \\ &= \epsilon_{Ct} + (1 - \epsilon_{CY})\frac{\dot{Y}}{Y} \end{aligned} \tag{4.3}$$

as shown in Morrison [1989b], where $\dot{C} = dC/dt$ so $\dot{C}/C = d\ln C/dt$ and similarly for Y, the superscript R represents "adjusted for Returns to scale", and the second equality in (4.3) stems from the Ohta [1975] derivation showing the equality of the cost- and primal-side measures of productivity growth outlined in Chapter 2 and developed

[2]This assumes homotheticity, as was shown in Chapter 3.

in equations (2.11 - 2.12).[3] The last term of (4.3) captures the error bias; ϵ_{Ct} differs from the corrected version ϵ_{Ct}^R by $(1-\epsilon_{CY})(d\ln Y/dt)$. This correction shows to what degree standard procedures for measurement of technical change are invalid when scale economies exist.

This adaptation can be interpreted as reflecting the fact that marginal and average costs no longer coincide, and valuation of output changes should be at marginal rather than average costs. Since

$$\epsilon_{CY} = MC \cdot Y/C = MC \cdot Y/AC \cdot Y = MC/AC,$$

the adjustment by ϵ_{CY} restates the change in output in terms of its correct marginal value. Thus, $1/\epsilon_{CY}$ measures returns to scale; it represents the proportional change in output possible from a given percentage change in costs. If this exceeds one, average costs decline with a scale expansion so there is potential for a proportionately greater output than cost increase.

A second difference from the more restricted technical change specification also occurs, however, because now even with the error adjustment there is a difference between the primal and cost measures. In particular, since the primal measure is

$$\epsilon_{Yt} = d\ln Y/dt - \sum_j (p_j v_j/p_Y Y) d\ln v_j/dt,$$

and with perfect competition $\epsilon_{CY} = MC{\cdot}Y/C = p_Y Y/C$, the equality between ϵ_{Yt} and ϵ_{Ct} now must be adapted to read $\epsilon_{Yt} = -\epsilon_{Ct}^R/\epsilon_{CY} = -\epsilon_{Ct}^{R'}$, (where the R superscript reflects the error bias adjustment of the cost measure, and " ' " represents the adaptation of the cost to the primal measure, both due to returns to scale).

This adaptation stems from the fact that the shares weighting the output growth rates in the cost measure are in terms of costs, and with nonconstant returns to scale costs no longer equal returns (revenue, $p_Y Y$). In fact, from the equality $\epsilon_{CY} = MC \cdot Y/C$ it is clear that $p_Y Y = C \cdot \epsilon_{CY} = MC \cdot Y \neq AC \cdot Y = C$. Thus, if the denominator of (4.3) is multiplied by ϵ_{CY}, which necessitates dividing

[3] Note that ϵ_{Ct} is a negative number, since productivity growth in the cost sense is represented by a *diminution* of costs. Thus if the adjustment term is negative, productivity growth appears better with the adjustment.

the entire expression by ϵ_{CY}, the equivalence of the cost and primal measures again emerges.

This modification is due to Ohta [1975]. It is only appropriate, however, if the cost-side measure has already been corrected so there is no error bias. Conceptually the construction of $\epsilon_{Ct}^{R'}$, as a product of two cost derivatives is a decomposition of the primal measure[4] into two parts, the effects of technical change and of scale, since the output value reflects both characteristics of production.

If $\epsilon_{CY} \neq 1$ because of fixity and therefore non-optimal capacity utilization, additional sources of error must be recognized. In this case the valuation of fixed inputs is incorrect using standard measures, since shadow and market values for these inputs deviate. More specifically, (4.1) depends on instantaneous adjustment through Shephard's lemma, which is used to substitute v_j, the cost minimizing demand for input j, for $\partial C/\partial p_j$ for all inputs.[5] If any input k (x_k) is fixed, however, this is not valid because in the short run the firm will not be able to choose a cost minimizing demand for x_k. Therefore, variable and total costs do not change proportionately with output even with constant returns to scale (CRTS) in the long run; costs change extra-proportionately in the short run because of non-optimal use of the fixed inputs.

This can be formalized through the expression for ϵ_{CY} developed in Chapter 3 for the case of fixity and CRTS; $\epsilon_{CY} = 1 - \Sigma_k \epsilon_{Ck}$ for multiple quasi-fixed inputs, or $\epsilon_{CY} = 1 - \epsilon_{CK}$ if only capital is fixed. Incorporating this difference in short run costs from that which is feasible in the long run so that technical change is correctly measured requires adjusting the weight on the growth in output analogously to the case of scale economies.

In addition, as with the scale measure, the dual and primal measures no longer coincide; reproducing the primal from the cost-side expression requires defining the shares in terms of the shadow values of the fixed inputs. Since $\epsilon_{CY} = 1 - \epsilon_{CK} = C^*/C$ with only capital fixed,

[4]Note that the primal measure does not have a bias correction because the assumption $\epsilon_{CY} = 1$ was not used for construction of the measure.

[5]See Chapter 5 for development of the theoretical basis for this substitution.

dividing the shares by ϵ_{CY} results in specifying the shares in terms of C^* instead of C, and in decomposing the primal measure into its individually identifiable technical change and capacity utilization impacts.

This treatment for the problem of fixity, however, has another implication that did not occur in the case of long run nonconstant returns to scale (NCRTS). If the quasi-fixed input shares (both cost and revenue) are evaluated at p_k, observed changes in these inputs are not being weighted at their correct marginal value. In fact, they should be valued at the shadow value Z_k for both the dual and primal measures.

This shadow value is captured in the *ex-post* measure of capital, which can be computed as a residual of revenues less variable costs if the assumptions of only one quasi-fixed input, perfect competition and constant returns to scale are made, as will be discussed further in Chapter 6. However, if this is not the case the Z_k values must be estimated parametrically; the returns to different characteristics of the production process cannot be untangled by just data manipulation. This is true in general for the ϵ_{CY} value, since this cost elasticity is not likely to be observable even if only one extension is being accommodated.

In sum, if the assumption that market prices approximate the marginal products of inputs is not made,

$$\epsilon_{CY} = 1 - \sum_k \epsilon_{Ck} = CU_c \neq 1$$

because $Z_k \neq p_k$, and the shadow values Z_k rather than p_k are valid for analysis. Then the corrected dual cost productivity measure computed from the variable cost function becomes:

$$\begin{aligned} \epsilon_{Ct}^F &= \left(1 - \sum_k \epsilon_{Ck}\right)\frac{\dot{Y}}{Y} - \sum_k \frac{Z_k x_k}{C}\frac{\dot{x}_k}{x_k} - \sum_j \frac{p_j v_j}{C}\frac{\dot{v}_j}{v_j} \\ &= \epsilon_{Ct} + \sum_k \epsilon_{Ck}\left(\frac{\dot{Y}}{Y} - \frac{\dot{x}_k}{x_k}\right), \end{aligned} \tag{4.4}$$

using the second equality of (4.3), which reduces to

$$\begin{aligned}\epsilon_{Ct}^{F} &= (1-\epsilon_{CK})\frac{\dot{Y}}{Y} - \frac{Z_k K}{C}\frac{\dot{K}}{K} - \sum_j \frac{p_j v_j}{C}\frac{\dot{v}_j}{v_j} \\ &= \epsilon_{Ct} + \epsilon_{CK}\left(\frac{\dot{Y}}{Y} - \frac{\dot{K}}{K}\right), \qquad (4.5)\end{aligned}$$

with only capital fixed, and where the superscript F represents "adjusted for Fixity".[6] As before, the last term in this expression can be thought of as an error bias that occurs in this case if instantaneous adjustment is assumed when subequilibrium (not being able to reach a steady state because of fixity) really exists. Note that the bias depends on the relative growth rates of output and the quasi-fixed inputs since the standard assumption that $\epsilon_{Ck} = 0$ affects the weights on both these components of the overall measure.[7]

After the error bias correction is made, if in addition one wishes to determine full potential productivity growth if the effects of disequilibrium were removed, it is possible to calculate

$$\epsilon_{Ct}^{F'} = \frac{\epsilon_{Ct}^{F}}{(1-\sum_k \epsilon_{Ck})} = \frac{\dot{Y}}{Y} - \sum_k \frac{Z_k x_k}{C^*}\frac{\dot{x}_k}{x_k} - \sum_j \frac{p_j v_j}{C^*}\frac{\dot{v}_j}{v_j} = \epsilon_{Yt}, \quad (4.6)$$

which can be summarized as

$$\epsilon_{Ct}^{F'} = \epsilon_{Ct}^{F} / \left(1 - \sum_k \epsilon_{Ck}\right) = \epsilon_{Yt}.$$

To recapitulate this similarly to the returns to scale case: after the error bias adjustment is made to correct the original measure, the adaptation of the base of the share expression generates the full primal measure. In reverse, this motivates a decomposition of the primal

[6]This is developed in more detail in Morrison [1989b].

[7]Equations (4.3) and (4.4) are based on an output-side computation of the cost measure, where $d\ln C/dt$ has been substituted. Alternatively, the cost side measure can be calculated directly, although the adjustment is not as straightforward. See Morrison [1989b] for further elaboration and additional adaptations to include dynamic adjustment.

measure to identify independently the impacts of technical change (ϵ_{Ct}^{F}) and fixity ($CU_c = 1 - \Sigma_k \epsilon_{Ck}$).

If both NCRTS and fixity exist, then adjustments must be made for both of these aspects of the production structure. Weighting the output growth term by ϵ_{CY} as in (4.3) (where now $\epsilon_{CY} = \eta \cdot CU_c$) adjusts for changes in output that should not be attributed to technical change, whether they result from scale economies or subequilibrium, by revaluing the output change appropriately at its marginal value. Valuing the quasi-fixed inputs at their shadow values similarly specifies the changes in these inputs at their true marginal products.

It is important to recognize that, although the first type of adjustment made here corrects for erroneous assumptions and therefore errors in the unadjusted measure, the second adjustment instead facilitates interpretation. Depending on the context and interpretation desired, either ϵ_{Ct}^{F} (ϵ_{Ct}^{R} if scale economies exist instead of fixity) or $\epsilon_{Yt} = \epsilon_{Ct}^{F'} (= \epsilon_{Ct}^{R'})$ might be more appropriate to use as a productivity growth measure. The point of the adjustment to generate a primal-side equivalent is to highlight the two independent factors incorporated in multifactor productivity measures rather than to identify the "best" or "correct" measure.

In other words, in some circumstances one might think short run constraints due to fixity (or cost changes from scale economies) are a valid element of productivity growth that should be included in the measure. However, in most cases it would seem desirable to identify the individual contributions of technical change and utilization or fixity (scale). In such a case the decomposition of ϵ_{Yt} provides more interpretative potential. If only the technical impact is desired the $\epsilon_{Ct}^{F}(\epsilon_{Ct}^{R})$ measure could be used alone or one could employ the primal measure ϵ_{Yt} multiplied by ϵ_{CY}.[8]

Finally, we can illustrate these adjustments diagramatically. Figure 4.1 identifies the three different types of cost changes that may be

[8] Note that *dividing* ϵ_{Ct} by ϵ_{CY} is equivalent to *multiplying* C by ϵ_{CY}, and vice versa for ϵ_{Yt} and $p_Y Y$. This can create some confusion since at first glance this may appear to reverse the adjustments discussed above.

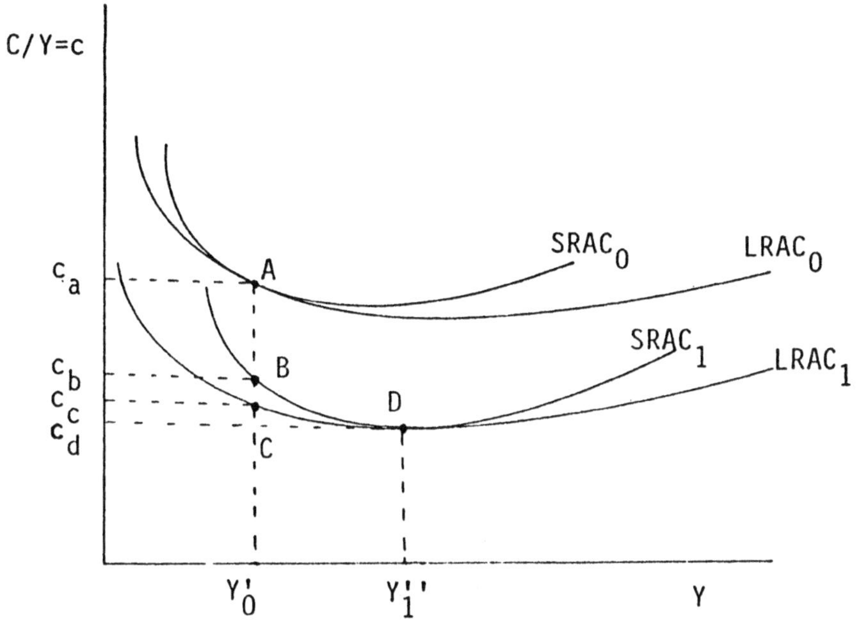

Fig.4.1. Illustrations of the adjustments

picked up as productivity change when the impacts of subequilibrium and scale are ignored.

Assume the firm was initially in equilibrium at point A in time period 0 at the tangency of the short run average cost curve $SRAC_0$ (defined for a fixed capital stock K_0) and the long run average cost curve $LRAC_0$. Between time periods 0 and 1 the cost curves fell, due to technical change, to $SRAC_1$ and $LRAC_1$. The primal side response given the same input use as before is to produce Y_1'' at average cost c_d. This average cost is lower than c_a due both to technical change and scale economies. However, cost-side measures will not reflect this full change unless the constraints due to fixity, and the potential cost changes from scale economics are appropriately measured and the initial technical change impact is augmented by the cost changes due to other factors.

The first issue about reflecting the change correctly – the error bias adjustment – is not easy to motivate using this diagram because the existence of NCRTS (through the slope of the $LRAC$ curve) and fixity (from the greater slope of the $SRAC$ curve) implicitly is incorporated in the construction of the figure. However, if it were assumed that the $LRAC$ curve were flat, for example, and that full adjustment could be made, points B, C and D would clearly not be represented correctly; the diagram and the corresponding analytics would be erroneous. The error bias corrections, therefore, simply generate the correct diagram.

Even if the points were correctly measured, however, the second issue – relating dual and primal measures – implies that ambiguous conclusions could result from direct evaluation of output levels and costs. For example, in the short run at the given output level Y_0' the measured cost decline would be only to c_b. If the assumptions of full equilibrium and $CRTS$ were made, it would appear from cost measures that the change from c_a to c_b was the full potential decline. However, when subequilibrium and $NCRTS$ are recognized, the interpretation changes. Movement from B to C (c_b to c_c) stems from adjustment of the fixed inputs (full change to a steady state), and to D (c_d) is permitted by taking advantage of scale economies (with a change in output). The complete potential primal side change and its corresponding cost impacts will therefore not be captured unless these assumptions are relaxed and the movement of output is incorporated.

In terms of the primal measure, if instantaneous adjustment is assumed when it is unjustified, the movement from Y_0' to Y_1'' will be misrepresented because the market price of capital will be higher than its shadow value in the short run. Therefore, the weight on capital growth will be incorrect, resulting in over- or under- representation of productivity growth depending on whether the growth of capital during this period was positive or negative. Assuming constant returns also limits interpretation, because the movement from A to D will be assumed to be completely a result of technical change, rather than recognizing that part of the potential augmentation of output is a consequence of scale economies.

Combining (4.6) and the analogous definition of $\epsilon_{Ct}^{R'}$ results in an expression incorporating both error bias corrections for fixity and scale (representation of the correct diagram), and decomposition of the full potential productivity change into its technical change, capacity utilization and returns to scale components.[9] This facilitates interpretation of the resulting measured indexes. It remains to see how these adjustments can be implemented empirically. Before moving to this step in the next chapter, however, we will first explore further several related theoretical developments which provide additional interpretative power.

4.2 The Measurement of Biases with Respect to Technical Change

Most measures and indicators characterizing production processes and economic performance can be defined in the context of cost changes. Productivity growth measures, for example, are fundamentally based on the change in the cost of a given output level with a change in technology, $\partial C/\partial t$, generally expressed in elasticity form as $\epsilon_{Ct} = \partial \ln C/\partial t$. Shadow values and capacity utilization indexes are dependent on the idea of the potential cost savings with a change in the level of a quasi-fixed input at a given output level, $\partial G/\partial x_k$, or $\partial \ln C/\partial \ln x_k = \epsilon_{Ck}$. Returns to scale are defined in terms of the derivative $\partial C/\partial Y$ $(\partial G/\partial Y)$ or elasticity $\epsilon_{CY} = \partial \ln C/\partial \ln Y$. Even the expressions for optimal input factor demand depend in a sense on the change in costs with variations in input prices; through Shephard's Lemma, $v_j = \partial C/\partial p_j$ as formalilzed in the next chapter, so the share is $S_j = \partial \ln C/\partial \ln p_j$.

These cost elasticities represent overall changes in costs. However, they also embody information on the contributions of the individual factors to the total cost change. Attempts to increase the interpretation potential of these measures have led to development of the concept of biases with respect to changes in exogenous variables. These bias measures distinguish input-specific effects from the overall im-

---

[9]Alternative decomposition frameworks such as that proposed by Fuss and Waverman [1986] have also been used. Although clearly analogous to that used here, the motivation and interpretation differ somewhat.

pact. Measurement procedures carried out using parametric methods allow empirical distinction between these differential effects, although these effects cannot be identified directly from the data.

The most commonly discussed bias measure is that with respect to technical change. Overall neutrality (often termed Hicks neutrality) of technical change implies that all inputs are affected equiproportionately by technical change. This is not, however, likely to be the case in general, since different types of technical advances may be more likely to conserve on a particular input, such as labor or energy. These differentials, in fact, may even be induced by changes in relative prices; if the price of energy increases dramatically it might be thought that technology would be developed to save energy relative to other inputs. Technical change biases capture these disparate possibilities for conservation of inputs with a change in technology. Technical change may be input j-using, -saving or -neutral depending on whether the change in the use of input j is larger, smaller or the same as the average change over all inputs.

Biases are computed as second derivatives of the cost function, or, equivalently, derivatives of the pertinent cost elasticities. A technical change bias with respect to input j, for example, is calculated as the cross-partial derivative of the logarithm of the cost function with respect to $\ln p_j$ and t. The resulting bias reflects the change in demand for input j with a change in technology relative to other input responses, and thus indicates its relative contribution to cost fluctuations. These biases represent the varying impact of technical change on different inputs, which may be important for evaluating efficiency with respect to particular inputs over time.

Note that since this derivative must be computable, a precise functional form must be specified for the cost function and econometric estimation must be carried out to generate the bias measures; parametric procedures are necessary. This is particularly the case if the exogenous determinants of the biases are of interest. Arguments of the cost function in general become determinants of its derivatives, although certain functional forms simply yield a parameter as the bias estimate. Data analysis alone, therefore, does not allow for identification or assessment of biases because the independent impact of technical change on different inputs cannot be distinguished without further structure.

It is also important to recognize that these biases reflect *relative* changes in input use, since technical change may well reduce the use of all inputs. The bias is often, therefore, thought of in terms of changes in input shares; a decline in the share of an input reflects *proportionally* greater reduced demand for that input than for others.

Formal expressions for biases can readily be constructed based on the development of technical change biases by Sato [1970] and Binswanger [1974].[10] These treatments are based on the Hicksian concept that, with a value-added production function, technical change is labor-saving -using or -neutral depending on whether the marginal rate of substitution increases, decreases, or stays constant with a change in t while holding the capital-labor ratio constant. Resulting adjustments in factor shares are the basis of the definition of technical change biases.

A Hicksian-style definition of a technical change bias for the dual cost framework with multiple inputs is based on the relative factor share change allowing for substitution effects:

$$B_{jt} = \frac{\partial S_j}{\partial t} = \frac{p_j v_j}{C}\left(\frac{\dot{v}_j}{v_j} - \frac{\dot{C}}{C}\right) = S_j(\epsilon_{jt} - \epsilon_{Ct}), \tag{4.7}$$

where $S_j = p_j v_j / C = \epsilon_{Cj}$, the short run share of variable j in total costs,

$$\begin{aligned} \epsilon_{jt} &= \partial \ln v_j/\partial t,\ C = G(\cdot) + \sum_k p_k x_k = \sum_j p_j v_j(\cdot) + \sum_k p_k x_k, \\ \dot{v}_j &= \partial v_j/\partial t \end{aligned}$$

and $\dot{C} = \partial C/\partial t$. Since C is specified in terms of the restricted cost function $G(p, x, Y, t)$, (4.7) is based on constant variable input prices as well as on fixed input and output levels, and therefore explicitly reflects a short run bias. It could, however, also be developed in

[10] See Berndt and Wood [1982] for a good discussion of technical biases. Also see Gollop and Roberts [1983] for a related discussion including consideration of regulatory variables.

terms of the instantaneous adjustment cost function $C(p, Y, t)$, which would yield a long run measure.

The expression in parentheses on the right hand side of (4.7) is the primal-side Uzawa-Watanabe substitution term $B_{jt}^U = \partial \ln S_j / \partial t$, which is used to define a technical innovation as input j-saving - neutral or -using when B_{jt}^U is less than, equal to, or greater than zero. Clearly since $S_j > 0$ this also implies the same relationship for B_{jt}.

There are two identifiable components to the total input share response to technical change (for a given level of output) represented by this measure. These components are the average percentage reduction in inputs $\dot{C}/C$ and the percentage change in demand for the jth input $\dot{v}_j/v_j$. Thus, if $B_{jt} < 0$ the reduction in v_j from a change in t is greater than average; technical innovation is relatively input j-saving, and thus decreases costs particularly at the expense of employment of input j.

This highlights the interpretation of the bias as a relative change in input use. The second term in the parentheses, ϵ_{Ct}, is the neutral term – the overall proportional change in costs with technical change. The first expression in parentheses, ϵ_{jt}, signifies the input-specific change which may be greater or less than the neutral impact. If ϵ_{jt} and ϵ_{Ct} are equal, the proportional changes are equal and technical change is neutral with respect to input j. If this is true for all inputs, technical change has no biases; it is Hicks neutral. Even if technical change is non-neutral, however, the sum of these biases must be zero because overall the relative changes must cancel out; "on average" technical change must be neutral and shares must always sum to one by definition.

The empirical complexity of these bias terms depends on the functional form used for the cost function and therefore demand (or share) expressions, and whether the function used is a restricted cost function, allowing for the difference between short and long run. The simplest specification of biases arises when the functional form is such that the share equation is the natural expression for analysis, and when the model is specified in terms of instantaneous adjustment the short run-long-run distinction that requires imputation of movement to the long run does not cause complications.

This implies that the long run translog functional form, which is a second order Taylor series expansion of $C(\cdot)$ in logarithms, is useful for this type of analysis. (This form will be specified in more detail in Chapter 7). Since the translog form is written in logarithms, so $\ln C = f(\ln p_j, \ln Y, t)$, a natural adaption of the specification of demand equations is to construct the model in terms of shares (recall that, as mentioned above, Shephard's lemma implies $\partial \ln C / \partial \ln p_j = (\partial C / \partial p_j) p_j / C = v_j p_j / C = S_j$). It turns out, in fact, that the specific expression for this share with the translog is quite simple; depending on the exact form of the function it looks something like

$$S_j = \frac{\partial \ln C}{\partial \ln p_j} = \alpha_j + \sum_{i \neq j} \gamma_{ij} \ln p_i + \gamma_{jj} \ln p_j + \delta_{jY} \ln Y + \delta_{jt} t, \quad (4.8)$$

where the $\alpha_j, \gamma_{ij}, \gamma_{jj}, \delta_{jY}$, and δ_{jt} terms are parameters, and $\partial S_j / \partial t = \delta_{jt}$; the bias term is just a parameter.[11] Therefore, the measurement of biases is quite straightforward in the translog case, although econometric estimation is required to estimate δ_{jt}, and analysis of the determinants of the bias is not possible because it does not depend on the data, as alluded to above.

If a restricted cost function $G(\cdot)$ is used, however, as in Morrison [1988b], the cost function is specified in terms of just variable inputs. Although a second logarithmic derivative of this function is again simply a parameter, the derivative $\partial^2 \ln G / \partial \ln p_j \partial t$ does not represent the relevant bias measure because the appropriate cost elasticity

[11] When concavity is imposed this expression becomes even simpler but is less likely to represent the production process correctly because often this requires restricting factor substitution parameters to zero. See Berndt and Wood [1982] for further elaboration. This simplification of the model to force it to satisfy regulatory conditions has often been imposed by Jorgenson and Fraumeni [1981], as discussed in more detail in Chapter 8. It may be useful to note for now that the most troublesome input factor in terms of curvature violations is capital; 33 of the 36 industries violate curvature in the Jorgenson-Fraumeni framework. This may imply that the treatment of capital is invalid in the instantaneous adjustment framework and a short run model such as those suggested for measuring capacity utilization would be preferable.

is based on total instead of variable costs. This causes the full bias expression to be more complex and therefore somewhat less interpretable directly, but more conducive to analysis of its determinants.

It is useful to note also that bias measures have a converse interpretation. $\partial S_j/\partial t = B_{jt}$ can be redefined as[12]

$$\partial^2 \ln C/\partial \ln p_j \partial t = \partial^2 \ln C/\partial t \partial \ln p_j = \partial \epsilon_{Ct}/\partial \ln p_j = B_{tj};$$

B_{jt} can thus alternatively be expressed as the effect on total cost diminution of a change in p_j. More specifically, when technical progress occurs, $\partial \ln C/\partial t$ is negative. Now if p_j increases and B_{jt} is positive (negative) then the effect of this price change is to reduce (increase) the rate of cost diminution from that which would have prevailed had neutrality existed.

This justifies the assertion often made in studies of biased technical change that an increase in the price of input j diminishes the rate of (multifactor) productivity growth if technical change is input j-using. Thus, if technical change is labor- capital- and energy-using, as has been found by Jorgenson-Fraumeni [1981],[13] increased prices for any of these three inputs will reduce multifactor productivity growth. However, increases in materials prices, since the bias is negative (materials-saving), will augment productivity growth.

This converse interpretation of the biases can be illustrated more explicitly by using the translog form to identify the dependence of the dual cost rate of technical change, $\partial \ln C/dt = \epsilon_{Ct}$, on the biases. For the translog function this cost elasticity becomes

$$\epsilon_{Ct} = \frac{\partial \ln C}{\partial t} = \delta_t + \sum_j \delta_{jt} \ln p_j + \delta_{tt} t, \tag{4.9}$$

where the δ_{jt} terms are the biases as noted above. Thus, since $\partial \epsilon_{Ct}/\partial \ln p_j = \partial S_j/\partial t = \delta_{jt}$, the bias term represents both the change in productivity growth with a change in the price and a change in the share of input j in response to technical change.

[12] Note that this equality uses Young's theorem on the symmetry of second derivatives.

[13] See the discussion of bias measures in Chapter 8 for further elaboration.

4.3 Extensions to the Theory of Technical Change Biases

To provide additional understanding of technical change biases it is worthwhile briefly to explore the linkages between biases and factor-augmenting technical change, since the distinctions between the two are sometimes confused. Augmentation of a factor occurs when technical change causes the "effective" amount of that factor to increase given the measured level of the factor; in terms of efficiency units more of the input exists. Conversely, this can be interpreted as a decreased price of a certain amount of services from the more efficient input. Since augmentation is generally expressed as a constant exponential rate, this implies

$$v'_{jt} = v_{jt}\exp^{\lambda_j t}, \quad \text{or} \quad p'_{jt} = p_{jt}\exp^{-\lambda_j t} \tag{4.10}$$

where "'" refers to augmented or effective units and λ_j is the exponential rate of augmentation for input j.

This imposes a particular form on the dependence of the production or cost function on t if augmentation exists. As shown by Berndt and Wood [1982], for example, if factor augmentation is incorporated into the instantaneous adjustment translog function mentioned in the previous section, the δ parameters showing technical change impacts are related to the augmentation rates according to:

$$\begin{aligned}\delta_t &= -\sum_i \alpha_i\lambda_i, \quad \delta_{jt} = -\sum_i \gamma_{ij}\lambda_i, \quad \delta_{Mt} = -\sum \gamma_{jt} \quad \text{and} \\ \delta_{tt} &= -\sum_i \gamma_{it}\lambda_i,\end{aligned}$$

where i indexes all inputs under consideration but j denotes all inputs except intermediate-material inputs.[14] Therefore the bias and augmentation terms are related, but not in a directly or easily inter-

[14]This assumes the materials share equation is the one deleted from the system of estimation equations. This arises because one equation must be chosen to be deleted; the system is singular due to the requirement that shares sum to one. See Chapter 7 for further discussion of this issue.

pretable fashion; the bias coefficients are a complicated combination of both augmentation and substitution among inputs.[15]

In this framework Hicks neutral technical change – where the shares of inputs do not vary with technical change because the inputs are affected proportionately – exists when all augmentation rates are equal. Harrod-neutral and Solow-neutral technical change are alternative versions of neutrality in which only labor- and only capital-augmenting technical change occur, respectively. These imply, given the relationships above, that with λ_L only deviating from zero for the Harrod neutral case, $\delta_t = -\alpha_L \lambda_L$, $\delta_{jt} = -\gamma_{jL} \lambda_L$, $\delta_{tt} = -\gamma_{Lt} \lambda_L$. Therefore the biases δ_{jt} depend on the augmentation rate of labor and the substitution possibilities between input j and labor. Analogous conditions are inferred by the assumption of Solow neutrality.

"Value-added" neutrality is also sometimes distinguished. In this case only capital and labor are augmented while energy and materials (and any other identifiable intermediate inputs) are not; Leontief neutral technical change occurs when capital and labor augmentation rates differ and Leontief/Hicks neutrality occurs when the rates are the same. In this case the biases depend on the augmentation rates and the substitutability of labor and capital with the other inputs.[16]

Therefore, except in the case of Hicks neutral technical change, the relationship between biases and augmentation is reasonably complex to untangle and interpret. However, the concepts are closely related and intimately linked to the notion of overall technical change. That this latter assertion is true for biases is obvious from equation (4.9); ϵ_{Ct} can be expressed directly in terms of δ_t, δ_{tt} and the bias terms. A similar association holds for the augmentation parameters, since the augmentation rates directly capture the change in effective input use between two time periods. As Berndt and Wood [1982] show, the relationship between ϵ_{Ct} and the augmentation rates is straightforward;

---

[15] For an early treatment of biases and the relationship between augmentation and biases see David and van de Klundert [1965]. They show that whether augmentation of capital more than labor implies a capital-using bias, for example, depends on whether the elasticity of substitution between capital and labor exceeds or falls short of one.

[16] See Berndt and Wood [1982] for a more detailed analysis of augmentation.

$$\epsilon_{Ct} = -\Sigma_j S_j \lambda_j, \text{ where } S_j \text{ is the share of input } j.$$

Finally, it should be noted that the augmentation framework is not unique to a specification of technical change. Any quality adjustment that might be relevant to an input can be written in a form similar to (4.10). In particular, if (4.10) is rewritten as:

$$\ln v'_{jt} = \ln v_{jt} + \lambda_j t, \quad \text{and} \quad \ln p'_{jt} = \ln p_{jt} - \lambda_j t, \tag{4.11}$$

it looks very much like the simple hedonic expression for capital introduced in Chapter 3. In fact, the factor augmentation model is a simple quality-adjustment or hedonic model that just takes the impact of t into account. If utilization, or any other quality-adjustment is made, it can be developed similarly in this framework.[17]

Obsolescence (from energy price changes) as well as technical change and vintage, for example, can be analogously incorporated as in Berndt and Wood [1984] and Morrison and Nelson [1989]; these effects can then be distinguished from utilization. Once more than one quality-adjustment is taken into account, however, it may be useful to expand the functional form to take cross-effects into account rather than simply specifying a log-linear framework, as is done in Morrison-Nelson.[18] This extension is considered in more detail in Chapter 9.

[17]Of course, as in the case of utilization, appropriate care must be taken to avoid double counting, which will arise if the effect of the quality determinant is accomodated in more than one way.

[18]It should be emphasized here that this type of approach begins to build in a type of "embodied" technical change in addition to the standard "disembodied" technical change that has implicitly been assumed here. The distinction between the two has important consequences, as noted briefly in Chapter 3. Most multifactor productivity research, however, assumes technical change is disembodied, which in effect means that its effects are assumed not to depend on the vintage structure of the inputs. This type of technical change, which is simply assumed to proceed along with time rather than depending on the composition of inputs, is represented by the "t" in the cost function specification. For further discussion of the importance of this distinction, see Berndt and Kolstad [1987].

4.4 The Theory and Interpretation of Utilization and Scale Biases

Another useful set of biases to construct when focusing on performance and the difference between short and long run behavior is utilization (fixed input) biases. Utilization biases can be motivated similarly to technical change biases, as in Morrison [1988b], but have not received much attention in the literature. They reflect the (relative) change in variable input demand when a fixed input constraint is relaxed. It may be the case, for example, that when it becomes possible to reduce the capital stock (disinvest) in an industry where capacity utilization is low, this causes the share of energy to decline. Investment is therefore energy-using relative to other inputs.

More generally, say capital is quasi-fixed and the share of input j decreases when capital increases. Then increased availability of capital may be said to be input-j-saving in the sense that adding more capital reduces the short run demand for input j relative to other inputs. Alternatively, this suggests that if the stock of capital is a binding constraint (demand is too high for a steady state given the capital stock), there is over-utilization of capital by extra-normal use of input j.

A "subequilibrium" or utilization bias can be defined similarly to that for technical change as:

$$B_{jk} = \frac{\partial S_j}{\partial \ln x_k} = \frac{p_j v_j}{C}\left(\frac{\partial v_j/\partial x_k}{v_j/x_k} - \frac{\partial C/\partial x_k}{C/x_k}\right) = S_j(\epsilon_{jk} - \epsilon_{Ck}), \tag{4.12}$$

where $\epsilon_{jk} = \partial \ln v_j/\partial \ln x_k$. ϵ_{Ck} will be negative if $Z_k > p_k$ so more of input x_k would be desired to reach a steady state, and vice versa for $p_k > Z_k$. In the former case, $B_{jk} < 0$ implies that ϵ_{jk} must be strongly negative; inputs k and j must be substitutes. Thus an increase in x_k relaxes the fixed input constraint but reduces costs extra-proportionately with respect to v_j; it is input j-saving because the constraint on input k was accommodated by using substitutes. This reasoning is reversed if x_k and v_j are complements. Note again, however, that this is a relative rather than absolute direction of change. All variable inputs might be "saved" in terms of reducing their levels; the bias has to do with the relative or proportionate change.

Equation (4.12) can be interpreted as a utilization bias because over-utilization of fixed x_k imposes extra costs on the firm for substitutes. Over-utilization of capital equipment, for example, may cause substitution of extra labor-hours relative to other inputs to accommodate the lack of capital, or increase the use of partly processed raw materials so constraints on machinery are less binding. In reverse, under-utilization of capital may thus impinge particularly on employment of labor in the short run because there will be a tendency to substitute toward the excessive existing capital. Conversely, if labor is a gross complement with capital, as suggested by the existence of short run increasing returns to labor in some industries,[19] labor may benefit in the short run (in relative terms) from output stagnation and resulting excess capacity.

The symmetry of biases mentioned above also, of course, holds in the case of utilization biases. This facilitates interpretation of the terms. For example, $\partial S_j/\partial \ln K(= \partial^2 \ln C/\partial \ln p_j \partial \ln K)$ can be re-defined as $\partial \epsilon_{CK}/\partial \ln p_j(= \partial^2 \ln C/\partial \ln K \partial \ln p_j)$; a variable input bias with respect to fixed capital also represents the impact of a change in p_j on the cost elasticity with respect to capital. Since the elasticity $\epsilon_{CK} = \partial \ln C/\partial \ln K$ is the basis for the measure of capacity utilization CU_c, as discussed in Chapter 3, this further substantiates the interpretation of these biases as utilization biases. In this case, for example, if the utilization bias implies that investment is energy-using, this not only says that increasing capital causes the share of energy to rise, but also that higher energy prices reduce capacity utilization. This can be further illustrated using the translog function by constructing an explicit expression for ϵ_{CK}, analogously to that for ϵ_{Ct} in (4.9).

It is worthwhile noting that utilization biases can only be specified in terms of an augmentation framework, as in (4.10) or (4.11), when utilization is characterized as a determinant of capital quality directly – as in an hedonic expression. When utilization is more aptly recog-

[19]See Morrison and Berndt [1981]. Note that this is most likely to be the case for skilled workers, and substitution may exist for production workers, although in total complementarity may be observed.

nized to be directly a result of the constraints on behavior imposed by fixity of factors, this specification is inapplicable.[20]

The differential impact of short run output fluctuations on individual inputs can be represented analogously to technical change and utilization biases, by determining the change in the share given a change in output demand. The Hicksian output- or "scale"-bias is:

$$B_{jY} = \frac{\partial S_j}{\partial \ln Y} = \frac{p_j v_j}{C}\left(\frac{\partial v_j/\partial Y}{v_j/Y} - \frac{\partial C/\partial Y}{C/Y}\right) = S_j(\epsilon_{jY} - \epsilon_{CY}), \tag{4.13}$$

where $\epsilon_{jY} = \partial \ln v_j/\partial \ln Y$. This can be expressed alternatively as the Uzawa output bias: $B^U_{jY} = \partial \ln S_j/\partial \ln Y = \epsilon_{jY} - \epsilon_{CY}$. Although this bias may be thought of as a scale bias, when it is measured based on a restricted cost function, it reflects a short run change and thus does not represent true scale but instead returns to only the variable inputs. This results because ϵ_{CY} incorporates both capacity utilization and returns to scale.

The scale bias can be interpreted similarly to the technical change bias; ϵ_{CY} represents the average output effect, and ϵ_{jY} indicates the input-specific output effect. If, for example v_j is labor (L) and ϵ_{LY} is very small so $B_{jY} < 0$, this implies increasing returns to labor relative to other inputs. Short run increases in output are therefore input j (labor) saving. In this case stagnation of output demand, such as in the steel industry, implies an expansion in the share of labor, which will (directly) hurt workers less than if the decline in all inputs were proportional. Symmetry of bias terms further implies that $\partial S_j/\partial \ln Y$ can be redefined as $\partial \epsilon_{CY}/\partial \ln p_j$.

Finally, note that since all these biases are defined in terms of cost elasticities, the linkages among technical change, utilization and scale can be formalized similarly to the construction of bias measures. For example, a "bias" term could be defined as $B_{Yt} = \partial \epsilon_{CY}/\partial t$. This measure will show how ϵ_{CY} changes with a change in technology, which indicates the combined change in capacity utilization and scale

[20] As noted in Chapter 3, this type of exercise has implicitly been carried out by Griliches and Jorgenson [1967], but problems exist with respect to how the utilization index is computed; it must be an exogenous index to be used in this way, which causes interpretational difficulties.

economies when technical change occurs. The effect on capacity utilization can be isolated by computing $B_{Kt} = \partial\epsilon_{CK}/\partial t$ (with capital only fixed). Similar "biases" can be defined in terms of changes in $\epsilon_{CY}, \epsilon_{Ct}$ or ϵ_{Ck} with respect to Y and x_k. Although these measures have interesting implications for analysis, however, it is more justifiable to motivate them in the context of elasticities of the cost elasticities, or second order elasticities; they are structurally analogous to standard biases, but the bias interpretation is somewhat ambiguous.

* * * * *

Overall, technical change, utilization and scale effects can be expressed in a number of ways which facilitate different types of analyses. Although straightforward data manipulation is sufficient to construct the accounting measures of productivity growth presented in Chapter 2, and is sometimes used (with qualifications) to construct capacity utilization indexes such as those discussed in Chapter 3, the multiple adaptations discussed in this chapter generally require econometric modeling. Econometric modeling is also necessary to estimate biases or augmentation rates to provide further interpretation of technical change. In the next chapter we will proceed further to pursue the problems involved in construction and econometric implementation of empirically implementable production theory models that summarize economic performance and productivity growth.

Chapter 5

Empirical Implementation of Productivity Growth Measures and Adjustments

In the past few chapters we have specified a framework for analysis of productivity growth. This framework highlights the linkages among some different aspects of productivity that are necessary to unravel to present a clear picture of the impacts that affect a firm's economic performance. Unfortunately, empirical identification of these different aspects is not straightforward.

Various attempts at constructing empirically implementable models to represent production processes and developing the measures necessary for untangling the impacts have been made. Some efforts to adapt standard accounting-type measures of productivity growth to recognize these different impacts have employed nonparametric or simple parametric methods. However, generating measures consistent with those used for productivity growth measurement itself, and with representations of other types of firm behavior, is inherently complex. This is particularly true when a number of different facets of firm behavior must be represented simultaneously.

Distinguishing, for example, technical change (a shift in the production function) from returns to scale (incorporated in the shape of the production function) and markups (from market power) is not possible to accomplish through direct data manipulation. Similarly, untangling the differential impacts of technical change on inputs, which requires consideration of the "twist" of an isoquant as it shifts (biases), is not discernible from direct observation. Instead, dealing with these issues requires more complete analysis of the structure of costs and production, which is possible to do only with additional information on the form of the cost and production functions. Therefore, specification of these functions and use of econometric, parametric methods are required.

Developing such a parametric approach requires consideration of the underlying economic theory relating these functions, the estimation of such functions, and (based on the results) the manipulations necessary to compute economic indicators to address these types of issues. This chapter outlines the building blocks required for this development. Section 5.1 begins with an overview of attempts to deal with the issues raised by our theoretical treatment in the previous chapters, which are based on nonparametric and simple parametric methods. Then in the following sections the important theoretical and empirical developments necessary to generate justifiable and consistent parametric measures of economic performance measures are sketched, as a basis for further elaboration in the following chapters. Section 5.2 outlines what is meant by a parametric approach to analysis of productive processes and productivity. In Section 5.3 the theoretical basis necessary for developing such models, introduced sketchily in the past two chapters, is developed more formally in the context of results based on duality theory. Finally, in the last section, the use of these models for generating measures of economic behavior and performance, and the interpretation possibilities stemming from this type of analysis, are highlighted.

5.1 Nonparametric and Simple Parametric Measurement Methods

It is difficult to compute the measures necessary for adaptation of productivity growth measures to take utilization and scale impacts into account using nonparametric or other simple methods. The problem is disentangling returns to these different characteristics of the production process to obtain valid economic measures of capacity utilization and returns to scale, or of the shadow value of the fixed inputs (Z_k) and marginal costs (MC) which provide the economic basis for these measures. Even if the impact of one deviation from the traditional framework can be distinguished, this may often only be accomplished by assuming all remaining restrictive assumptions are valid, since the raw data is capable of identifying only a limited number of more general relationships.

A number of attempts to compute ϵ_{CY} (MC) or ϵ_{Ck} (Z_k) to undertake scale and subequilibrium adjustments have been pursued empirically, using various approaches and with differing degrees of success. Some of these, even given the limitations of simple forms of analysis for this type of extension, have been insightful and fruitful.

Researchers such as Berndt and Fuss [1986] and Hulten [1986], for example, have attempted to compute the shadow value of capital (Z_K) without a parametric specification. These nonparametric approaches rely on some version of the shadow value of the capital stock being captured in the measured value of the firm. This is implemented in Berndt and Fuss by using Tobin's q as a basis, and in Hulten by computing the *ex-post* value of capital from the value of output. Both of these measures are, to some extent, based on the notion of a residual measure so they may include returns to something other than the capital stock.

Berndt and Fuss, for example, rely on the Tobin's q idea that the market value of a firm (represented by the stock market valuation), as compared to the actual value of the firm's capital (reflected in the firm's replacement value), captures the difference between the shadow and market prices of capital. The resulting measure, however, constructed as a ratio of these two values, includes many things that might not be thought of as elements of a pure shadow value, such as goodwill. This approach relies also, of course, on the assumption of only one quasi-fixed input.

Hulten instead computes the *ex-post* residual value of capital as $p_Y Y - G(\cdot) = Z_K K$ and then focuses on how difficult a valid *ex-ante* measure of the price of capital (p_K) is to compute relative to this *ex-post* measure. The problem with the residual measure, however, is that if nonconstant returns to scale, multiple quasi-fixed inputs, market power or other aspects of the production structure exist that are not explicitly recognized, returns to these technological and market characteristics are included in addition to the true return to capital in the residual. Therefore, maintaining the restrictive assumptions of constant returns to scale, perfect competition, and one quasi-fixed input is necessary to measure the shadow value of capital nonparametrically.

Another possible approach to isolating the impact of subequilibrium, suggested by the development of capacity utilization adjustments in the previous chapter, is to use published measures of capacity utilization. Specifically, the error adjustment for fixity (of capital only) can be expressed from (4.5) as $\epsilon_{Ct} + \epsilon_{CK}(d \ln Y/dt - d \ln K/dt)$ where the second term is the generally ignored error bias. Thus, since $CU_c = (1 - \epsilon_{CK})$ implies $\epsilon_{CK} = 1 - CU_c$, the error adjustment can be made using only a capacity utilization measure. The adaptation of the cost measure to decompose the primal productivity growth index is also possible since this simply requires dividing by the capacity utilization measure CU_c, as in (4.5).

Unfortunately, this approach also is subject to serious problems. In addition to requiring the assumption of one quasi-fixed input (from the error bias correction in (4.3) it is clear that the different ϵ_{Ck} components cannot be untangled without further information), published capacity utilization measures are not consistent with economic theory. As outlined in Chapter 3, these measures never allow overutilization of fixed inputs and therefore always fall short of one. It is evident, however, that there will be many cases where overutilization of an existing amount of fixed stocks occurs. This could result, for example, from the inability of investment to keep up with a sudden growth in demand. In this case economic CU measures would exceed one. Thus, since the physical notion of capacity utilization has little interpretative power in terms of economic values and thus shadow values of fixed inputs, use of these measures does not appear constructive in this context.[1]

It seems, therefore, that although it would be ideal to generate a nonparametric measure of the shadow value of capital and use this directly to adjust productivity growth measures for fixity, no really justifiable measure exists for this purpose. Parametric methods which use a specific form of the variable cost function and thus imply an explicit functional form for $Z_K = -\partial G/\partial K$ will in most cases be preferable to determine the bias resulting from subequilibrium.

Attempts to measure scale economies also face great obstacles. A fundamental difficulty is the lack of a theoretical framework for identification of scale economies from raw data, which of course results in a paucity of published measures. Therefore, although the theory developed in Chapter 4 suggests returns to scale measures may be used directly to adjust for scale economies, the scope for appropriate application of this theory is very limited.

Several approaches to this do, however, have some potential. First, a number of parametric studies have been carried out which attempt to measure returns to scale for different industries, and these might be used (with some hand-waving) in productivity studies of the same industry.[2] These separately generated measures will not be fully con-

---

[1]If fluctuations are the issue rather than the level of productivity growth, using standard measures which are highly correlated with economic measures might be justifiable. Although it is difficult to determine which measures might be suited to this, Morrison [1985b] showed that the FRB measures tend to more closely track economic measures than measures like the Wharton index. One potentially useful although somewhat *ad-hoc* adaptation to this is to try to identify the level of capacity utilization where investment and inflationary pressures are likely to begin, and normalize this value to one to correct somewhat for problems with levels in the published CU measures.

[2]This is the type of procedure used often, for example, in empirical general equilibrium studies where the model is too complex to measure elasticities necessary for the analysis. Measures from other studies or some "average" measure from a set of studies are often simply inserted into the analysis.

sistent with the theoretical structure or the data (unless they are based on the same data set) in any particular study, but may at least provide some insights. For example, a study by Christensen and Greene [1976] on electric utilities plants suggests returns to scale were "used up" by 1970. This in turn implies η, the inverse of the returns to scale measure, became higher than one after 1970, whereas it exceeded one before 1970. For a productivity study on electric utilities this information could be useful for interpreting changes in productivity during this period, even if the theoretical structure and data used were not identical.

Another possible approach depends on unsophisticated parametric methods and therefore imposes little structure on the interactions among different characteristics of the production structure. This procedure is based on a simple formalization of the idea that scale economies exist when costs do not rise as fast as output growth; when average cost curves are downward sloping $\partial \ln C/\partial \ln Y = \epsilon_{CY}$ is less than one. Therefore if any measure of the dependence of C on Y, and thus of the shape of the cost curves, can be constructed, this may be sufficient even without a full structure to provide interpretation.

This idea may be implemented by imposing a simple functional form as an approximation to the cost function $C(p,Y,t)$. One possibility is to assume a log-linear approximation such as:

$$\ln C = \alpha + \beta \ln Y + \gamma t + \sum_j \delta_j \ln p_j, \tag{5.1}$$

where β directly represents the cost elasticity with respect to output ϵ_{CY}. Thus, if this equation is estimated, the parameter estimate for β can be used to adjust for scale.

This method also has implications for separating (again in an *ad-hoc* way) the impacts of scale and fixity by assuming the alternative approximation

$$\ln G = \alpha + \beta \ln Y + \gamma t + \sum_j \delta_j \ln p_j + \phi \ln K, \tag{5.2}$$

where the p vector does not include p_K. This is, of course, an approximation to the short run cost function represented by $G(Y,t,p,K)$.

Since ϕ here measures $\partial \ln G/\partial \ln K = -Z_K \cdot (K/G) = \epsilon_{GK}$, which determines $\partial \ln C/\partial \ln K = \partial \ln(G + Z_K K)/\partial \ln K = \epsilon_{CK}$, this has implications for adjusting for both returns to scale and subequilibrium. However, the structure for linking ϵ_{GK}, ϵ_{CK} and ϵ_{CY}, as well as recognition of any other cross effects, is ignored in this unsophisticated specification, so it is not very well justified theoretically.

A final approach toward measurement of marginal cost to mention is an adaptation used by Robert Hall [1986], which was actually designed to take markups into account.[3] Since this process is designed particularly to capture marginal costs independently of average costs, it can potentially be used not only for measuring markups (the difference between output price and marginal cost), but also scale economies (the difference between average and marginal cost). Since Hall's methodology is based on a quite ingenious but simple parametric modeling approach and has had wide-ranging applications in the literature, it is worth digressing a moment to consider it in more detail.

The contribution by Hall provided a framework in which to measure marginal cost within the original Solow [1958] tradition. Hall's specification depends on the expression for marginal cost $MC = p_L \Delta L/(\Delta Y - \tau Y)$ (using our notation and assuming L is labor and τ is the rate of technical change).[4] This can be manipulated to read:

$$\frac{\Delta Y}{Y} = \mu \left(\frac{p_L L}{p_Y Y} \frac{\Delta L}{L} \right) + \tau + u_t, \tag{5.3}$$

where $\mu = p_Y/MC$, and $\tau_t = \tau + u_t$ is analogous to our ϵ_{Yt} measure.

The assumptions about τ_t are very important for Hall's analysis. One implication of the model is that technical progress can be "viewed as random deviations from an underlying constant rate" (Hall [1986], p.290). In addition, u_t is assumed uncorrelated with the business

[3]This extension is outlined in Chapter 9.

[4]This stems from the idea that capital is fixed, so short run changes in costs ($p_L L$) from an output change (ΔY) result only from changes in labor (ΔL). In addition, this reflects the idea that the change in output should be adjusted for the amount that output would have risen simply from technical change with no change in labor input (τY). See Hall [1986] for further details.

cycle, which is based on the idea that "true" productivity growth should not be correlated with the business cycle. In this scenario, productivity growth measures that indicate procyclical productivity, for example, are picking up some aspects of the production process other than just technical change.

The justification for this is straightforward; technical change should not decline in a cyclical downturn because technology does not just disappear. Instead, other changes firms make during cycles or other characteristics of the technology, such as utilization changes, the ability to take advantage of scale economies, and markups, instead drive the observed productivity fluctuations. Hall attributes all this cyclical variability to markup behavior, and estimates μ assuming τ is an average technical change variable and relying on the lack of correlation between u_t and cyclical behavior.[5]

The Hall specification assumes that Y is value added output, L is the only input under consideration, and L and p_L are based on measures of hourly labor input and price. Hall makes some comments about how additional inputs can be incorporated, retaining the assumption that Y refers to value added output and that the technological relationship between capital and labor is very simple.

In our case, since we have been working in previous chapters with gross output (including all inputs), we could use our development of the productivity growth measure to substitute a weighted average of all the inputs rather than just labor into (5.3). This extension of the

[5]This is the reverse of the approach used by Solow, who assumed MC could be measured by p_Y (perfect competition) and then solved for τ. As we have already stated, Solow's approach results in a residual that includes changes in all aspects of observed productivity, including markups, utilization, etc., as our estimate of "productivity", rather than just technical change. It might also be noted here that in Hall's treatment arguments are presented about how other cyclical factors might affect the markup, and characteristics of the production process such as labor hoarding are isolated. In our context this can be thought of as changing utilization of a quasi-fixed labor stock, which will be reflected in a full economic measure of capacity utilization.

Hall expression results in:

$$\frac{\Delta Y}{Y} = \mu \left(\sum_j \frac{p_j v_j}{p_Y Y} \frac{dv_j/dt}{v_j} \right) + \tau + u_t. \tag{5.3'}$$

Hall's empirical implementation based on equation (5.3') is quite straightforward, although it does require a simple form of econometric structure. The estimation method is to construct measures of $\Delta Y/Y$ for the left hand side of the expression and the share-weighted changes in the $v_j s$ for the right hand side (these would already have been computed for the traditional productivity growth measure), calculate the average of the traditional technical change measure for τ (or just use a constant since it does not have a time trend – multiplicatively scaling the constant does not make any difference) and run a regression to estimate μ. Once this estimate of μ is obtained it can be used to compute $MC = p_Y/\mu$ from the definition $\mu = p_Y/MC$.

The idea motivating this procedure is to choose as an estimator of μ the value just high enough to leave the residual uncorrelated with the business cycle. Although single equation methods are sufficient to carry this out, one qualification makes the procedure too complex to be dealt with simply by using an OLS (ordinary least squares) estimation technique. To impose the assumption that u is uncorrelated with the business cycle in the estimating process, instrumental variables instead of OLS techniques should be used, with measures of the business cycle as instruments. Hall uses a measure of the rate of growth of real GNP (Gross National Product) ($\Delta GNP/GNP$) as an instrument in his initial work, but for later studies constructs a complex instrumental variable taking changes in defense spending, oil price changes, and other things into account to create a variable that more clearly should exhibit the desired correlation characteristics.

In sum, there are a number of nonparametric and simple parametric approaches that may be pursued to measure the cost elasticities necessary to adjust productivity growth indexes to reflect returns to scale and fixity. However, none of them is able appropriately to identify the structure that is implied by a production process that simultaneously has all these characteristics. Therefore, many researchers have turned to more complete structural models based on production theory to provide the framework in which to measure indicators of economic performance. In the next sub-section we begin to consider how such a framework could be developed and implemented.

5.2 The Fundamentals of the Parametric Production Theory Approach

Parametric production theory-based empirical models of productivity growth and capacity utilization require a specific representation of the production technology through production functions or, more often, dual cost or profit functions. As alluded to several times while our framework for productivity growth analysis was formulated in previous chapters, this structure is possible to develop using production theory methods that allow specification of implementable cost functions incorporating the optimization processes of firms. In this section we will pull together some of the ideas and results underlying the development of such a structure.

Cost functions to be used as the basis for analysis may rely on the assumption of instantaneous adjustment, such as in specification $C(p,Y,t)$ from previous chapters. Optimization behavior, and thus optimum demand for all inputs, is explicitly included in this specification because of the underlying behavioral assumption of cost minimization. The resulting models therefore allow for the dependence of input demand, and costs with respect to any particular exogenous variable, to be affected by the levels of all other exogenous variables.

For example, demand equations for factors of production are derived from this function using Shephard's lemma (a duality result motivated in the next section) to obtain the long run optimal demand for input $j; \partial C(p_j,p',Y,t)/\partial p_j = v_j(p_j;p',Y,t)$, where the input price vector p' here excludes the price of input j. This function explicitly includes all arguments other than p_j as shift variables.[6] Similarly,

[6]Note that this full specification of the arguments of the function is usually simplified by writing $v_j(p_j,p,Y,t), v(\cdot)$, or even just v_j, leaving the functional nature of the demand expression from the optimization process implicit. These less

the (long run) total cost function may be written as $C(Y;p,t)$, which implies a marginal cost function $\partial C(Y;p,t)/\partial Y$ and average cost function $C(Y;p,t)/Y$, both of which are explicitly dependent on the levels of the input prices and technology. This provides a rich basis for the analysis of shifts in, movements along and shapes of input demand and long run cost functions.

Alternatively, cost functions may incorporate the existence of fixed factors by including the levels rather than the prices of the fixed factors as arguments, resulting in $G(p,Y,t,x)$, as seen in Chapter 3. These restricted or variable cost functions represent subequilibrium in the sense that they explicitly reflect short run constraints that keep the firm from reaching a steady state, and therefore they capture the difference between short and long run behavior. Short run cost curves can directly be measured using these functions, and in most cases one can capture the long run "desired" levels of fixed inputs by imputing the long run envelope of the short run curves. This expands further the behavior of firms that can be represented by the model.

For example, as briefly developed in previous chapters, given this explicit dependence on fixed factors capacity output and shadow values can directly be measured. Thus this framework provides an implementable structure that can be used to compute capacity utilization measures to adjust productivity growth indexes for subequilibrium. Returns to scale can also be measured in this framework, since the shapes of both the short and long run cost functions can be assessed. This allows the impacts of returns to scale on productivity growth indexes to be determined.

More specifically, once a functional form for $G(p,Y,t,x)$ is assumed, an explicit form for $Z_K(\cdot) = -\partial G(\cdot)/\partial K$ is implied.[7] If the parameters of the cost function can be estimated, therefore, a measure of Z_K can be constructed to substitute into the shares used for

explicit forms will primarily be used in this manuscript in order to keep complex notation at a minimum. It should be recognized, however, that since the cost functions represent minimized values, any expression characterized using these functions, such as an input demand or shadow value function, or from combining these with other information, such as a capacity utilization measure, depends directly on the arguments of the functions used as a basis of analysis.

[7]For some functional forms a closed form solution, however, may not exist.

the productivity growth computation. $CU_c(p,Y,t,x) = C^*/C$ can then be computed and used to calculate error biases and to show the difference between the primal and dual, or full and observed short run, measures of productivity growth, as outlined in Chapter 4. Similarly, the cost function can be used to construct estimates of $\epsilon_{CY}(p,Y,t,x) = [\partial C(\cdot)/\partial Y] \cdot Y/C = [\partial G(\cdot)/\partial Y] \cdot Y/C$, once a functional form for G and thus an explicit form for $\epsilon_{CY}(\cdot)$ is specified. As shown in the last chapter, this measure can be used to assess the impact of scale economies.

Some models may also allow for profit maximization, by explicitly specifying output quantity as a response to observed product price. Imperfect competition may even be recognized by incorporating an output demand and therefore marginal revenue function in the optimization framework. In addition, the framework can include dependence on various other economic factors that might affect the firm, such as regulations, costs of adjustment, inventory holdings, or other determinants of behavior, by including them as arguments of the function representing optimal behavior. This facilitates evaluation of the effects of these types of behavior on the production process, and thus on economic performance.

In the next sections we further elaborate this outline of a structure for analysis of production processes and productivity.

5.3 An Overview of the Relevant Duality Theory

Recent developments in production theory have provided a framework that facilitates summarizing the structure of the production process and therefore of productivity growth. This framework is primarily due to the methodology provided by duality theory. The basics of duality theory are effectively summarized in Diewert [1984]. This section provides a somewhat simplified overview of Diewert's treatment, which gathers together and formalizes a number of results referred to in previous sections of this text. The treatment here highlights the theoretical concepts necessary to support empirical implementation of models used for extension and refinement of productivity growth measurement and interpretation.[8]

The fundamental idea of duality theory is that the technology represented by the firm's production function $Y = Y(v,t) = f(v,t)$ (where, as before, t is a time counter or other representation of changing technology over time, Y is output and v is a vector of J variable inputs) can be described equivalently in other forms, most of which also incorporate optimizing behavior.

One of these forms is the cost function since it reflects the minimum total cost of producing a particular output level (Y), given the production technology (t) and input prices (p). Since the production function is by definition a constraint on this minimization problem, the cost function $C(p,Y,t)$ not only reflects cost minimization but also completely describes the technology of the firm. In reverse, this implies that in certain circumstances $C(\cdot)$ can be used to reproduce the original production function. Similarly, in the short run with, say, capital fixed, this duality can be developed in terms of a production function distinguishing variable (v) from fixed (x) inputs, $Y(v,x,t)$, and the corresponding restricted or variable cost function $G(p,t,Y,x)$.

Other dual functions can also provide a useful structure for analysis. Profit maximization, for example, not only incorporates all the information contained in the cost function, but also reflects output choice. These choices can be formalized as a profit function $\Pi(p,p_Y,t)$ or restricted profit function $\Pi(p,p_Y,t,x)$, where p_Y instead of Y is exogenous to the firm so output choice is captured.

Since this represents a more general optimization problem than the cost function, in some cases the profit function is preferable for analysis. However, if it can be assumed that the observed cost minimization point sufficiently closely approximates the optimal, not much information is lost by using a cost function approach. In addition, if output regulation precludes the firm from choosing output to maxi-

[8] Although this provides theoretical justification for some of the results asserted in other parts of this text, the reader who is not interested in, or well versed in, the theoretical details can skip this with little impact on the understanding of the rest of the text.

mize profits, the cost function, even if somewhat more restricted, may be more relevant. We will, therefore, focus on the use of cost functions, although in most cases straightforward extension allows the analysis to be remotivated in terms of the profit function or other dual functions.[9]

To formalize the cost function and motivate its application we start by defining the total cost function as

$$C(Y,p,t) = \min_v(p^T v : f(v,t) \geq Y) \tag{5.4}$$

where $(p_1, p_2, \ldots, p_J) = p >> 0_J$ is a vector of J positive input prices, no monopsony exists, the production function is defined as before, "T" indicates a transposed vector, and $>>$ means strictly positive (every element is greater than zero).

If a solution to this cost minimization problem exists, we can state a number of regularity conditions that the resulting function must satisfy. These properties are (in less rigorous form than that presented in Diewert [1984]):

(i) $C(\cdot)$ is a nonnegative function $(C(Y,t,p) \geq 0)$;

(ii) $C(\cdot)$ is (positively) linearly homogeneous in input prices for any fixed output level $(C(Y,t,\mu p) \equiv \mu C(Y,t,p)$ for $\mu > 0)$;

(iii) $C(\cdot)$ is increasing in prices $(C(Y,t,p_1) > C(Y,t,p_0)$ if $p_1 > p_0$, or $\partial C/\partial p_j > 0)$;

(iv) $C(\cdot)$ is a concave function of p (informally, $\partial^2 C/\partial p_j^2 \leq 0$);[10]

(v) $C(\cdot)$ is continuous in p and continuous from below in Y; and

(vi) C is nondecreasing in Y for fixed p $(C(Y^0,t,p) \leq C(Y^1,t,p)$ for $Y^0 \leq Y^1$, or $\partial C/\partial Y > 0)$.

[9]Functions such as the indirect production function or distance functions can also be used for analysis, but are not as often used because they are less intuitive representations of firm behavior.

[10]More formally, if $C(Y,p^0,t) = \min_X(p^{0T}X : f(X,t) \geq Y) = p^{0T}X^0$, and $C(Y,p^1,t) = \min_X(p^{1T}X : f_0(X,t) \geq Y) = p^{1T}X^1$, then $C(Y,t,\lambda p_0 + (1-\lambda)p^1) \geq \lambda p^{0T}X^0 + (1-\lambda)p^{1T}X^1 = \lambda C(Y,t,p^0) + (1-\lambda)C(Y,t,p^1)$.

Most of these conditions are quite intuitive. (i), for example, simply reflects the fact that costs are positive for productive firms. If not, if output price were positive production would be infinite. (ii) indicates that the units of measurement for costs do not matter; if all prices increase by a particular factor, minimum possible total costs of production for a given output level must change by the same proportion. (iii) implies that if a price increases, costs must also increase; if this is not the case costs could not have been minimized in the first place. (iv) is less obvious but still has some interpretation potential. As an input price rises minimum costs also go up, but this increase will not be proportional because substitution occurs. The marginal product of input j drops with increased use, so the demand curve for this input slopes down. A proportionate increase in costs is therefore an upper bound on the increase.[11] (v) in effect says that inputs must be divisible. This is required for derivatives to be defined for analysis, although discontinuities could result if indivisibilities exist. (vi) ensures that marginal cost as well as total cost is positive, which is necessary for optimization to make sense. If this does not hold and marginal revenue is positive, optimal production will not be defined.

Only if a function satisfies all of these (quite reasonable) properties will it be a valid cost function for theoretical and empirical work. This implies that many types of functions that have been assumed for empirical analysis cannot be justified theoretically. For example, the linear cost function $C(Y,p,t) = \alpha + \beta^T p + \gamma t + \delta Y$, where α, γ, and δ are constants and β is a vector of constants violates property (ii) (linear homogeneity in input prices).

Once a valid cost function is specified, the conceptual process underlying this duality theory result can be reversed to reconstruct the firm's underlying production function by setting up the optimization

[11] Since this result is relatively nonintuitive and is important for many duality theory results, Diewert [1984] provides a useful geometric illustration of why it occurs. In brief, this shows that if two cost minimizing situations are considered with two different price vectors but the same isoquant, the average of these minimum costs at the average price between the two periods will be lower than can be reached at the average price level between the two periods. This implies the intuition mentioned here. For further details, consult Diewert [1984].

problem

$$f^*(v,t) = \max_Y(Y : p^T v \geq C(Y,p,t) \text{ for every } p >> 0_J). \qquad (5.5)$$

This will reproduce the convex hull of the isoquants reflecting the production technology, so if the production function, and therefore the isoquants, fulfill standard regulatory conditions,[12] $f^*(v,t) = f(v,t)$.

This follows because cost minimization will never reflect nonconvexities or incorrect slopes in isoquants because they will be irrelevant for behavior, but these will not exist if regularity conditions on the original function are globally satisfied. In addition, this suggests that for empirical application it does not really matter whether the technology truly is represented by $f^*(\cdot)$ or $f(\cdot)$, because observable market data will never allow us to identify the difference. The nonconvex areas will be ignored by rational economic agents.

The cost function therefore completely represents the information on the technology contained in the production function, and reflects optimization behavior since its construction is based on the solution to an optimization problem. Thus all the information on factor or input demand patterns can be inferred from the cost function.

This implication stems from the result called Shephard's lemma, employed in the previous two chapters, which states that if $C(Y,p,t)$ satisfies all regularity properties mentioned above, it will be the case that $v_j(Y,p,t) = \partial C(Y,p,t)/\partial p_j$, for all j, where $v_j(Y,p,t)$ is the cost minimizing input quantity of input j needed to produce Y units of output given input prices p and the level of technology t. This can be motivated very loosely by noting that since $C(Y,p,t)$ represents minimum costs, and therefore $C(Y,p,t) = \Sigma p_j v_j^*$ where $v_j^* = v_j(\cdot)$ is the optimal demand for input v_j, it must be true that $\partial C/\partial p_j = v_j^* = v_j(\cdot)$.

Using the duality theory foundation we can also illustrate that some theoretically required properties of demand functions are met by the $v_j(\cdot)$ functions. For example, as long as $C(\cdot)$ is twice differentiable, property (iv) implies that input demand decreases with input price

[12] See Diewert [1984] for a rigorous treatment of regulatory conditions for different types of functions.

increases, so the requirement that demand curves be downward sloping is satisfied by construction. In addition, homogeneity of degree zero in prices[13] is satisfied by construction; a standard duality result asserts that if a function, say $C(Y,p,t)$ is homogeneous of degree n in an argument, say p, then the derivative function $\partial C/\partial p_j$ is homogeneous of degree $n-1$. Since property (ii) requires $C(\cdot)$ to be linearly homogeneous in prices, $\partial C/\partial p_j$ will be homogeneous of degree zero.

Finally, it can also be shown that not all inputs can be inferior – another standard theoretical result. This is somewhat more complex to illustrate, but can be derived in three steps. First note that the linear homogeneity in prices property of $C(\cdot)$ from (ii) will also hold for a derivative of this function with respect to another argument of the function, and thus will be true for $\partial C/\partial Y$.[14] Using this, Euler's theorem implies that summing up the derivatives of $\partial C/\partial Y$ with respect to the different components of p, multiplied by the corresponding price, and adding, reproduces the function: $\Sigma_j p_j \partial^2 C/\partial Y \partial p_j = \partial C/\partial Y$. Since $\partial^2 C/\partial Y \partial p_j = \partial^2 C/\partial p_j \partial Y = \partial v_j/\partial Y$ by the symmetry of the Hessian matrix and Shephard's lemma, this implies $\Sigma_j p_j \partial v_j/\partial Y = \partial C/\partial Y > 0$ from (vi). Therefore not all $\partial v_j/\partial Y$ can be negative.

As already implied, therefore, the cost function is a theoretically justifiable basis for empirical analysis of the entire pattern of firm behavior. Due to the construction of the cost function, theoretically consistent and valid input demands may directly be represented. Once these demand functions are derived from a specific functional form for $C(Y,p,t)$, the demand functions themselves and changes in input demand resulting from changes in any arguments of the function can be specified and assessed.

In addition, adding other arguments into the function does not in general cause these overall properties to be violated. In particular, as stated before, a variable cost function subject to K fixed inputs,

---

[13]The definition of homogeneity of degree zero in prices for this function is that if all prices change by a certain proportion, the demand function is not affected. This, of course, is the same as saying the demand function may be specified in terms of relative prices.

[14]This is also a standard duality theory result. See Diewert [1984].

represented by the vector x, can be defined as $G(Y, x, t, p)$, where the p vector now does not include the price of any x_k variable. This formally results from a minimization problem analogous to (5.4) where in this case the relevant production function constraint $Y(v, x, t)$ represents only the trade-offs among variable inputs possible to produce a given output level using the given stocks of x_k.

Lau [1978] has shown that the standard cost function properties are maintained for the variable cost function when this procedure is used. In particular, Shephard's lemma still holds (for the variable inputs) and the properties of the resulting input demand functions are maintained. An additional property of the function results in the shadow value expression we have used to represent how variable costs can be reduced with a relaxation of the fixity constraint on $x_k : -\partial G(\cdot)/\partial x_k = Z_k(\cdot)$. Also, regularity conditions require G to be decreasing ($\partial G/\partial x_k < 0$) and convex ($\partial^2 G/\partial x_k^2 < 0$) in x_k; the shadow value is positive and declines with increases in the stock of x_k. Using these properties along with the Shephard's lemma property of optimal variable input demands allows for a rich specification of the firm's behavior in the short and long run.

To extend the interpretive potential of the cost function further, we can add a vector r, which denotes N other arguments of the function which may be choice or fixed variables but do not have any impact on returns to scale. In this case, the technology can be summarized by a restricted cost function of the form $G(x, p, t, Y, r)$.[15] The r_n variables, defined as "environmental or behavioral parameters" by McFadden [1978], may be any determinants of costs (and therefore firm behavior) other than commodity levels. These variables represent one version of McFadden's [1978] "z" variables which may not be subject to curvature restrictions.

For example, regulation could be a constraint on the firm's choices. This may be incorporated into the r vector by a variable representing the amount of regulatory capital (say pollution abatement capital) owned by the firm, that is not a factor in production of the measured

[15] Note that this can also be extended to the case of multiple outputs, although representation of capacity utilization is problematic in this case, as shown by Berndt and Fuss [1989].

output and is likely not a choice variable for the firm.[16] Another type of variable that could be contained in r is investment in stocks of x_k, $dx_k/dt = \dot{x}_k$. If this is included in r it represents adjustment costs on the quasi-fixed factors, formalized by $\partial G/\partial|x_k| > 0$; variable costs increase according to the amount of investment or disinvestment.[17]

Although many other duality theory results have been generated, these provide the foundation for constructing the empirically implementable models of firm behavior that are often used for analysis of the structure of production.

5.4 Specification of Empirically Implementable Restricted Factor Demand Models

Using this duality theory as a basis, factor demand models employing the cost function framework have often been developed and used for empirical implementation. The resulting analysis of the production structure, including that for productivity growth and capacity utilization, therefore by definition has a cost orientation. In this section we formalize more completely the use of cost functions to generate estimable equations representing firm behavior and other computable measures reflecting production processes and performance.

To begin, let us say that the technology can be summarized by the extended version of the restricted cost function referred to above, $G(x,p,t,Y,r)$. Since this dual cost function reflects the existing technology by construction and also incorporates optimization behavior, Shephard's lemma can be used to represent optimal (cost minimizing) variable input demands:

$$v_j(p_j;x,p,t,Y,r) = \frac{\partial G(x,p,t,Y,r)}{\partial p_j}. \tag{5.6}$$

[16]See Morrison [1988b]. This extension will be developed further in Chapter 9.
[17]For one example of this, see Morrison [1988c].

This derivative by definition holds all other arguments of the $G(\cdot)$ function fixed so they become shift variables for the demand function. Once a functional form for $G(\cdot)$ is assumed, therefore, a specific form of the input demand function is imposed, and the system of J estimating equations implied by (5.6) reflects variable input demand behavior conditional on all the other arguments of the function.

Other choices may also be implied by the G function, and therefore motivate additional equations summarizing firm decisions. For example, if $\dot{x}$ is in the r vector, investment equations are implied. The optimization problem facing the firm in this case is to choose the path of x_k, or $\dot{x}_k$, in addition to the vector of variable inputs at each time period to minimize the present value of the stream of costs from producing output Y at each future period, or, in continuous time:

$$\text{Min}_{x,\dot{x}} C(0) = \int_0^{\infty} e^{-rt} \left(G(p, x, \dot{x}, r, t, Y) + \sum_k p_k x_k \right) dt + \sum_k q_k x_k(0), \tag{5.7}$$

where $p_k = q_k(r + \delta_k) =$ the rental price of x_k, q_k are the asset prices of new quasi-fixed inputs, the firm knows the initial stocks of quasi-fixed inputs $x(0), r$ includes all the components of r other than x, and G captures minimization at each point in time over all variable inputs given any x, Y levels.[18] Minimization of this yields the Euler first order conditions:

$$-G_x - rG_{\dot{x}} - p_x + G_{\dot{x}\dot{x}}\ddot{x} + G_{x\dot{x}}\dot{x} = 0, \tag{5.8}$$

as in Berndt, Fuss and Waverman [1980], where $\ddot{x}$ denotes the second derivative of x with respect to time and p_x represents the K prices of the fixed factors x_k.

This set of equations implicitly represents investment, and therefore adjustment toward long run equilibrium, of the firm. In this form they can be estimated as in Pindyck and Rotemberg [1983] and Morrison [1988c,d]. Depending on the functional form it may also be possible analytically to solve for the x_k levels. For example, in Berndt, Fuss and Waverman [1980] this is accomplished by using a quadratic form

[18] See Berndt-Fuss-Waverman [1980] or Morrison and Berndt [1981] for clarification of the underlying steps.

for $G(\cdot)$, so that the second derivatives do not depend on the data. The Berndt *et.al.* development results in a partial adjustment framework where the adjustment parameter depends on the discount rate and parameters of the model. These investment equations, however, become intractable to solve with multiple quasi-fixed inputs unless some independence is assumed, as discussed in Morrison and Berndt [1981].

Note that for either of these investment specifications, expectations become an issue since the firm is explicitly making current decisions depending on future expected exogenous variables. This can be dealt with in a number of ways, none of which is completely satisfactory. For example, Berndt, Fuss and Waverman [1980] simply assume static expectations so only current variables are relevant for the decision making process. Pindyck and Rotemberg [1983] rely instead on the analytical equivalence of rational expectations and the "cleansing of errors" resulting from using three stage least squares as an estimating technique. Morrison [1986b] outlines the use of "partial" rational expectations or adaptive expectations frameworks based on constructing time series analysis ARIMA specifications of price paths, and concludes that the adaptive expectations framework is preferable for representing expectations formation.[19] Implementation of this, which implies estimating additional equations representing the expectations process, will be discussed further in Chapter 7.

Equations representing pricing behavior may also be incorporated into the analysis, if one assumes the observed output is the profit maximizing level of output, or if profit maximization is explicitly built into the analysis. Mork [1978], for example, used the profit maximization equality $p_Y = MC = \partial G/\partial Y$ to construct an estimating equation based on the assumptions that observed output coincides with short run profit maximization and perfect competition exists.[20]

[19] See Chapter 7 for further details.

[20] Once this is included the cost function approach represents the same optimization process and output choice decision as that captured by a profit function. This, therefore, provides an alternative approach to use when output choice is thought to be important. Results will differ at least somewhat, however, since the output level is an argument of the cost function-based equations instead of the output price. The stochastic specification is therefore different.

Morrison [1988c,d] instead includes a demand equation $Y = D(p_Y, \rho)$, where ρ is a vector of variables affecting the output demand curve, which implies an inverse demand equation $p_Y = D^{-1}(Y, \rho)$ to derive the estimating equation

$$D^{-1}(Y,\rho) = p_Y = -\frac{\partial D(Y,\rho)^{-1}}{\partial Y} Y + \frac{\partial G}{\partial Y} \tag{5.9}$$

from the expression

$$MR = Y \cdot \frac{\partial D(Y,\rho)^{-1}}{\partial Y} + D(Y,\rho)^{-1} = \frac{\partial G}{\partial Y} = MC, \tag{5.10}$$

where MR denotes marginal revenue. This allows profit maximization with imperfect competition and motivates not only an additional potential estimating equation but also the computation of the price elasticity of output demand facing the firm and the markup of price over marginal cost.

These equations completely represent the input demand, investment, and (in a profit maximization context) output supply decisions for a firm. These decisions are provided with an explicit representation by assuming a functional form for $G(\cdot)$ (and $D(\cdot)$, if used) and estimating a system of equations including all these expressions. Using the resulting parameter estimates, patterns of behavior may be assessed using elasticities of demand (and other decisions) with respect to changes in exogenous variables (discussed further in Chapter 7), and indexes representing productivity, capacity utilization, shadow values, or other indicators.

For example, this model implies that a measure of the impact of technical change may be imputed explicitly from the functional relationship; $\partial C/\partial t$ can be measured directly from the cost function itself. This measure is not often used, however, as a basis for analysis, because the focus of technical change analysis is generally on explaining the swings in the standard accounting measure of productivity growth and this direct measure by construction smooths those swings.

Shadow value and capacity utilization measures, however, stem directly from the estimated parameters of these equations. Since the shadow values of the quasi-fixed inputs have been defined as $-G_k = Z_k$ for each k, once the parameters of $G(\cdot)$ have been estimated this derivative may directly be taken, resulting in an explicit form for Z_k. The dual capacity utilization measure may than be calculated easily as

$$CU_c = C^*/C = \left(G + \sum_k Z_k x_k\right)/C.$$

Alternatively, depending on the interpretation of the measure desired and what variables are included in the r vector, this could be measured as

$$CU_c = \left(G + \sum_k Z_k x_k + \sum_n Z_n r_n\right)/C.$$

For example, if the $r_n s$ measured regulatory variables, it might be useful to consider their impact on the perceived level of capacity utilization, even though these are not choice variables for the firm. Due to this constraint, in this case equilibrium capacity utilization CU_c will not equal one.

Although these measures (and any others based on a restricted cost function) represent only short run behavior, long run or steady state responses may also be determined. Movement to a long run point may be implicit or explicit depending on whether investment equations are actually derived and used. If they are not, then the firm is assumed to be optimizing only in the short run based on the given levels of the fixed factors, whereas if they are, an adjustment process is implied. In either case, however, the "desired" or long run equilibrium levels of the quasi-fixed factors may be imputed as mentioned in Chapter 3; this now can be formalized further.

More specifically, the investment equations above depend on the market prices of the fixed inputs, p_x, and the shadow values of the x_k inputs, $-G_x = Z_x$. The explicit representation of desired fixed input stocks, therefore, also depends on these values, since in equilibrium when $\dot{x} = \ddot{x} = 0$ and adjustment costs $rG_{\dot{x}}(0)$ are zero (no net investment is being carried out) equation (5.8) reduces to $-G_x = p_x$. This set of K equalities can therefore be solved for the K steady state levels of the quasi-fixed inputs as $x^*(p,t,Y,r)$.[21] This ability to ascertain long run behavior from the model permits measurement of long run elasticities, including the scale elasticity ϵ_{CY}^{LR} determining returns to scale.

Alternatively, these long run equilibrium equations can be solved, as outlined before, for the steady state (capacity) level of output, Y^*, given the levels of quasi-fixed factors determining available capacity. Again, note that this capacity level of output is not a "desired" level in the sense that adjustment of output is not implied; Y^* is simply that level of output production that would cause the firm to have no desire to adjust its fixed factors. As developed in Chapter 3, the primal measure of capacity utilization Y/Y^* is based on this computed value for Y^*.

From this formalization of the fundamentals of a production theory-based empirically implementable model of firm behavior it is clear that such a model provides a rich basis for analysis of production structures and productivity. In particular, it not only allows representation of demand, supply and investment patterns, but provides an integrated structure for measurement of indexes representing subequilibrium, scale economies and other characteristics of the production process that one might want to identify separately from productivity growth.

* * * * *

The actual empirical implementation of such a framework is not sraightforward. First, as with all measures of production structure and productivity growth, including those based on accounting or simsple parametric methods, the question of how to construct relevant data immediately arises. This is especially problematic for the capital variable, since the durability of capital poses difficulties for measurement and the economic theory underlying the notion of capital has no direct counterpart in standard balance sheet or income statement entries for firms. This is a particularly important obstacle in

[21] Note that if multiple quasi-fixed inputs exist, these equations must be solved simultaneously to generate expressions for full long run equilibrium in all fixed inputs.

the restricted cost function context because of the emphasis on capital in measures of capacity utilization. In addition, questions about functional forms that might be useful for analysis emerge because of the significance of short- and long-run substitution patterns. Econometric issues are also important to confront, since the framework is complex. Systems estimation, simultaneity and nonlinearity problems often abound in these models, for example. The following two chapters deal with these implementation difficulties.

Chapter 6

Data Construction for Estimation and Measurement

The data generally used for estimation of production theory models, or generating accounting measures of productivity growth, include as many outputs and inputs of the firms as possible in order to reflect all production and costs. Output is usually measured as an aggregate of all types of production. The categories of inputs generally distinguished are capital (K), labor (L), energy (E), non-energy intermediate materials (M), and sometimes purchased services (S). Inputs such as land and inventories are often included in the measure of capital. Others, like pollution abatement capital, are often implicitly included, and some, such as $R\&D$ (research and development) expenses, are generally ignored.

The two potentially most problematic issues that arise in data construction involve the measurement of capital and aggregation. The construction of capital data is difficult because it requires re-thinking the idea of current input use. As a durable input the *services* from the available stock of capital, and the *rental* or user prices of these services, are the relevant values for construction of productivity growth measures, and neither of these are readily observable. Developing capital measures also requires consideration of what types of inputs should be included as components of the capital stock, which is sometimes unclear. Aggregation issues arise because none of the data categories, except possibly labor, can generally be measured in terms of one type of unit. Therefore, quantity indexes aggregating "apples and oranges" (like tons of iron ore and yards of cloth in the materials category) must be constructed. It is often difficult to accomplish this in a relevant, and thus interpretable, manner.

In this chapter these and related issues about appropriate data development for representation of production processes and productivity growth are addressed. The following Section (6.1) overviews the construction of the necessary noncapital data series. Then the next two sections focus on capital data measurement; the conceptual issues underlying construction of capital are overviewed in Section 6.2, and then formalization of the measurement procedures is carried out in Section 6.3. Finally, Section 6.4 elaborates some of the aggregation issues that arise in data construction.

6.1 Developing Non-Capital Data for Empirical Implementation

A number of issues emerge when attempting to construct appropriate price and quantity measures of non-capital inputs and outputs. These issues are wide-ranging but generally involve adjusting for quality change and aggregating across heterogeneous commodities. In this section we will consider a fairly standard division of output and input into one aggregate output, and labor, energy and intermediate materials inputs,[1] and separately identify how these difficulties arise for these individual factors in turn.

Output (Y) measurement for a single-output firm is fairly straightforward, since for a single output there is only one type of unit involved, say numbers of pairs of shoes or tons of steel. In this case, therefore, an (average) price per pair or ton (or other quantity units) can

[1] This is, for example, the division used by the Bureau of Labor Statistics in the U.S.

generally be specified in dollars (or other monetary units) as total sales divided by the quantity of the commodity, and thus quantity and price indexes can directly be measured.

Even in this simple case, however, questions begin to emerge. For example, it is not immediately clear how changes in quality can be handled. In a few cases (tons of steel might be an example) this is not a critical issue since the product is quite homogeneous. However, in most cases (e.g. thousands of computers produced) the quality of a particular unit might change dramatically over time or across companies; the product is very heterogeneous. These problems are not in general dealt with well using conventional data gathering procedures, but some researchers have attempted to deal with them using hedonic measurement techniques. Although I will not pursue this further here, a number of studies have pointed out this problem, its possible consequences, and alternative methods of dealing with it.[2]

Inventories also pose difficulties for output measurement because data is generally reported in terms of sales, whereas actual production is the relevant output; these will differ by the change in output inventories. For productivity measurement, therefore, sales data must be adjusted by net inventory change. Other questions might arise with firm level data about how to deal with promotional "giveaways" or other sales promotions that affect the value of the output produced, and purchases of final goods for resale. Again, while these problems are often "swept under the rug", they should not be forgotten.

Additional dilemmas arise if the firm is a multi-product firm. How to add together goods that are measured in different units is a standard index-number problem. It is not an easy problem to deal with; although determining the total value of production is relatively straightforward, dividing this value into its aggregate quantity and price (deflator) components is not. Index number theories are generally relied on to provide the best guide to the type of index to compute, but even theoretically founded measures are not truly justifiable unless relative price or quantity changes across commodities are "very" similar, or relative marginal products do not change with changes in other input

[2]These types of issues are raised again in Chapter 9 and Chapter 10 in more detail.

prices.[3] These problems, of course, become more severe when aggregation to the level of an industry or country is attempted. These aggregation and index number issues will be dealt with further in Section 6.4.

Labor input (L) is relatively easy to measure compared to other inputs, since labor statistics are generally presented in terms of wage bill paid (total expenditure) and number of workers or worker-hours (quantity). This implies a direct division of the expenditure into quantity and price. Similar problems arise for labor as for output, however.

First, although hours worked would be better as a measure of true labor input than the number of workers, many firms do not have the necessary data to determine the hours. In addition, there may be important differences between salaried (nonproduction) and wage (production) employees, that is not reflected in the number of hours worked, suggesting that aggregation difficulties are important to address. Another separately identifiable category of labor, entrepreneurial input, is generally not even included in the data. The quality of labor might also change over time, which has caused some researchers[4] to generate "effective" labor indexes to account for education, training and other quality components that might affect the efficiency of workers independently of overall technical change. The common existence of contract or temporary labor demand poses an additional problem. This component of labor is often reported differently than standard labor expenses on income statements of firms, provoking questions about whether this input should be considered part of labor or of purchased services. These diverse types of issues

---

[3]The sufficient conditions of proportionate (constant relative) prices and quantities are due to Hicks and Leontief, respectively, and are discussed by Parks [1971]. Even if these conditions do not hold, however, separability allows aggregation. One of the simplest separability requirements is that the relationship between two commodities, represented by the ratio of their marginal products, does not change with alterations in relative prices of other commodities.

[4]See Jorgenson, Gollop and Fraumeni [1987] for a discussion of how such labor data might be constructed. This reference also provides important information on measurement of other inputs. Adjustment of labor data for quality changes might also take the form of hedonic measurement, similarly to that for output.

need to be dealt with to construct relevant and interpretable measures of labor input and price.

Energy input (E) is sometimes measured in units which facilitate direct summation of different types of energy use – either $BTUs$ or Megawatt Hours, for example. In this case simple summation of $BTUs(MWHs)$ generates a quantity measure, and summation of the expenditures on these energy sources and division of this value by the quantity of $BTUs(MWHs)$ results in a direct average price per $BTU(MWH)$ measure.

Although this appears reasonably straightforward, questions arise about whether input- or output-BTU's are a more appropriate measure for the quantity of energy demanded, since conversion efficiencies differ;[5] this may invalidate this simple aggregation of the input components. Also, sometimes it is not completely clear whether a particular input is an energy or non-energy material input. For example, is crude petroleum in the refining or plastics industry an energy or material input?[6] Finally, if energy sources are measured in different units, a quantity index must instead be developed based on index number theory, since substitution between energy sources is not perfect. Ultimately, therefore, individual judgment and assumptions are built into the data by the researcher.

Non-energy intermediate materials (M) and purchased services (S) tend to be "catch-all" categories which include data on various inputs with different units. Quality changes over time are especially difficult to deal with in this case. Another problem with constructing these data is distinguishing what should belong in these categories rather than in others. Justification of aggregation procedures of course also remains an issue.

An important obstacle in terms of practical application is that many inputs in these categories which appear on a firm's income statement are only presented in terms of the value of the input, with no measure of quantity or price. Since it is important to determine how much change in value can justifiably be considered a result of changes in

[5]See Berndt [1978] for further discussion of this problem.

[6]In the U.S. Census surveys crude petroleum is treated as a materials input; energy is restricted to those inputs used directly for heat, light and power.

unit price over time rather than in the quantity units themselves, relevant price indexes or deflators must be found to use for aggregation purposes. Only then can quantity and price indexes be individually identified.

Accomplishing this is sometimes difficult. Some researchers have argued that an overall *GDP* deflator is useful for many purposes,[7] or that if an input might be thought of as labor-intensive an overall labor cost deflator might be better. It is, however, also often possible to find output deflators for specific industries,[8] and these in many cases might be preferable. For example, if a certain type of chemical is used for production, it might be most justifiable to use a chemical-industries deflator (or a further breakdown into industry sub-sectors if available) than an overall *GDP* deflator.

Overall, although much of the necessary information for noncapital data construction is available from balance sheets and income statements of firms, and from the aggregated data on these firms available from government statistics, many issues arise concerning the interpretation and use of these data. These issues should be kept in mind when constructing data series or using available data sources, and when interpreting results generated from these numbers.

6.2 Difficult Issues Surrounding Capital Data Construction: The Concepts

Construction of data series for capital poses fundamental and somewhat unique difficulties, although some are also similar to those we confronted in the last section concerning other inputs and outputs.

---

[7] Schankerman and Nadiri [1986] have used this for *R&D* expenditures, for example.

[8] These correspond to the otput prices used for productivity computations to deflate output values for particular industries. Some government statistical organizations, for example, such as the Bureau of Labor Statistics in the U.S., provide productivity growth measures for fairly disaggregated industrial sectors, and the corresponding output price and quantity data used is often made publicly available.

First, the categories are not clearly defined. Although capital plant, equipment and structures (buildings) provide the essential basis of the measure, as mentioned in Chapter 3, other categories might also be important. For example, some inputs such as *R&D* (research and development) might be considered a long-term investment, and therefore a component of the capital stock, whereas capital inputs such as pollution abatement capital which do not produce measurable output might be thought to be irrelevant for measurement of productivity and therefore not included as part of capital.

Evaluation of the treatment of even more standard components of the capital stock raises troublesome questions. Land, for example, may bestow widely ranging capital gains on its owner, which causes problems valuing it as a component of capital; i.e., its rental price may be negative if large unexpected capital gains counteract the direct costs of the asset. Inventories are also often specified as an element of the capital stock, but arguably do not provide productive services, and therefore might be left out for productivity computations. Maintenance could also be included as part of total capital holdings, since it in a sense adds to the stock (or at least the durability) of capital equipment.[9]

Also, once data on these different components of the capital stock are developed and the relevant components determined, aggregation of these into an overall capital measure is required, so the aggregation difficulties mentioned for the non-capital inputs again arise.

The types of issues mentioned so far have similar counterparts for other data categories. However, fundamental distinctions involving the durable nature of capital also exist. Specifically, the primary difficulty that distinguishes the measurement of capital from that for other inputs involves how to deal with measurement of a good

[9]It might be useful to mention here that if one is working with firm data, only some of the components of the balance sheet are consistent with an economist's notion of capital stock. Categories that might be included, for example, include both tangible and intangible fixed assets, "investments", inventories, and accounts receivable. The point is, however, to measure productive assets rather than financial assets, so "investments" in bonds or accounts receivables would not be considered part of the capital stock. Sometimes some categories of financial capital, however, are included under the heading of "working capital".

that provides a stream of services over time, and which is often not considered part of the "costs" faced by the firm.

The non-capital inputs (L, E, M and S) are generally treated by accountants as encompassing virtually all the "valid" costs of production. The only categories on standard balance sheets that might not be contained in the labor, materials, energy and purchased services categories of the non-capital inputs (and therefore are considered as part of costs in an accounting definition) are depreciation (the amount allowed by the taxation authorities, which may have no economic basis), taxes, $R\&D$, rentals of equipment and structures, and maintenance. Any revenue over and above these yearly expenditures on capital and the non-capital costs are considered accounting "profits".

Economists often go to the other extreme in computing the "expenditure" on capital. From the economist's perspective, if perfect competition and constant returns to scale prevail, all the "profits" measured by accountants are really returns to capital; they are necessary payments for capital because they represent opportunity costs. If this is true, a "residual" method of constructing the price of capital may be used which imputes an internal rate of return to capital and assumes this ex-post rate of return is the capital stock's legitimate cost.[10]

For most productivity growth computations, neither of these concepts of capital's quantity, price and value is valid. The accountant's definition ignores the fact that there is a real cost of putting funds into a durable capital stock. This real cost includes not only the (economic) rate of depreciation, but also the loss of the return one could obtain on the money elsewhere, given the risk incurred – what is often called the "user cost" of capital. The firm (or the investor who provided the necessary funds) therefore *should* receive a certain amount of return to compensate for these costs; to an economist these are costs, not part of the profits for the firm.

[10]This is computed by taking the dollar value of sales (revenues), subtracting expenditures on variable inputs (non-capital costs) to obtain the value of or "returns to" capital, and then computing the capital price by dividing these returns by a measure of the quantity of capital. This procedure is discussed in further detail below.

The economist's residual conception of capital, however, also has some shortcomings. Some returns picked up in a measure of the *ex-post* or internal rate of return generated by a residual method may be due to technological and market characteristics like returns to scale and market power (imperfect competition or monopoly). For the former, it may be justifiable for the firm to absorb this return, since a larger firm is more efficient in terms of lower unit cost; this is in a sense a return to greater efficiency. In terms of imperfect competition, returns or profits generated simply because of a firm's market power do not reflect efficiency. They should be identified to correctly impute a value to capital, since the loss to society from the monopoly element affects overall welfare.

Determining what portion of revenues should be considered "pure" profits, and what part is truly a return to capital, is crucial for correctly evaluating the contribution of capital to production. These capital measurement issues are thus important for productivity analysts to take into account to assess effectively whether productivity or efficiency has increased. Methods used to measure capital quantity and price must deal with these issues.

Ideally the capital stock can be measured by adding up investment in capital goods over time for each component of the stock, allowing for inflation in the price of capital, physical depreciation of the stock, maintenance, obsolescence and anything else that alters the usefulness of a given dollar's worth of capital investment over time. This generates a constant dollar (or other monetary unit) level of capital for each asset which can be considered the effective stock available for production. The flow of capital services (quantity of capital used each year) is then generally assumed to be a constant proportion of the corresponding capital stock. The associated price of capital services for each capital input is measured as the price of investment goods (the "asset" price), adjusted for taxes, discount rates, depreciation and capital gains to generate a "rental price" or "user price" for each component of the capital stock. These procedures generate *ex ante* measures of the service quantity and rental price of each type of capital which can then be aggregated using index number methods such as Divisia aggregation to generate measures of the quantity and price of the capital input as a whole.

Generally, however, the necessary data are not available in a convenient form for carrying out these procedures appropriately. For example, aggregation problems abound, quality changes occur over time, and appropriate price deflators, measures of obsolescence and other crucial determinants of the effective available stock of capital, are often not available. Therefore, many researchers measure the value of capital available to the firm as the value of the firm's sales minus all variable costs (usually including labor, intermediate materials and energy), compute a capital stock estimate from data on investment, and generate an "internal rate of return" for computation of the price of capital such that the price times quantity of capital is equal to the value originally computed. This is essentially the "residual" method.

The resulting quantity and price measures are considered *ex-post* in the sense that all returns observed in retrospect are included, rather than those expected *a priori*. This type of procedure, however, includes many returns to the capital stock that might more correctly be imputed to other characteristics of production or the market, such as returns to scale or market power, or to other omitted inputs such as inventories, purchased services, selling expenses, land or other costs. The *ex-ante* measure, by contrast, is independent of the impacts of these additional characteristics of production and the market. The basic ideas underlying the computations are similar; the main differences are the rate of return calculation and the treatment of capital gains. Since the *ex-ante* measure does not include returns to factors such as market power,[11] capacity utilization and returns to scale, and the *ex-post* measure includes them all. Identifying these aspects of efficiency ultimately requires econometric techniques, as will be discussed further in Chapter 7.

Keeping this overall summary of the issues involved in constructing capital stock measures in mind, let us proceed by developing the different "pieces of the puzzle" more formally and in greater detail, first focusing on the computation of capital stock measures.

[11]This could be an issue for output or input markets; imperfect competition can arise because of monopoly (oligopoly or monopolistic competition) power, monopsony, or, say, wage policies agreed on with labor unions.

6.3 Difficult Issues Surrounding Capital Data Construction: A Formalization

As mentioned already briefly, a relevant measure of the available capital stock is computed as "what is left" of the investment in past time periods for the firm. This is generally written for each capital asset x_k as

$$x_{k,t} = \sum_{\tau=0}^{T} x_{k,t,t-\tau} = \sum_{\tau=0}^{T} s_{k,t,\tau} z_{k,t-\tau} \tag{6.1}$$

(from equation (6.2) in Berndt [1990], and motivated in Christensen and Jorgenson [1969]), where T is the life of the durable good, $x_{k,t,t-\tau}$ is the stock of x_k in time period t still remaining from investment in period $t-\tau$, $s_{k,t,\tau}$ is defined as the physical survival rate for age τ investment in time period t for asset k, and $z_{k,t-\tau}$ is gross investment in asset k at time $t-\tau$. This summation must be done for each asset individually, and then the assets must be aggregated based on their user costs, as discussed below.

Determining the level of $x_{k,t}$ for each asset therefore requires finding a "benchmark" level of the stock in period 0 (if only one firm is being considered and the startup period is included in the data this could be zero, otherwise another basis must be found), deflating the value of investment by relevant deflators (to make the units comparable over time – get the numbers into constant dollars) and cumulating the investment from that point on based on some assumption about survival rates.[12]

Finding a benchmark sometimes is difficult (requiring some judgement, past data, numbers from other studies or hand-waving). Generating deflators for the different assets also can pose problems, although, as noted for the materials quantity deflators, sometimes output price series for the supplying industries involved (office equipment, for example) are available and may be justifiable to use.[13] In

[12]This can often be done using "canned" programs. For example, the econometric software package TSP (Time Series Processor) has a CAPITL command that cumulates a series of investment values when given a benchmark and a depreciation rate.

[13]This is somewhat questionable, however, since sales or exise taxes are generally

addition, for output and materials inventories (if included) it may be legitimate to use the output and materials deflators generated for the non-capital inputs. The survival rate problem is perhaps the trickiest of all; we must determine how to characterize $s_{k,t,\tau}$, which is theoretically motivated in terms of physical deterioration, but generally is referred to as a depreciation rate.

There are a number of standard assumptions for $s_{k,t,\tau}$ including:

(i) one-hoss shay (the machine runs at full tilt until it dies, and the dying time often is based on a Winfrey distribution of observed service lives);

(ii) constant exponential decay (δ% / time period, implying $s_\tau = (1-\delta)^\tau$);

(iii) straight line or linear depreciation (e.g., 5 % of the original in each period);
and

(iv) decelerated depreciation (any method where the age-price profile declines slower than concave – one hoss shay may be included here due to the shape of the mortality distribution).[14]

None of these measures is consistent with accounting methods generally used to compute depreciation, which are based primarily on statutory taxation provisions concerning the writing off of investments. The depreciation numbers found on most company's balance sheets are, therefore, not very useful for construction of economic theory-based capital measures.

The assumption most commonly used to compute economic depreciation is a form of exponential decay called the perpetual inventory method, based on geometric deterioration. This assumption implies

omitted in such data. It also may be useful to note here that the capital gains computation will depend on these deflators since capital gains is measured as the increase in price (value) of the stock one already has, which is the change in the deflator between time periods.

[14]See Berndt [1990], Ch. 6, Hulten and Wykoff [1980, 1981a, 1981b], or Hansson [1988] for more information.

services never actually reach zero so every unit of investment is perpetually part of the inventory of capital. The perpetual inventory method essentially assumes that

$$K_t = (1 - \delta_t)K_{t-1} + I_{t-1}, \tag{6.2}$$

where K_t is the capital stock at the beginning of time t and I_{t-1} is investment in period $t-1$. Often a constant exponential rate is assumed for δ_t, as implied by (ii) above. A somewhat extended version of this is the method used by the BLS in the U.S., which is based on an hyperbolic function. Other assumptions may also be imposed on the time pattern of δ_t to generate different shapes of depreciation functions.

Hulten and Wykoff [1981a,b] tested which assumptions about depreciation patterns appeared justifiable. They set up a general representation for the survival function called the Box-Cox form, which can take on different depreciation assumptions as special cases, and then employed data on second-hand asset prices to assess which pattern seems best to approximate observed data trends. They concluded that geometric decline appears justifiable, and that constant exponential (perpetual inventory or geometric with $\delta_t = \delta$) is a valid assumption, although straight-line also approximates the data patterns reasonably well. Even though special cases of geometric functions were sometimes statistically rejected, sensitivity analyses suggested that the stock levels computed with different assumptions about the time path of δ_t were virtually identical.

Many researchers have interpreted these results as a justification for computing depreciation using a constant exponential method. A common assumption for δ is 12-15 % for equipment and 6-7 % for structures, although the OECD tends to use 10 % and 5 %, respectively. Alternatively, sometimes it is possible simply to obtain supplementary information on use and scrapping of machinery and the assumed life of structures and make some assumptions. This approach is sometimes used for aggregate data (almost exclusively for some countries such as Sweden, as is elaborated in Blades [1983]), although it would seem more appropriate when more detailed disaggregated data is available.

This discussion of capital stock data construction has implications about development of the capital price measure. Since the underlying theory specifies the service flow from capital as the relevant input to measure, it is necessary to construct corresponding data series measuring the service flow price. This concept is the basis for the notion of the user cost of capital, which not only includes the investment price, but adjusts it by the interest and depreciation rates, capital gains and taxes. The idea is that the only portion of capital costs the firm pays is an implicit rental price each year, which is the interest rate on the investment price, plus the deterioration involved, less capital gains, adjusted by taxes (corporate income taxes, depreciation deductions, etc.).

This is represented by the equation

$$c_t = TX_t[r_t J_{t-1} + \delta J_t - \Delta J_t] + b_t \tag{6.3}$$

(from Berndt [1990]), where b_t represents the effective property tax rate, J_t is the asset price in time $t, \Delta J_t$ is $(J_t - J_{t-1})$ representing capital gains, r_t is the interest rate, δ is the depreciation rate, and TX_t is the "effective" rate of taxation on capital income given by

$$TX_t = (1 - T_t\Theta_t - \kappa_t)/(1 - T_t), \tag{6.4}$$

where T_t is the effective corporate income tax rate, Θ_t is the present value of depreciation deductions for tax purposes on a dollar's investment over the lifetime of the good, and κ_t is the effective rate of the investment tax credit.[15] All of these variables must be measured in order to compute the user cost.

There are a number of qualifications about this formula, although most are minor. First, it is important whether available deflators are based on end-of-the-year or beginning-of-the-year prices, because of the time dimension and lags implied in this formula. This formula implicitly assumes that "t" refers to the end of the current time period, while other variables are measured as current year totals. In addition, in some cases the distinction between J_t and J_{t-1} is not

[15] As in Berndt [1990], p.6.39 – See Hall and Jorgenson [1967] and Christensen and Jorgenson [1969] for further elaboration of this.

made, so (6.3) reduces to

$$c_t = TX_t[J_t(r_t+\delta) - \Delta J_t] + b_t, \quad \text{or} \quad c_t = TX_tJ_t(r_t+\delta) + b_t, \tag{6.5}$$

if capital gains are also ignored.

The latter assumption is imposed especially for *ex-ante* measures, although in the U.S. the official BLS figures include a modified version of them in their *ex-post* measure. They compute a three-year moving average of capital gains (J_t^* becomes $(J_t + J_{t-1} + J_{t-1})/3$ and $\Delta J_t = (J_t^* - J_{t-1}^*)$) instead of the standard first difference, since capital gains, especially on land, have fluctuated so much in the past decade. This procedure smooths these wide variations.

Another issue is whether r_t is computed as an internal rate of return (*ex-post*), as discussed above, or a market rate (*ex-ante*). Computing the internal rate of return essentially involves taking the capital stock data, data on all other variables such as depreciation, and the total value of capital from the residual calculation and working backwards to solve for the implied r_t. In other words, take the expression for the user cost of capital from the last section multiplied by K_t to obtain net value:

$$NR_t = K_tc_t = K_t\{TX_t[r_tJ_{t-1} + \delta J_t - \Delta J_t] + b_t\} \tag{6.6}$$

where NR_t is net revenues (revenues less variable (non-capital) costs) and K_t is the sum of the x_ks. If more than one asset is included, therefore, this becomes a summation

$$\sum_k x_{k,t}c_{k,t},$$

as outlined in Harper, Berndt and Wood [1989]. Once K_t is computed, data on all the other variables including NR_t from the residual calculation are available to use to solve for r_t. This results in the internal rate of return (implicitly assumed the same for all assets) that imputes all revenues not paid out in terms of variable costs to the capital stock.[16]

[16]Note that this rate of return may only be computed for the entire capital

By contrast, for the market or *ex-ante* rate, instead of assuming the value of capital is known and r_t should be solved for, r_t is assumed and the price of capital (and therefore its value) is calculated. In the U.S. a Moody's Bond Yield (Baa bonds) is often used for r_t in the construction of capital data for the manufacturing sector.

One concern here is whether this measure of r_t should be considered an after- or before- tax return, since the former is relevant when the taxation adjustments in (6.5) are made. Another problem is that when dealing with an individual firm, firm-specific risk should be taken into account. This can be dealt with either by determining the average risk of related companies, or by trying to take into account firm-specific risk, assuming that the expectations of risk formed by the firm's managers are "rational".

More specifically, risk is often incorporated into the rate of return simply by assuming a larger discount rate than that for bond yields (generally imposed in an ad-hoc manner). Alternatively one can rely on using a rate of return for some more risky assets – possibly a weighted average of rates of return in the industry in which the firm produces.[17] One way these data may be used to accommodate risk is by using the Capital Asset Pricing Model from finance theory, as suggested by Auerbach [1983].[18]

---

stock, not individual assets, since net revenue cannot be allocated across assets. If a number of assets exist, as is generally the case, different depreciation and rates of return must be substituted and a more complex equation results. The methodology and final expression for dealing with this is derivable from the development in Harper, Berndt and Wood [1989].

[17]This information is often available through standard data tapes like CitiBank in the U.S.

[18]One approach to this is to use a CAPM model, which isolates firm-specific risk. Essentially, the "beta" (β) from a CAPM model identifies the riskiness of an asset compared to the market, since it is based on the equation:

$$r_H - r_f = \alpha + \beta(r_M - r_f),$$

where r_H is the rate of return to the individual firm, r_f is the risk-free return, β is the firm-specific "beta", and r_M is the market rate of return. Clearly, if the return to the firm is exactly the market rate, $\beta = 1$ and $\alpha = 0$. If the asset is less risky than the market as a whole $\beta < 1$ and if it is more risky $\beta > 1$. This can be used to adjust the information on the rate of return to more closely approximate that faced by the firm.

This adjustment for risk may deal in part with the problem of expectations, an issue that arises because of the capital gains term in the rental price formula. Harper et al [1989], for example, note that ideally ΔJ_t should be *expected* capital gains, particularly for *ex-ante* measures. However, it is very difficult to determine what the expected level of returns might be. Thus many researchers use realized levels or drop this component entirely.

Finally, data on taxes and their use must be clarified. Determining a value for b_t is straightforward (average and marginal might differ); it is available on income statements in the form of land and asset tax information. Identifying how to measure TX_t is, however, more complicated.

The desired procedure is to employ statutory marginal tax rates to approximate T_t, and assume this is the appropriate rate facing the firm for returns to any capital asset. However, applying this may be somewhat complicated for firms who pay taxes in different jurisdictions. It is also complex simply because determining the marginal tax rate is not straightforward. In addition, once the level of T_t is established, data on depreciation deductions and investment tax credits are also required and may not be available. A useful alternative, therefore, is to rely on the notion of an "effective tax rate" used by Christensen and Jorgenson [1969], which is simply measured as taxes paid divided by property income before taxes; call this T_t'. Although this measures an average tax rate, there is much precedent in the literature for using this value to summarize all the tax parameters, resulting in $TX_t = 1/(1 - T_t')$ instead of (6.4).

This discussion has summarized many issues to be recognized when constructing capital data measures. A problem that remains, however, and which is also pervasive in any type of data construction, is how to aggregate the different components of the total capital measure, once measures for individual assets have been developed. This issue is the subject of the next section.

6.4 Aggregation Issues Arising in Data Construction

Aggregation of different outputs and inputs is a very difficult issue for empirical implementation. Although the theory is quite well developed (albeit somewhat complex), problems arise because in practice aggregation of the data, and some types of aggregation procedures, often cannot be theoretically rationalized. The question of aggregation therefore is often broken down into two parts. It must be determined whether aggregation is justified (separability theory), and also what methods are valid to carry out the aggregation (index number theory).[19]

The initial question about aggregation is whether it is valid to add various goods into a "Hicksian composite" that summarizes the quantity of all the goods consistently – as if it were a single commodity. The conditions necessary are complicated, but a sufficient property of the data is that relative prices of the goods to be aggregated do not change over time, as shown by Hicks [1946]. Fixed proportions (constant relative quantities) of goods is also sufficient to justify aggregation, as discussed by Parks [1971]. A simple test of whether these conditions are satisfied is to compare price and quantity indexes of different commodities. Although it is rarely the case that this procedure provides strong evidence justifying aggregation, it may at least generate information on what commodities come closest to satisfying the conditions.[20]

Alternatively, conditions for aggregating two goods as a composite good which is distinct from another – justifying separability of two goods from a third – are satisfied if the relative marginal products of the two goods to be combined do not alter with a change in the price the other good. Assessing whether this separability requirement is satisfied requires more structure than simple data analysis. If it

[19]See Caves, Christensen and Diewert [1982], Diewert [1976, 1980, 1984, 1986], and Blackorby, Primont and Russell [1978] for further elaboration of index number and separability theory. Another classic study to peruse is Green [1964].

[20]Parks [1971] uses this method to evaluate aggregation and outlines other studies that have also considered these conditions empirically.

can be shown to be satisfied, however, aggregation of the two goods is defensible; the aggregated goods "move together" as a combined substitute (or complement) for other inputs.[21]

If this is not true, or if the technology is not correctly represented by the procedures used for aggregation, the aggregate index (or aggregator function) will not be "consistent". The question of consistency initially involves separability considerations, but also has to do with how to represent the aggregate, the latter of which involves index number theory. Problems with either of these aspects of the aggregation problem can cause loss of information, and thus errors. Before elaborating possible methods for construction of an aggregator function, therefore, it is useful to consider what it means for an index not to be consistent.

Denny [1980] provided a useful and simple way of showing the loss of information that arises with errors in aggregation.[22] His approach was to consider an example which can be illustrated by an isoquant diagram, where two types of capital, K_1 and K_2, are used along with labor for production. The resulting production function summarizing this production structure is $Y = f(K_1, K_2, L)$, and an "aggregator function" for total capital is specified as $K = g(K_1, K_2)$, suggesting that the production function can be written as $Y = f(K, L)$.

Problems may exist with this, however, because the correct representation of the K_1, K_2 combination may depend on the levels of L and Y, in which case the aggregator function cannot consistently be defined. In addition, in order to minimize errors of aggregation, the aggregator must appropriately represent the technology – the correct amount of effective capital input necessary to combine with L to produce output.

To illustrate these points, say that one level of aggregate capital can

---

[21] Berndt and Christensen [1973] discuss ways to determine whether aggregation is justified in a parametric framework. See Blackorby, Primont and Russell [1978] for a more elaborate discussion of separability conditions. Since these conditions may be complex and are difficult to check and to satisfy, further consideration of them will not be pursued here. It is useful, however, to at least recognize the issues raised by separability theory when considering aggregation.

[22] For further details of the following discussion, see Denny [1980].

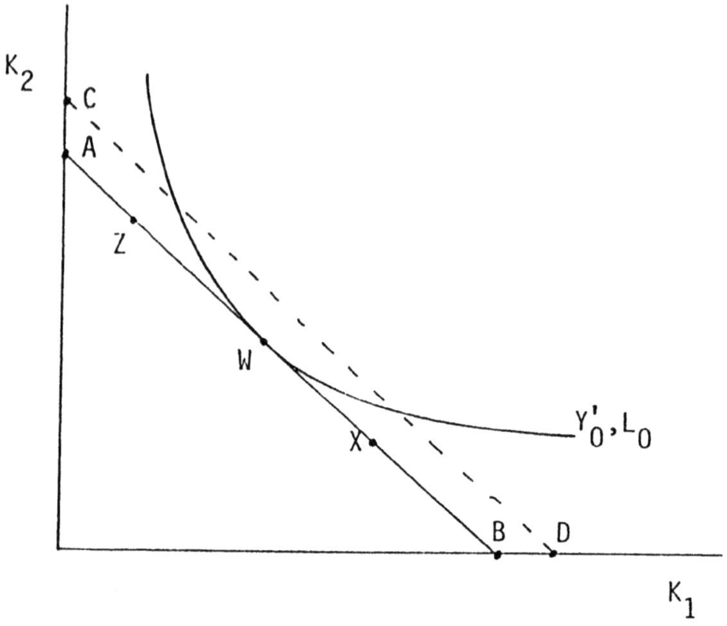

Fig.6.1. Aggregation and loss of information

be represented by the line AB, a larger value is reflected in the line CD, and the isoquant tangent to AB (defined for given quantities of output and labor) can be drawn as (Y_0, L_0) in Figure 6.1. This assumes a simple linear version of the aggregator function $g(K_1, K_2)$. The loss of information from this version of the aggregator function results because any point on line AB, say Z, is indistinguishable from another point, say X, on the same line once aggregation is accomplished. However, it may not be the case that these points all have the same implications for technical efficiency.

Further interpretation of this problem can be obtained from consideration of the implications from the (Y_0, L_0) isoquant. Given the production function, the only point at which the aggregator correctly represents the combination of inputs producing Y_0 is at the tangency point W. The only case in which the aggregation is correct, therefore, is when the aggregator function is consistent with the production function – if the line AB can be "bent" so that it coincides with the (Y_0, L_0) isoquant; the aggregator function must correctly represent the relationship between K_1 and K_2 embodied in the given technology. In addition, for this consistency to hold in general, this aggregator function must be appropriate for any (Y, L) combination.

For the latter condition to hold, it must be the case that the AB curve may justifiably be drawn in K_1, K_2 space without any dependence on the levels of Y and L. This implies that the marginal rate of substitution between K_1 and K_2 does not depend on L; the production function can legitimately be written as $Y = f(K, L) = f(g(K_1, K_2), L)$.[23] Even when the rental prices of K_1 and K_2 do not vary proportionally, therefore, this "weak separability" condition[24] as well as homotheticity[25] of $g(K_1, K_2)$ allows a capital aggregator function to exist. In addition, to aggregate across production sectors, it must also be the case that these conditions hold for each production sector, and the sectors must have "almost" identical isoquants.

Although errors will exist any time these stringent conditions do not in practice hold, there are special circumstances in which the index number procedure used for aggregation will cause less errors than otherwise. In particular, we can specify conditions that should be true for an aggregator function and see which types of index numbers satisfy these conditions and therefore are more acceptable. This is the basis for what is called the *test* or *axiomatic* approach to index number theory, as elaborated in Diewert [1980].

Further, if the index number procedure were consistent with the existing production function – the relationship between K_1 and K_2, for

---

[23]To see this, recall that the marginal rate of substitution in this case is $(\partial f/\partial K_1)/(\partial f/\partial K_2)$, which can be rewritten using the chain rule as $(\partial f/\partial g \cdot \partial g/\partial K_1)/(\partial f/\partial g \cdot \partial g/\partial K_2) = (\partial g/\partial K_1)/(\partial g/\partial K_2)$. Since the g function does not depend on L, therefore, neither does this ratio, and the tradeoffs between K_1 and K_2 are not affected by changes in labor. In this sense they are inpedendent of L.

[24]Variants on these separability conditions such as "strong separability" and "recursive separability" are defined and used in more rigorous developments of this aggregation problem. For a formal treatment of separability conditions, see Blackorby, Primont and Russell [1978].

[25]The index must also be independent of scale for the aggregator to be well defined.

example, were appropriately represented for the given technology – the aggregation procedure would be reasonably defensible. This is the basic idea underlying the theory of exact and superlative index numbers presented in Diewert [1976, 1984], where an index number is exact to a particular functional form if the index number generated exactly replicates the ratio of the relevant functions at the two sets of prices.

For example, consider an input price index such as that for capital. After a price change for any of the components, the measure of the difference in the overall input price should incorporate substitution between the components consistent with that implied by the complete cost function representing behavior. If this is the case, the capital price index will reproduce the ratio of the capital-cost functions ($g(\cdot)$) at the two price combinations.[26] In addition, the change in the cost of inputs in general will equal to ratio of the two total cost functions ($C(\cdot)$) for the two price conditions. This is a primary result of the *microeconomic* approach to index number generation, involving justification of index number procedures based on their capability to appropriately measure actual economic variables and thus to reproduce the true technological relationships among these variables.

Since it is clear that aggregation procedures will seriously affect empirical estimates of inputs and outputs, and therefore any econometric estimation or index number generation (such as for indexes of productivity growth), it is worthwhile pursuing this further to see which types of index numbers have been proposed, which seem most justifiable, and what they imply.

6.5 Index Numbers and Aggregation

The fundamental index number problem is to take the value of a number of different commodities and partition the combined value into a price and quantity index representative of the entire group of commodities. Since dollars (or other monetary value units) are a

[26] For a more formal treatment, see Diewert's papers, cited above.

common measure of any commodities, once the total value of (expenditure on or revenue from) the commodities and either a price or quantity index has been found, the corresponding quantity or price index can be determined implicitly. Computing the implicit index simply requires dividing the value by the computed index.

Formally, we can express this problem as in Diewert [1989a],[27] where the prices and quantities of the I commodities we wish to aggregate for each time period $t = 1, \ldots, T$ (t could also be different economic units instead of time) are represented by the vectors

$$p_t \equiv (p_{1,t}, \ldots, p_{I,t}) \quad \text{and} \quad x_t \equiv (x_{1,t}, \ldots, x_{I,t}).$$

Based on this, the index number problem can be expressed as the problem of condensing this information to find T values of aggregate prices (P_t) and quantities (V_t) of all I commodities such that

$$P_t V_t = \sum_i p_{i,t} v_{i,t}. \tag{6.7}$$

The quantity and price indexes V_t and P_t therefore each summarize all the price and quantity information in one aggregate number for each time period t.

One might initially think that this could be accomplished quite simply using some type of average. Three alternative versions of this were suggested in the 18th and 19th centuries.[28] One possibility is to compute the arithmetic average of the period t prices divided by the arithmetic average of the period $t-1$ prices as

$$P_t/P_{t-1} = \left(\sum_i p_{i,t}/N\right) / \left(\sum_i p_{i,t-1}/N\right)$$

where P_t/P_{t-1} is interpreted as the ratio of aggregated prices in periods $t-1$ and t. Similarly, instead of taking a ratio of the averages, one could take the average of the price ratios themselves, using either an arithmetic or geometric mean. However, problems emerge with any

[27] See this paper for further elaboration of the following index number discussion and proofs of the assertions made.

[28] See Diewert [1989a] for further references and elaboration.

of these formulas; the first is not invariant to changes in the units of measurement, and the others run into problems because prices are not randomly distributed but instead are systematically related.

This simple beginning to index number theory eventually led to a large literature where different indexes were suggested and then subjected to tests of their consistency with intuitively reasonable axioms and with microeconomic theory. Some of the most commonly recognized indexes, for example, are the Laspeyres, Paasche, Fisher Ideal, and Törnqvist (or Divisia, the continuous version of the discrete Törnqvist index).

The Laspeyres and Paasche indexes embody an attempt to deal with the relationship between prices by basing their comparison on quantities, which explicitly holds quantities constant (the reverse can be done to generate a quantity index based on prices, in which case prices are assumed constant). The basic idea of this approach is to weight the prices by a given set of quantities, v_i, generating indexes of the form

$$P_t/P_{t-1} = \sum_i p_{i,t}v_i / \sum_i p_{i,t-1}v_i.$$

The Laspeyres index (P_L) uses the quantities from the base period (period $t-1$) and the Paasche (P_P) from period t. The Fisher ideal index is a geometric mean of the Paasche and Laspeyres indexes, $P_t/P_{t-1} = (P_L P_P)^{1/2}$. Finally, the Törnqvist index is a geometric mean of the price ratios,

$$P_t/P_{t-1} = \Pi_i \left(p_{i,t}/p_{i,t-1}\right)^{\overline{S}_i}, \tag{6.8}$$

where

$$\overline{S}_i \equiv (\frac{1}{2}) \left(p_{i,t-1}v_{i,t-1} / \sum_i p_{i,t-1}v_{i,t-1} \right) + (\frac{1}{2}) \left(p_{i,t}v_{i,t} / \sum_i p_{i,t}v_{i,t} \right)$$
$$= (\frac{1}{2})(S_{i,t-1} + S_{i,t})$$

is the average expenditure share on good i for $i = 1, \ldots, I$, and Π_i represents the product of all the i values.

Perhaps the most popular index currently used by economists is this last index – the Törnqvist index, commonly referred to as a Divisia even when measured in its discrete form.[29] This has resulted at least partly because of the support provided this index by the microeconomic approach to justifying index number formulas; the Törnqvist index is consistent with the popular translog functional form. Since this is a "flexible" functional form which provides a second order approximation to an arbitrary function (as discussed further in the next chapter) the Törnqvist formula is quite general.

Specifically, the Törnqvist index allows for substitution among inputs, which is assumed away in the Laspeyres and Paasche forms. The assumption of no substitution between periods implies that the P_L and P_P indexes are upper and lower bounds to the true index, which provides some rationalization for using the combination of the two contained in the Fisher index.[30] Although the theoretical support for the more complete representation of the technology provided by the Törnqvist index has been persuasive in the view of many researchers, in practice, if changes between years are small, the deviations between the indexes tend to be negligible.

One somewhat minor implication of using the Törnqvist (Divisia) index for aggregation is that if growth rates are computed for the resulting index, consistency requires a different method of computing these rates than is commonly used. This issue of consistency between formulas used, however, can make a significant difference in practice if changes between years is large, which may be the case if one is using data for an individual firm.

Specifically, a standard way to think of computing growth rates for some aggregate input V (or some output Y) between years t and $t-1$, is the growth rate $(V_t - V_{t-1})/V_{t-1}$. This assumes the base to compute the percentage from is the quantity in the first year. However, when aggregation is done in terms of index numbers, the formula is, instead, $\ln(V_t/V_{t-1})$. This is because the standard command to create a Törnqvist quantity index equivalently to the price index above

[29] Some standard statistical programs have a command that directly estimates this index. In TSP the DIVIND command will carry out these manipulations.

[30] This is outlined in a number of standard texts, including Hirschleifer [1980].

is based on the formula

$$\ln(V_t/V_{t-1}) = \sum_i \overline{S}_i \ln(v_{i,t}/v_{i,t-1}), \tag{6.9}$$

where v_i is the quantity of the ith factor of the I to be aggregated, and V represents the aggregated quantity vector, as stated. If this expression is exponentiated (as is often the case), causing it to appear more similar to (6.8), (6.9) becomes

$$V_t/V_{t-1} = \Pi_i \left(v_{i,t}/v_{i,t-1}\right)^{\overline{S}_i}, \quad \text{so} \quad V_t = V_{t-1}\left[\Pi_i \left(v_{i,t}/v_{i,t-1}\right)^{\overline{S}_i}\right]. \tag{6.10}$$

Two points from this formula are worth elaborating. First, what this implies for the interpretation of the growth rate compared to that commonly measured, and, second, what it suggests is the proper procedure for cumulating the resulting growth rates to obtain a quantity index.

To clarify the first point, we can rely on the definition of logarithms. Without going through the algebra, let me assert that this formula is equivalent to computing the growth rate as $(V_t - V_{t-1})/[(V_t + V_{t-1})/2]$, or evaluating the change in terms of the average of the two quantities instead of the first year only. If the quantity changes are not large (or are miniscule as suggested by the theory underlying the formulas which are based on continuous rather than discrete changes), the difference between the two formulas is small. However, with large changes this formula underestimates the growth rate compared to the more standard measure based on year $t-1$. The interpretation of the growth rate and the validity of comparisons with other growth rates are, therefore, affected.

This should not matter for computation of the levels (quantity index for V) if the corresponding formula is used for reconstructing the quantity index.[31] To illustrate this, note that if the "standard" growth rate formula $(V_t - V_{t-1})/V_{t-1} = GR$ (GR = Growth Rate) is

[31] For a homogeneous output or input these manipulations are not even necessary, but since in most applications all outputs and inputs are not homogeneous and even those which are provide the basis for further aggregation, they therefore should be consistent with the other computations.

relied on for computations, this implies that $V_t - V_{t-1} = GR \cdot V_{t-1}$, so $V_t = GR \cdot V_{t-1} + V_{t-1} = (GR + 1) \cdot V_{t-1}$. Thus, standard procedures for computing levels from a series of growth rates are valid. However, when the $\ln(V_t/V_{t-1}) = GR$ formula is used, the procedure for cumulating the growth rates is somewhat altered; $V_t/V_{t-1} = \exp(GR)$ (where exp means exponentiated), so $V_t = \exp(GR) \cdot V_{t-1}$. Therefore, instead of adding one and cumulating, the growth rate should be exponentiated and then cumulation should proceed.

A final point to note is that the Törnqvist index, when written in logarithmic form as in 6.9, looks very similar to the primal productivity growth formula (2.1), reproduced here as

$$\epsilon_{Yt} = d\ln Y/dt - \sum_j S_j d\ln v_j/dt, \tag{2.1'}$$

which can be rewritten more in the style of (6.9) as:

$$\epsilon_{Yt} = \ln(Y_t/Y_{t-1}) - \sum_j \overline{S}_j \ln(v_{j,t}/v_{j,t-1}). \tag{6.11}$$

Thus the share-weighted aggregate input measure generally used for productivity growth computations is simply a Törnqvist index of the various inputs specified. This might be thought of as a further motivation for using Törnqvist indexes for aggregation of input components; consistency is maintained between aggregation for each input and for overall aggregation of the inputs.

* * * * *

Once the data for output and inputs are constructed using these methods, accounting measures of productivity growth and Tobin's q indexes of the residual value of capital as compared to its *ex-ante* value (if the residual method has not been used to generate capital data) may directly be computed. However, for analysis that directly pertains to the cost or production function, such as of biases, marginal shadow values, adaptation of productivity growth measures to take scale economies into account, or any other elaboration, econometric methods are necessary. Issues arising when the analysis is extended to econometric modeling are the subject of the next chapter.

Chapter 7

Issues of Econometric Implementation

The production theory and data construction discussions in the previous two chapters laid the foundation for combining the two to provide an empirical representation of production processes. Accomplishing this is important to explore more fully the structure of production for a firm or industry than is possible using data analysis only. Many issues, however, arise when attempting to carry out such econometric measurement.

One of the first issues to consider when moving toward econometric estimation is what function might be the most useful to represent the production structure. Answering this question requires considering two parts of the problem; what *type* of function best represents the behavior one might assume would be relevant for the firm or industry in question, and what *form* that function might take. The first of these sub-questions concerns the choice of whether a production, cost, profit or other type of function will be most useful for analysis, and what arguments of the function should be included. This is the focus of the first section of this chapter. The second has to do with approximating the true function by a specific functional form which must be sufficiently "flexible" to represent the important relationships among decision variables of the firm. This is pursued in Section 7.2.

Once the deterministic structure of the model is specified, it is important to establish the appropriate econometric model for estimation. This involves ascertaining what assumptions are relevant for the stochastic structure, and thus what sorts of statistical procedures might be used. For example, a complete model of production processes is represented by a system of equations, in which simultaneity, expectations of the future, autoregressive errors, and other complications might appear. The appropriate econometric specification must therefore allow for these types of complexities. In the third section of this chapter, Section 7.3, we overview some of the more common difficulties encountered in empirical implementation, and how they might be resolved.

After estimation is carried out, the theoretical structure and parameter estimates must be used to compute measures summarizing the important relationships among inputs and outputs, such as elasticities and indexes used as indicators of economic performance. In the final section, Section 7.4, we provide an overview of the types of indicators that can be estimated using these models.

7.1 The Choice of Functions to Use for Empirical Analysis

The choice of the relevant function to use for analysis is important since it determines what types of equations represent the production technology and behavior, and what indicators may be generated directly from these equations.

A production function might initially be thought to be the most useful to specify and work with, since it directly represents the production technology, and indicators such as productivity growth indexes are generally motivated in this context. However, as a basis for representing the behavior of firms, the production function has some shortcomings. The main problem with the production function specification, which was recognized early in the development of empirically implementable production theory models and provided initiative to move to other specifications, involves the endogeneity versus exogeneity of right-hand side variables.

Essentially, if the production function is used directly for estimation, input quantities are on the right hand side of the equation and therefore are treated at least implicitly as exogeneous variables. Similarly, since this function defines the marginal products, if profit maximization equations are used to represent behavior the input price (or price ratio p_j/p_Y) turns up on the left hand side of the estimating equation and the marginal product expression (which is a function of the v_js and t through the chosen functional form for the production function) appears on the right hand side.[1] Although manipulation of these equations may be done so the implications for the stochastic disturbance term are changed somewhat, this commonly used specification implies that the v_js are exogeneous (independent variables) and the prices endogenous (dependent variables). This is not desirable if one thinks firms work the other way; they observe the market price and then made decisions about input demand.[2]

More generally, in many cases the natural way to consider firms' behavior is in terms of costs rather than output levels, and thus in terms of a cost rather than a production function. The primary reason to use a cost function for estimation purposes is that the demand functions can be derived simply by taking derivatives of the function from Stephard's Lemma; $\partial C/\partial p_j = v_j$. This means also that input demand is by definition the endogenous (dependent) variable, which facilitates using these expressions as a system of estimation equations.[3] Further, if one wishes to consider input demand elastici-

[1]The first-order conditions providing the foundation for the system of estimating equations stem from the equality $p_j/p_Y = MP_j \equiv \partial Y(v,t)/\partial v_j$. This equality of the value of the marginal product ($p_Y MP_j$) and the price of the input (p_j) is a standard representation of optimal input demand resulting from profit maximization.

[2]A classic paper about the stochastic specification of models based on the production function is that by Zellner, Kmenta and Dreze [1966].

[3]Note that the assumption of input prices being exogenous and input demand quantities endogenous is more relevant at the firm level, but for an aggregate economy the opposite might be thought to be the case. Therefore, for some applications this could cause a production function approach to be preferable.

ties and biases it would seem to make more sense to base analysis on demand functions themselves.

The cost focus also is directly amenable to specification and interpretation of economic indicators. For example, as we have seen, the primal (output) concept of productivity growth has a natural cost counterpart in terms of the cost of a particular output level, as does capacity utilization since utilization ultimately depends on deviations between the shadow values and market prices of inputs.

In addition, use of the cost function avoids some messy issues of long run behavior of firms, since with constant returns to scale and perfect competition (which in many cases are maintained hypotheses) profit maximization in the long run is not defined although cost minimization for a given output level is. Cost functions are also the natural choice for any type of firm which really does not have a choice over its output supply, such as some types of regulated firms.[4] A cost-based framework therefore may have important advantages for analysis, as outlined in a somewhat different context in Chapter 5.

Specifying and implementing a cost function model does, however, pose some problems. In particular, although many econometricians have found more robust estimates are generated from estimation of cost functions than profit functions, the built-in assumption of a given output level for the firm in a cost function framework is questionable, particularly when these functions are used to represent an aggregate of firms. Some researchers have attempted to deal with this problem somewhat by "instrumenting" the output level, which in a sense endogenizes it.[5] This might be thought of as a bit of an *ad-hoc* solution, however, if one thinks the impact of the endogeneity of output is significant. In this case a profit function might be preferable.

A profit function, specified by $\pi(p, p_Y, t)$ as constrasted to the cost function $C(p, Y, t)$, embodies the assumption of profit maximization

---

[4]See Nerlove [1963] as one of the first examples of such a cost function study, which focused on the electric utilities industry.

[5]This will be discussed further in the last Section of this Chapter.

subject to a given output price and therefore is dependent on the price instead of quantity of output. This suggests an additional Hotelling's lemma result to use as part of the system of estimating equations; $\partial\pi/\partial p_Y = Y$ can be thought of as the output supply equation, as noted by Lau [1978] among others.

Although the profit maximization framework therefore appears to be a more complete specification of firm decisions, some important restrictive assumptions about behavior remain. For example, the assumption of perfect competition is directly built in, whereas one might think imperfections in the market could cause difficulties with such a specification.[6] Also, as mentioned in the context of the production function, some types of indicators appear more naturally to be specified in terms of costs, such as capacity utilization, which is based on a cost derivative. Thus the cost function tends to be a popular basis for analysis of production processes.

The following discussion of functional forms therefore focuses on cost functions, as did the theoretical development of Chapter 5. Clearly analogous functional forms may be assumed for the other functions mentioned here, or even other less immediately obvious functions such as the distance function of duality theory, mentioned in Chapter 5.

A final point to emphasize concerning the specification of functional forms is that a number of different arguments might also be included in these functions, as discussed in Chapter 5. To reiterate, although an instantaneous cost function, for example, is often specified in its simplest form as $C(p, Y, t)$, one might include various quasi-fixed factors represented by x_k or other "environmental or behavioral parameters other than commodity levels"[7] such as regulation or adjustment costs (investment) as r_n in any functional form. These functions can therefore be adapted to take a number of different market factors into account if they appear important for the analysis.

---

[6]This can be dealt with to a certain extent by adding a marginal revenue function to the analysis. Such an approach will be outlined in Chapter 9.

[7]See Chapter 5 where this is introduced, and McFadden [1978], where it is elaborated in more detail.

7.2 Possible Functional Forms to Use for Measurement

Many different functional forms have been used for econometric implementation of factor demand models and subsequent parametric estimation of productivity, adjustments and biases. The choice among the different functional forms is generally based on the type of analysis to be carried out. I.e., some functions simplify computation of elasticity formulas and specification of constraints such as constant returns to scale, some facilitate consideration of dynamic interactions, some allow curvature conditions to be directly imposed, and some enhance the ability to identify the difference between short and long run behavior. Most modern studies of production technology, however, do rely on some type of "flexible" functional form, which allows generality in terms of interactions among arguments of the function, such as substitution among inputs.[8]

"Flexible" functional forms by definition impose no *a-priori* restrictions on these interactions, which implies that these functional forms "provide a second order (differential) approximation to an arbitrary twice continuously differentiable function" as Diewert [1974] (as well as others) has shown. Thus, using a flexible functional form for, say, a cost function, allows a close approximation to the true function. Although I will not pursue the theory behind flexibility further, the interested reader can find further development of the theory as well as a more detailed discussion of different functional forms in Lau [1978], Diewert [1974], and Diewert and Wales [1987].

One example of a flexible functional form which has been used extensively for analysis of production is the translog function. The translog cost function, assuming instantaneous adjustment of all inputs is of the form:

$$\begin{aligned} \ln C(Y,p,t) &\equiv \alpha_0 + \sum_j \alpha_j \ln p_j + .5 \sum_j \sum_j \gamma_{ij} \ln p_i \ln p_j \\ &+ \delta_Y \ln Y + \sum_j \delta_{jY} \ln p_j \ln Y + .5\delta_{YY} (\ln Y)^2, \end{aligned}$$

[8] A useful, much more detailed and rigorous reference in this area is Lau [1986].

$$+ \quad \delta_t t + \sum_j \delta_{jt} \ln p_j t + .5\delta_{tt} t^2, \tag{7.1}$$

where p_j represents the price of the jth input, and regularity conditions (linear homogeneity in prices and symmetry) require

$$\sum_j \alpha_j = 1, \ \sum_i \gamma_{ij} = 0 \ \text{for} \ j = 1, 2, \ldots J,$$

$$\sum_j \delta_{jt} = 0, \ \sum_j \delta_{jY} = 0, \ \text{and} \ \gamma_{ij} = \gamma_{ji} \ \text{for all} \ i, j.$$

Translog production or profit functions can similarly be defined by constructing a second order Taylor series expansion in logarithms of the general function. Since the translog is a second order function with no constraints, it includes all cross effects between arguments of the function, and is therefore flexible.

It is clear from observation that this function is a generalization of the Cobb-Douglas functional form mentioned in Chapter 2. The Cobb-Douglas form, as discussed there, is restrictive in terms of the substitution assumptions incorporated in the form; elasticities of substitution between all inputs are one and shares of the inputs are constant. Extending this first order logarithmic function to a second order function, the translog, allows these constraints to be relaxed because cross-effects between inputs are recognized and the function can therefore represent more complex substitution patterns.[9]

Direct manipulation of equation (7.1) can easily be used to show that the standard regularity conditions for cost functions outlined in Chapter 5 can be satisfied by this translog function. However, whether some of the conditions hold at a particular observation depends on the parameter estimates. In particular, monotonicity conditions depend on the sign of the fitted shares; they must be positive.

[9]It should be noted that although simple functional forms like the Cobb-Douglas are self-dual, in the sense that a Cobb-Douglas cost function can be derived by cost minimization based on a Cobb-Douglas production function, this is not true for many more general forms. This cost minimization procedure, in fact, cannot analytically be accomplished using flexible forms. Therefore, the properties of a particular type of functional form are applied directly to the general function $C(P, Y, t)$ rather than derived through cost minimization.

The concavity conditions are more complex. They depend on the γ_{jj} parameters and cost shares and in general are not globally satisfied; they must be checked at each point to make sure they are not violated.

Note also that this function, although linear homogeneous in the prices as is required for regularity conditions to be satisfied, is not lineary homogeneous in output. The question of homogeneity in output has to do with the question of returns to scale. If $\delta_{jY} = 0$ for all j, for example, the translog function is homothetic. If, in addition, $\delta_{YY} = 0$, this reduces to homogeneity, and if, further, $\delta_Y = 1$, linear homogeneity in output (constant returns to scale), exists.[10]

The translog function has generally been used for studies of long run (instantaneous adjustment) factor demand, such as many produced by Dale Jorgenson,[11] although it is possible to construct a short run version of this function, as has been done by Brown and Christensen [1981]. The advantage of the translog functional form is that since it is defined in terms of logarithms many elasticities, as well as potential restrictions on the form, depend only on the parameter estimates rather than being a function of the data itself. When the extension to a short run function is made, however, the logarithmic form causes a problem; finding the long run demand for the fixed factor(s), which requires constructing and solving the expressions $p_k = Z_k = -\partial G/\partial x_k$, cannot be accomplished analytically even with only one quasi-fixed input. Instead, algorithms to solve the equations numerically are required.

To accomodate this, other studies, especially those which explicitly incorporate a dynamic adjustment process, have used a (normalized) quadratic function. The quadratic is a useful function to apply to these types of studies because second order derivatives do not depend on the data, so adjustment matrixes for the quasi-fixed inputs are much easier to derive than would otherwise be the case. For example, in Berndt, Fuss and Waverman [1980], the computation of a flexible

[10] In the process of estimation, these restrictions may be imposed on the function and hypothesis tests carried out to check whether the more restricted scale specifications are justified by the data.

[11] See Jorgenson [1988] and the references contained in that study.

accelerator investment equation which depends on the rate of interest and parameters of the model is possible because they rely on this type of function.

The normalized quadratic short run cost function with only capital (K) quasi-fixed can be expressed as

$$
\begin{aligned}
G(Y,p,K,\Delta K,t) = L &+ \sum_j p_j v_j = \alpha_0 + \alpha_t t + \sum_j \alpha_j p_j \\
&+ \alpha_Y Y + \alpha_K K + \alpha_K \Delta K \\
&+ .5\left(\sum_i \sum_j \gamma_{ij} p_{ij} + \gamma_{YY} Y^2 + \gamma_{KK} K^2\right. \\
&\quad \left. + \gamma_{\dot{K}\dot{K}} (\Delta K)^2 + \gamma_{tt} t^2\right) \\
&+ \gamma_{jY} p_j Y + \sum_j \gamma_{jK} p_j K + \sum_j \gamma_{j\dot{K}} p_j \Delta K \\
&+ \sum_j \gamma_{jt} p_j t + \gamma_{YK} Y K \gamma_{Y\dot{K}} Y \Delta K \\
&+ \gamma_{tK} tK + \gamma_{t\dot{K}} t\Delta K + \gamma_{K\dot{K}} K \Delta K \qquad (7.2)
\end{aligned}
$$

where j does not index capital (K) or labor (L), but represents all other inputs, the function is normalized by the price of labor, and adjustment costs for capital are included since $\Delta K \equiv K_t - K_{t-1}$ is an argument of the function.

Although this function facilitates analysis of the full adjustment process of capital (investment behavior), at least three problems exist with this function: (i) one input must be chosen for normalization (and the results are not invariant to which is chosen), (ii) with multiple quasi-fixed inputs the adjustment process becomes complex and simplifications must be made, and (iii) the function does not easily reduce to constant returns to scale. Therefore, although constant returns versions have been estimated,[12] testing the different possible returns to scale specifications is not straightforward.

Therefore, if short run-long run analysis is desired, but it is not

[12]By, for example, Morrison and Berndt [1981].

important explicitly to represent investment behavior,[13] or multiple quasi-fixed inputs or scale analysis are important to include, the Generalized Leontief function has provided a useful alternative. This functional form is also an appropriate choice for approximation of a restricted (rather than instantaneous adjustment) cost function because "desired" levels of input stocks x_k^* and capacity output Y^* can be analytically computed, whereas with the translog they must be numerically derived.

A variant of the restricted Generalized Leontief function was developed in Morrison [1988a] and has been used by Morrison [1988c], for example, to compare production processes in U.S. and Japanese manufacturing. The restricted or short run version of the Generalized Leontief cost function for multiple fixed inputs is given by:

$$\begin{aligned} G &= Y\left[\sum_i\sum_j \alpha_{ij}p_i^{.5}p_j^{.5} + \sum_j\sum_m \delta_{jm}p_j s_m^{.5} \right.\\ &\left. + \sum_j p_j \sum_m\sum_n \gamma_{mn}s_m^{.5}s_n^{.5}\right] \\ &+ Y^{.5}\left[\sum_j\sum_k \delta_{jk}p_j x_k^{.5} + \sum_j p_j \sum_m\sum_k \gamma_{mk}s_m^{.5}x_k^{.5}\right] \\ &+ \sum_j p_j \sum_k\sum_l \gamma_{lk}x_k^{.5}x_l^{.5} \end{aligned} \tag{7.3}$$

where p_i and p_j represent prices of all variable inputs, x_k and x_l denote fixed inputs, and s_m and s_n enumerate output (Y) and other exogenous arguments of G not included in the returns to scale specification, such as the state of technology (t) or investment in quasi-fixed inputs (Δx_k).

A final set of functions to be mentioned here, although more are obviously possible to specify,[14] are those which constrain curvature

[13]Note that although specifying investment behavior directly is more complex with functional forms other than a quadratic, a dynamic process can be incorporated with other functions using Euler equations as in Morrison [1988c].

[14]Some of the most recent and general are the generalized Box-Cox and the

conditions (restrictions on the signs of the first and second order derivatives of the function) to be satisfied. Although curvature conditions with respect to both prices and fixed inputs must hold for our production theory models to be relevant, as discussed in Chapter 5, with flexible functional forms these conditions cannot in general be imposed without destroying the flexibility of the function. Therefore, determining whether they hold requires computing the derivatives and checking their signs, as noted above for the translog.

Unfortunately, in many cases the conditions are violated. This is especially the case for fixed factors, where this failure tends to be reflected in negative estimated shadow values. A number of researchers have attempted to deal with this problem. One approach suggested by researchers such as Diewert and Wales [1987] is to specify a flexible functional form that is sufficiently complex to impose curvature without losing the flexibility property. This complexity, of course, increases the problems involved in estimating the parameters and constructing indicators.

An example of this type of functional form is the Generalized McFadden functional form presented by Diewert and Wales as:

$$\begin{aligned} C(p,Y,t) \;\equiv\; & g^1(p)Y + \sum_j b_{jj}p_jY + \sum_j b_jp_j + \sum_j b_{jt}p_jtY \\ & + \; b_t\left(\sum_j \alpha_jp_j\right)t + b_{YY}\left(\sum_j \beta_jp_j\right)^2 \\ & + \; b_{tt}\left(\sum_j \gamma_jp_j\right)t^2Y, \end{aligned} \tag{7.4}$$

where the function g^1 is defined as

$$g^1(p) \equiv .5p_1^{-1}\sum_{i=2}^{J}\sum_{j=2}^{J} c_{ij}p_ip_j, \quad c_{ij} = c_{ji} \text{ for } 2 \leq i,\ j \leq J, \tag{7.5}$$

Fourier functions. For further references and comments see Berndt [1989], Chapter 9. For a comparison of some flexible functional forms, see Guilkey, Lovell and Sickles [1983].

and the parameters α_j, β_j and γ_j are preselected by the researcher. Note that this functional form also requires an arbitrary normalization due to the construction of the g^1 expression.

Although numerous issues arise about functional forms, many of these can be taken into account using variations on the forms introduced here. All of the functions here can be transformed into short run instead of long run functions by making the quantities instead of prices of the fixed factors arguments of the functions. They also can allow for adjustment costs or environmental or regulation effects by including Δx_k or r_n as arguments of the function, and the interactions between these and all other arguments can be captured within the flexible functional form. Therefore, although only a limited number of possible functional forms have been presented, these types of functions provide a rich basis for empirical analysis of production processes.

7.3 Some Econometric Problems to Take into Consideration

In order empirically to implement models of production processes based on the functions and functional forms discussed in the previous sections, systems of equations representing the behavior summarized in the functions must be specified, and estimation of these systems of equations must proceed using relevant data. Although many issues emerge when carrying out this last step, in this section we concentrate only on some of the most prominent econometric considerations that have emerged in the literature. Also, although again cost functions are used as an example, it should be recognized that the issues encountered are similar for other functions.[15]

First, a system of equations which reflects the behavior of the firm

[15] I will not be expounding on the relevant econometric theory but only highlighting problems that should be taken into account. For further elaboration of the econometrics themselves, see any standard econometrics textbook. For a more focused discussion of estimation of factor demand models themselves and some exercises to carry out, see Chapter 9 of Berndt [1990].

and the technology must be constructed for estimation; as outlined in Chapter 5 this involves using versions of Shephard's and Hotelling's lemmas. The initial step required for empirical implementation, therefore, is to decide what equations will be included in this system. This decision depends on the focus of the analysis, the function used to represent the production process and econometric considerations.

The most fundamental equations that generally provide the basis for estimation are the optimized input demand equations, represented by $v_j = \partial C/\partial p_j$ for input j. For a total cost function assuming instantaneous adjustment, these equations summarize the full range of input substitution behavior of the firm; all the parameters necessary for construction of elasticities symbolizing this behavior are contained in the equations. For increased efficiency of estimation, however, researchers often also estimate the cost function itself.

If the function chosen for the analysis is instead a restricted or variable cost function, these demand equations may only be constructed for variable inputs. In this case, additional information may be provided by shadow value equations from the Hotelling's lemma expression $Z_k = -\partial G/\partial x_k$.[16] These equations are therefore sometimes also used for estimation purposes. Employing this approach generates a problem, however, because Z_k, the shadow or *ex-post* value for fixed input k, is not in general observable. Some researchers have assumed that a residual *ex-post* value $Z_K = (p_Y Y - G)/K$ may be computed for capital (if K is the only quasi-fixed input) and used as the dependent variable of the equation. However, this is not justifiable unless constant returns to scale and perfect competition exist, since otherwise returns to these factors will be included in the Z_K measure.

If the shadow value expression cannot be used, an alternative equation based again on the assumption of perfect competition (and implicitly assuming endogenous output), $p_Y = MC \equiv \partial G/\partial Y$, is sometimes invoked.[17] Adding this equation to the system of variable input

---

[16] Note that this implies the capital quantity measure may not be measured as an *ex-post* value, using a residual method, because then the shadow value is implicitly already incorporated in the measure of K.

[17] See Mork [1978] and Morrison [1988a] for examples of this in the perfect and imperfect competition case, respectively. Note, of course, that with imper-

demand and cost function equations often facilitates "tying down" estimates of the fixed input parameters; in practice these estimates may not be very robust unless the extra shadow value equation is included in the system.

The more complete the optimization process specified, the more optimization equations might be implied for estimation and analysis. For example, for a dynamic model such as those developed in Berndt, Fuss and Waverman [1980], Nadiri and Prucha [1989] and others, the shadow value equation expands into a complete investment equation based on the Euler equation discussed in Chapter 5. These investment equations can be specified in most cases for all quasi-fixed inputs, although once multiple quasi-fixed inputs are included some difficulties arise with cross-effects on the adjustment matrix.[18]

Once the system of estimating equation is specified, the question becomes what estimation method to use. For example, single equation least squares is not appropriate because of cross-equation restrictions; the same parameter will appear in different equations and must be constrained to be equal everywhere. Other issues might also arise to cause complications.

An initial point to note is that with some specifications it is not valid to estimate the entire system of equations because the errors are dependent on one another. In particular, when using the translog function share equations are natural to use for analysis because the function is specified in logarithms, and shares are equal to logarithmic derivatives. Since the sum of the shares of the inputs must equal one, the errors on the share equations sum to zero. Therefore, one of the equations must be dropped. Working backward from the adding up restrictions allows estimation of the parameters of the omitted equation. Although this sounds somewhat questionable at first glance, it turns out that the results are numerically invariant to which equation is deleted because of the linear dependence, as long as a maximum

---

fect competition this equality becomes $MR = MC$ where MR denotes marginal revenue. This therefore requires specifying also a revenue function.

[18]This is discussed in more detail in Morrison and Berndt [1981]. If the Euler equation is estimated directly rather than solving for the investment level, in most cases this difficulty does not appear.

likelihood estimation procedure is employed.[19] This has now become such a standard procedure to use that most researchers do not elaborate further but simply mention which of the equations was deleted.

Most resulting systems of equations specified for estimation contain no simultaneity; in this case "Zellner's Seemingly Unrelated" systems techniques are generally invoked to deal with the standard issues involved in systems estimation. To implement this procedure an additive disturbance term is appended to each estimation equation of the system, and it is assumed that the resulting disturbance vector is independently and identically normally distributed with mean vector zero and constant, non-singular covariance matrix Ω. The estimation method consists of using equation-by-equation ordinary least squares to obtain an estimate of Ω, and disturbance covariance matrix on the system of equations. This technique is often denoted Zellner-efficient (ZEF).[20] If the ZEF estimator is iterated until changes in the estimate of Ω from one estimation to the other becomes very small, the iterative Zellner (IZEF) estimator is obtained. This estimator generates results numerically equivalent to the maximum likelihood estimates.

There are a number of cases when it is questionable whether standard systems estimation techniques are valid. For example, if analysis is based on a dynamic adjustment model, the investment levels of quasi-fixed inputs are independent variables for most equations but

[19]Since iterative Zellner (seemingly unrelated) methods are equivalent to maximum likelihood estimation, using standard iterative systems estimation methods is sufficient for invariance to which equation is delated. As is outlined further in Berndt [1990, Chapter 9], however, if one-step Zellner efficient techniques are used, care must be taken that the first round estimate of the disturbance covariance matrix does not impose the symmetry restrictions.

[20]This is sometimes also called the minimum chi-square estimator. Most statistical programs used for econometric estimation have a package that does this type of estimation. In TSP the LSQ command carries out estimation on a system of equations, and has a number of options that may be chosen for different types of algorithms and numbers of iterations on both the parameters and variance-covariance matrix, for example. With only one iteration this reproduces the ZEF estimator, and when iterated to convergence it becomes the IZEF estimator. This command is also capable of dealing with nonlinear models, which occurs with some functional forms, although some other "canned" programs have difficulties with nonlinearities.

comprise the dependent variable in the investment equation. With only one quasi-fixed input this is not a problem because the system is structurally recursive; there are no two equations where the independent and dependent variables show up on opposite sides of the equation. However, if more than one quasi-fixed input exists, so that, for example, the Δx_j equation is a function of the Δx_k value (and vice versa) for any two quasi-fixed factors x_j and x_k, simultaneous equation estimation techniques must be used.

A common procedure for dealing with simultaneity which is available in most statistical packages used by econometricians is iterative three stage least squares (ITHSLS or THSLS). This systems estimation approach uses instrumental variables to "endogenize" the variables that appear as both independent and dependent variables. This technique is also often used to deal with the possibility of endogenous output, as mentioned before. In addition, Pindyck and Rotemberg [1983] have demonstrated that one way to alleviate the problem of nonstatic expectations of the future path of input prices is to "instrument" current prices (which represent the relevant stream of expected future prices with error) using THSLS.

The question of what variables to use as instruments often becomes an issue when estimation by THSLS is attempted. A standard approach is to use lagged values of the explanatory variables, as was done by Pindyck and Rotemberg [1983]. As they mention, various specifications of instruments might be thought to be more independent, but sometimes do not result in very reasonable estimates. Some choices could include overall macroeconomic variables like a cost of living index, rate of interest, unemployment rate, and Gross National Product (GNP). When using aggregated data, however, such as for an industry, it should be taken into consideration that these variables may be somewhat endogenous, in the sense that the industry may have a significant effect on the aggregate measure.

Full information maximum likelihood (FIML) methods may also be used to deal with simultaneity if the assumption of normality of errors is invoked – as it generally is – and the entire system is fully specified.[21] With a large model and nonlinearities, however, some

[21] By constrast, THSLS may be used for a subset of equations specifying a system, if all the relationships cannot be identified.

researchers have found that it is difficult to obtain convergence using FIML. Unfortunately, as Hausman [1975] has shown, it is also the case that the THSLS methods often used for estimation of systems (even when iterated) are not in general numerically equivalent to FIML, although their asymptotic properties are the same.[22]

Additional difficulties arise for estimation if one thinks the vector of disturbance terms on the estimation equations in the system cannot be assumed independently and identically multivariate normally distributed with mean vector zero and a constant non-singular covariance matrix.

For example, the simple assumption of additive disturbance terms is often justified by saying it represents random errors by firms. However, some researchers have questioned whether this is reasonable. McElroy [1987] argues that errors are not due to firms but to econometrician's errors, and she suggests the entire optimization process should be imbedded in a stochastic framework. In this case the pattern of errors can be very different, with additive or multiplicative error terms in the equations, which implies that standard systems techniques may not be used; more complex estimation procedures requiring formal specification of the likelihood function may be required. This also implies in some circumstances that the cost function should not be estimated along with the demand or share equations because all information from this function is redundant.[23]

Another instance for which the usual assumptions about errors are inappropriate is when heteroskedasticity exists. A simple example where this could occur is when demand equations are specified over a time series. In this case the variance of the disturbance term may not be constant but instead tend to grow as the scale of operations, and therefore both the levels of demand and output, increases. If one thinks the increase in variance could be proportional to the change in output level – output change in a sense indexes the scale increase

[22]See Berndt [1990, Chapter 9] for a more complete discussion, and Hausman [1975] for more details.

[23]See Berndt [1990, Chapter 9] for a more complete overview of the problem and McElroy [1987] for more details.

– then an adjustment for heteroskedasticity using output would seem to be relevant. In this case specifying the input demand levels in terms of input-output levels (v_j/Y) instead of just v_j would reduce the disturbance heteroskedosticity. The issue of heteroskedasticity has not, however, received very much attention in the literature.

A possibly more important generalization, particularly when investment equations are included in the models, involves an autoregressive specification.[24] This is fairly straightforward to motivate, although differences emerge when dealing with a singular system, like that for the translog function, as compared to a standard system. The basic procedure is to apply a Koyck transformation analogous to that often done for single equation systems. In matrix notation, this requires specifying the first-order autoregressive stochastic process as:

$$U_t = RU_{t-1} + \xi_t, \tag{7.6}$$

which is simply the systems version of the first order univariate autoregressive scheme $u_t = \rho u_{t-1} + \epsilon_t$, $t = 2, \ldots T$. Given the n-equation system of equations $Y_t = V_t\beta + U_t$, where Y_t is an $n \times 1$ vector, V_t is an $n \times J$ matrix and β is a $J \times 1$ vector of parameters, (7.6) can be used to transform the system to one which is consistent with normality assumptions by constructing the Koyck-transformed system:

$$Y_t = RY_{t-1} + (V_t - RV_{t-1})\beta + \xi_t, \tag{7.7}$$

which has its obvious counterpart in single equation models. This transformed system can then be estimated using system estimation methods incorporating nonlinear parameter restrictions. The special case when R is diagonal can be tested as a restriction on this general specification.

The exception that appears for the translog form stems from the dependence among the cost shares; because the shares must sum to one the disturbances must sum to zero at each observation, and the disturbance covariance and residual cross-products matrixes are singular. This implies the very strong restriction that each column of R sums to a given constant. For example, if R is diagonal, all elements

[24] For further details see Berndt [1990], Chapter 9.

of the diagonal matrix must be equal.[25] Care must therefore be taken when interpreting the results of applying autoregressive techniques to singular systems.

If nonstatic expectations of future exogenous variables are included in the models, additional empirical implementation difficulties arise. One way to deal with these issues was suggested by Pindyck and Rotemberg [1983], who argued that estimates will be consistent with rational expectations about future input prices if the current input prices are considered endogenous in a THSLS estimation, as mentioned above. This result is attributed to Hansen and Singleton [1982] who show that if one uses an instrumental variable procedure and chooses instruments that are likely to help determine the expectations of the decision makers in the firms under consideration, consistency with error orthogonality and rational expectations is ensured. The problem is that although the resulting estimates will be *consistent* with rational expectations, the procedure does not explicitly identify how expectations are formed and therefore does not provide any interpretation of the impact of expectations.

Morrison [1986b] has considered two alternative versions of non-static expectations that do not require a full econometric model of the expectations process used by firms (which would be required for a true rational expectations process) but do extend the analysis to allow some interpretation of the expectations formation processes. The two approaches considered, adaptive and "partially rational" expectations, rely on ARIMA models[26] to calculate the expected variables which are then inserted into the model for estimation instead of the current measured variables. Empirical estimation of such models suggests that the relatively straightforward adaptive expectations model, which simply requires modeling an IMA (1, 1) moving average process, reflects the important impacts of nonstatic expectations on decision making without causing volatile parameter estimates or necessitating complex ARIMA modeling.

These extensions are worth elaborating briefly. Assume an expected

[25] This has been shown by Berndt and Savin [1975].

[26] See the texts by Nelson [1973] or Pindyck and Rubinfeld [1981] for further elaboration of these types of models and their estimation.

value of the observed exogenous variable π_t, π_t^*, in a simple economic structural model can be represented by a rational distributed lag[27]

$$\pi_t^* = a + b[L(\cdot)/D(\cdot)]\pi_t + \eta_t, \tag{7.8}$$

where $L(\cdot)$ and $D(\cdot)$ are polynomials in the lag operator. Because of the properties of a rational distributed lag, the path of expected variables expressed in this manner is a form of general or unrestricted rational expectations, and can be characterized by time series techniques using a general ARIMA model. The adaptive expectations version of this is a special case of an IMA(1, 1) process, as shown by Charles Nelson [1973].

Because the adaptive expectations process is relatively simple, it can be shown that the series of anticipated variables can be substituted directly into the estimating equations. This generates structural parameters representing expectations formation which are consistent with the rest of the model. This happens because the entire impact on the change in expected prices is incorporated in the first shock, as is clear from the formalization of the adaptive expectations or IMA(1, 1) process as $\pi_{t+1} - \pi_t = (1-\beta)e_t$. Since the difference in the expected exogenous variables, $\pi_{t+1} - \pi_t$, appears in the investment equations of dynamic models, $(1-\beta)e_t$ can directly be substituted.

With a more complex ARIMA process, however, the order of the ARIMA process must be determined using time series analysis (TSA) methods, and the resulting "expected values" substituted into the analysis. This is equivalent to incorporating a compound parameter representing expectations errors in the estimating equations.

Many different econometric issues arise when one attempts empirically to estimate a production theory-based model to represent firm behavior. The limited discussion here is not meant to be comprehensive but to include those issues which appear most often in the literature. Once these are dealt with estimation can proceed, parameter estimates can be generated, and indicators reflecting the pattern of input and output responses can be constructed. The next section

[27] See Nerlove [1972] for one development of this. See also Morrison [1986b] for further details of this procedure and the manipulations outlined below.

provides a brief overview of the types of measures and indicators that can be computed for analysis of the production structure.

7.4 Representing Firm Behavior Using the Empirical Estimates

Numerous indicators of firm behavior can be produced using the parameter estimates that result from estimation of a system of equations representing production processes. Many have already been discussed in the context of technical change, returns to scale and capacity utilization indexes, and corresponding bias measures. Additional analyses are generally carried out in terms of demand elasticities, which are directly related to the cost elasticities on which the other indicators are based. Our next step will be a brief summary of results about indicators that have already been introduced, which provides the basis for a more comprehensive overview of potentially estimable indicators of firm behavior and performance.

A cost-side technical change measure has been motivated as the cost elasticity $\epsilon_{Ct} = \partial \ln C(\cdot)/\partial t$ where $C(\cdot)$ is the cost function. It is easy to see that if this derivative is constructed, the resulting index of technical change will depend on the exogenous variables facing the firm; these variables are arguments of the cost function itself and therefore of its derivative. Thus, determining how technical change is affected by exogenous variables simply requires computing the elasticity of ϵ_{Ct} with respect to one of these variables, which involves taking the second derivative of the cost function.

For example, computing $\partial \epsilon_{Ct}/\partial \ln p_j = \partial^2 \ln C/\partial t \ \partial \ln p_j$ indicates how technical change is affected by change in the price of input j. As mentioned in Chapter 4, this is equivalent to computing the bias B_{jt}, which is simply the symmetric second derivative $\partial^2 \ln C/\partial \ln p_j \partial t$, since $\partial \ln C/\partial \ln p_j = S_j$ (where S_j is the cost share of input j). These expressions can easily be computed using the functional forms assumed for $C(\cdot)$ and the estimated parameters of the equation system.

Returns to scale can just as readily be measured because this index is represented by the output derivative $\epsilon_{CY} = \partial \ln C / \partial \ln Y$.[28] If further analysis of scale economies is desired, a second derivative can be constructed as, for example, $\partial^2 \ln C / \partial \ln Y \partial \ln p_j = \partial \epsilon_{CY} / \partial p_j$; this shows how returns to scale are affected by changes in the price of input j. Clearly, similar derivatives can be constructed to assess the impacts of any other exogenous variable. Also, equivalently to the bias argument for technical change, this measure can be shown to be identical to the scale bias $\partial S_j / \partial \ln Y$.[29]

As discussed in Chapter 3, the ϵ_{CY} measure is a combination of capacity utilization and returns to scale. If constant returns to scale exists but fixity also prevails, the elasticities just outlined reflect capacity utilization and its variations with changes in exogenous variables, the latter of which are equivalent to the utilization biases discussed in Chapter 4. If both fixity and returns to scale exist, however, distinguishing the two becomes somewhat more difficult.

In this case the expressions

$$CU_c = C^*/C = \left(G + \sum_k Z_k x_k\right) / \left(G + \sum_k p_k x_k\right) = 1 - \sum_k \epsilon_{Ck}$$

must directly be constructed and their derivatives taken to determine capacity utilization and its changes. For returns to scale, the long run elasticity $\eta = \epsilon_{CY}^{LR}$ must be generated. This can be computed as a full long run elasticity, as outlined in Chapter 4, or by using the equality developed in Morrison [1989b], $\epsilon_{CY} = \epsilon_{CY}^{LR} CU_c = (MC \cdot Y/C^*) \cdot (C^*/C)$, where $MC = \partial C / \partial Y = \partial G / \partial Y$ in the short run. This results in the expression $\epsilon_{CY}^{LR} = MC \cdot Y/C^*$, which can be used to construct measures of returns to scale and its derivatives.

Therefore, once a functional form for the cost function is chosen and parameter estimates are obtained, taking derivatives and substituting the parameter estimates provides a rich representation of firm behavior in the context of changes in costs and relative input demands. Additional direct information on substitution responses of

[28] Returns to scale are measured by the inverse of this measure.

[29] See Morrison [1988b] for further details.

firms may be generated, however, in terms of demand elasticities; these are measured as $\partial \ln v_j / \partial \ln \rho = \epsilon_{j\rho}$, where ρ represents any exogenous variable.

For price elasticities, for example, this expression becomes $\epsilon_{ij} = \partial \ln v_i / \partial \ln p_j$. If $j = i$ this represents the own demand elasticity and if $j \neq i$ it is the cross elasticity. Output, utilization and other types of elasticities can be specified if Y, fixed inputs or other required variables are included as arguments of the cost function and thus of the demand equation $v_j(\cdot) = \partial C(\cdot)/\partial p_j$. For example, the elasticity of demand for input j with respect to a change in output is $\epsilon_{jY} = \partial \ln v_i / \partial \ln Y$. These elasticities are also the basis for computation of biases, as shown in Chapter 5. I.e., the short run scale or output bias, which captures only the input-specific part of the demand elasticity, is $\partial S_j / \partial \ln Y = B_{Yt} = S_j(\epsilon_{jY} - \epsilon_{CY})$.

Demand elasticities are also often presented as Allen partial elasticities of substitution (AES), which are combination of (total) cost derivatives and are symmetric ($\sigma_{ij} = \sigma_{ji}$).[30] Short run Allen elasticities are specified as:

$$\sigma_{ij} = \left. \frac{C \cdot C_{ij}}{C_i \cdot C_j} \right|_{x_k = \bar{x}_k}, \tag{7.9}$$

where i, j can denote variable input prices, x_k, t or Y. For the translog, for example, Allen elasticities for variable input price changes are

$$\begin{aligned} \sigma_{ij} &= \frac{(G/C)\gamma_{ij} + S_i S_j (C/G)}{S_i S_j}, \quad i \neq j, \qquad \text{and} \\ \sigma_{jj} &= \frac{(G/C)\gamma_{jj} + (S_j^2 - S_j)(C/G)}{S_j^2}, \end{aligned} \tag{7.10}$$

for $i, j = L, E, M$. Short run output elasticities can be written as:

$$\sigma_{jY} = \frac{(G/C)\gamma_{jY} + S_j \epsilon_{CY}(C/G)}{S_j \epsilon_{CY}}, \tag{7.11}$$

[30]This is particularly true when the translog function is used for estimation, since the formulas can easily be specified in terms of shares which are the basis of the translog demand system.

and elasticities with respect to t are analogous with t substituted for Y. The quasi-fixed input elasticities are slightly different because the x_k appear both in G and in the remainder of the C expression:

$$\sigma_{jk} = \frac{(G/C)\gamma_{jk} + S_j(\epsilon_{Ck}(C/G) - p_k(x_k/G))}{S_j\epsilon_{Ck}}. \tag{7.12}$$

The relationship between these AES expressions and demand elasticities is straightforward. For example, the short run cross price elasticities are $\partial \ln v_i / \partial \ln p_j \equiv \epsilon_{ij} = S_j \sigma_{ij}$. Similarly, the short run elasticity of demand with respect to technical change is $\partial \ln v_j / \partial t \equiv \epsilon_{jt} = \epsilon_{Ct}\sigma_{jt}$. The short run demand elasticities with respect to output, $\partial \ln v_j / \partial \ln Y$, and those for x_k, $\partial \ln v_j / \partial \ln x_k$, follow directly.

Two points should be noted about these elasticities. First, since elasticity measures depend on the data as well as on the parameters, they will vary by observation. For technical change, returns to scale and capacity utilization measures, changes in these measures are important for analysis and the measures are generally reported as indexes. However, for demand elasticities, some "average" value is more often of interest, so these measures are often reported for the observation where the deflators used for estimation are normalized to one, or for some "representative" observation.

In addition, since the parameters all have associated distributions, the elasticities also have a stochastic specification, so it is possible to compute standard errors. Depending on the complexity of the functional form, however, these standard errors may be very difficult to compute. One procedure, used by Morrison [1988a], is to specify the equations directly as functions of the parameters and compute the estimated covariance matrix for this set of functions by linearizing the functions around the estimated parameter values. This permits the use of standard formulas for the variance and covariance of linear functions of random variables.[31] Other procedures have been developed by, for example, Kulatilaka [1985].

[31] This can be done using econometric packages such as TSP, where this is accomplished using the ANALYZ command, although not much is then known about the distribution of the variance-covariance matrix.

* * * * *

This overview of implementation issues covers a number of problems that might arise when attempting to estimate production theory models for productivity growth analysis. These types of models have been used quite extensively to assess the economic performance of countries and industries. In the next chapter we summarize some of the results found for a number of such studies, focusing primarily on the literature about the productivity slowdown of the 1970s in the U.S. It thus provides some perspective on one of the most topical issues productivity growth researchers have pursued in the recent past, and on the experience of one country which has been extensively analyzed the U.S.

Chapter 8

Empirical Evidence on Productivity Growth and Capacity Utilization

Analyses of productivity growth and indicators of economic performance may provide insights about a number of different issues. The issue that has probably received the most attention in the recent productivity literature is the "productivity slowdown" that began in the early 1970s in most industrialized countries. This slowdown was documented and analyzed for the U.S. by a number of researchers, including Edward Denison [1979]. Denison presented a wide-ranging study using growth accounting measurement procedures (outlined in Chapter 2). His study concluded that "What happened is, to be blunt, a mystery".

Since that time many speculations have been offered and pursued in the search for an explanation for the productivity slowdown. Contributions to this literature have involved data construction refinements, methodological developments, and empirical comparisons of different countries and sectors.[1] After considering some empirical evidence about the existence of a slowdown, in this chapter we overview

[1] A useful summary of these arguments is provided in Baily and Chakrabarti [1988].

some potential explanations that have provided the motivation for such productivity analyses. This evidence both demonstrates why researchers might be interested and concerned about this issue, and provides insights about what types of theoretical and empirical developments might prove fruitful in a search for "explanations" of the slowdown. Although the numbers presented are primarily for the U.S. (due to ready availability of the data and the extensive literature), analogous indexes could clearly be constructed and analyses carried out for other countries.

In the first section we will see what evidence about the slowdown standard labor productivity growth measures offer, and then explore what types of information should be taken into consideration to interpret these overall measures further. For example, information about substitution between inputs and variations across years and industries may be essential for a constructive assessment of economic performance. Section 8.2 then begins to look at what the determinants of the apparent slowdown might be, by focusing on the possible impact of dramatically increasing energy prices in the early 1970s. The contributions of capacity utilization and scale economies are considered in Section 8.3, using the methodology developed in earlier chapters as a basis. Finally, the technical change bias measures introduced in Chapter 4, and their use in assessing productivity growth trends, are discussed in Section 8.4.

8.1 What is the "Productivity Growth Slowdown" and Does it Exist?

Since the early 1970s productivity analysts have found evidence of a decline in productivity growth in most industrialized countries. This decline became most evident after 1973, although it appears it may have started in the late 1960s for some countries. The slowdown is also the most pronounced when growth is computed for the aggregate economy, although manufacturing productivity also declined during

Table 8.1: Labor Productivity Growth Rates, percent

	1955-73	1973-86	Decline
United States	2.0	1.3	0.7
Japan	8.8	3.1	5.7
Germany	4.2	2.0	2.2
United Kingdom	2.5	0.9	1.6
Italy	4.9	2.0	2.9
France	4.6	1.9	2.7
Canada	3.0	2.0	1.0

Source: Table 1 in Fischer [1988]

the 1970s.[2] The apparent decline, or at least stagnation, has been quite prolonged as well as pervasive. Although manufacturing productivity growth has tended to "snap back" since the early 1980s, the slowdown now has been evident for almost two decades in the business sectors of most countries, and has been called the "most significant macroeconomic development of the last two decades" by Stanley Fischer [1988].

Documentation of the slowdown has often been presented in terms of labor productivity. Table 8.1, drawn from Fischer [1988], indicates the extent of the slowdown for different countries as reflected by this single factor measure.

These numbers suggest a dramatic post-1973 productivity growth slowdown, in most cases to less than half the growth rate compared to the first period. This is true even of countries such as Japan, and, to a lesser extent, Germany, Italy and France, which experienced formidable productivity growth earlier on.[3]

[2]Baily and Chakrabarti [1988] point out that productivity growth in manufacturing resumed former levels between 1979-85, although a large part of this resulted from the computer industry, which experienced dramatic growth.

[3]Note that all these countries were rebuilding after wartime destruction during this period and therefore a large growth rate, especially in the earlier years, would be expected. Also, productivity levels remained higher in the U.S. for most of this period than other countries, even though growth rates were smaller; a "catch-up" was occurring. Although such comparisons of levels rather than growth rates are not straightforward, this has been accomplished in terms of "productivity gaps" by, for example, Conrad and Jorgenson [1985] and Conrad and Unger [1989].

A host of questions naturally emerge when considering these numbers. One is how the underlying structure of the different countries compare. For example, what aspects of production processes in these countries might cause such similar patterns of productivity growth? In addition, when looking at the performance of an individual country, one might want to find out what is camouflaged by these overall numbers in terms of yearly fluctuations and variations across industries. It would also be useful to discover what happened with other inputs, using more comprehensive measures such as multifactor productivity and related indicators such as capacity utilization. These and other such issues are very important to address in order to interpret these numbers and isolate the impacts driving the productivity patterns. Many of these issues have been considered in the voluminous literature on the productivity slowdown.

Numerous studies have dealt with comparisons of productivity growth rates, gaps between productivity levels, statistical measurement procedures, and technical and behavioral aspects of the production structure which might cause similar patterns among different countries.[4] One interesting country comparison has been between the U.S. and Japan. Studies which have compared the production structure in these two countries and the impact on productivity include Norsworthy and Malmquist [1983], Jorgenson *et al* [1989] and Morrison [1989c].[5] An overview of some findings from these studies can be used to show what types of information are important to uncover to facilitate interpretation of the standard productivity growth indexes.

The studies all confirm that productivity growth in Japan was larger for almost all industries than in the U.S. Norsworthy and Malmquist pursue this further in terms of input patterns, to determine that this results largely from a higher rate of growth of capital and materials per worker. Jorgenson *et al*'s industry-specific analysis of technical

---

[4] For a useful of changes in productivity, costs and prices in different countries, see Moore and Cullity [1984] and other papers in the same volume. Another useful reference, although the data only go to 1973, is Christensen, Cummings and Jorgenson [1980].

[5] Most of the studies published in the volume containing Jorgenson *et al* and Morrison are of interest in this context.

change – considering twenty nine different industries – supports this. They find that industries which were slower in catching up with the U.S. included light consumer goods or investment goods industries. Those that fared best belonged to the raw material processing or intermediate goods manufacturing industries. Again, characteristics of production that seemed important for "explaining" these differences included the fact that Japanese industries tended to be less labor intensive than their U.S. counterparts, and more intensive in the use of capital and intermediate inputs. Expressing this in terms of technical change biases, both countries but especially Japan tended to be capital- and material- using and labor saving.

Morrison also determines that investment and adjustment of labor use was important for Japan; using a dynamic model it was shown that Japan managed to sustain post-1974 growth in productivity more effectively than the U.S. because of greater responsiveness of firms in terms of input demand and investment. Japan was therefore better able to recover and maintain growth from a more severe decline in 1973-74. This suggests that flexibility of demand and larger investment rates tend to enhance productivity growth, a finding consistent with other studies of productivity growth.[6]

The broader investigation of productivity growth determinants permitted by these types of studies indicates a number of extensions to analyses of simple labor productivity growth averages that need to be made to assess the numbers effectively. As evident from these and other studies, such factors as differences among industries, breakdowns of the averages into yearly changes, the role of other inputs and their adjustment (investment), and relationships among inputs and their responsiveness are important to consider to provide insights about what is happening and what the causes might be.

Differences across industries can be informative because they highlight which areas are the most affected. In U.S. manufacturing, for

[6]This is consistent with a different thread of literature which points to the impact of interest groups which interfere with the growth process by slowing the reaction of the economy to real shocks. In this sense it is an example of the proposition that the larger and more stable the country, the slower its growth will be. A useful discussion of this is found in Olson [1988].

example, productivity growth did not decline as much as for the overall economy; the Bureau of Labor Statistics reports a decline only to 2.1 % from 2.6 % for 1973-86 as compared to 1949-73. These numbers still conceal a significant amount of variation among industries. Durable manufacturing industries such as petroleum products, which experienced a post-1973 decline to an annual average labor productivity growth rate of 0.9 % from an pre-1973 average of 5.2 %, fared much worse than nondurable industries. This is also true when the partition of the data series is at 1979, although some nondurable industries did better since 1979 than pre-1979. This is shown in Table 8.2, where Bureau of Labor Statistics labor productivity growth indexes for a number of different manufacturing industries are listed.

This could suggest that more capital and energy-intensive industries did worse, so the role of these inputs should be highlighted. The numbers also imply that services and other non-manufacturing industries were at a disadvantage relative to manufacturing as a whole. These and other conclusions from the industry breakdown can be used to provide inspiration for interpretation of productivity growth fluctuations. They also, however, suggest additional questions and thus motivate further extensions to the analysis.

Fluctuations between individual years rather than just overall averages are also enlightening. This is particularly true when assessment of more comprehensive productivity growth measures as well as of different industries is carried out. For example, extensive variation across years is not as apparent for labor productivity, at least in the aggregate, as for other types of productivity measures and for more disaggregated industries. This is evident from the Bureau of Labor Statistics productivity growth indexes for labor and multifactor productivity for manufacturing, textiles and primary metals, reproduced in Table 8.3.

Although we will return to consider the multifactor productivity growth measure more in a moment, the point to note for now is that wide swings in productivity growth, especially for multifactor productivity and durable goods industries (with primary metals as the representative durable goods industry), are concealed in the summary annual averages. Although labor productivity does fluctuate

Table 8.2: U.S. Labor Productivity Growth Rates, percent*

	1949-73	1973-86	1949-79	1979-86
Manufacturing	2.6	2.1	2.4	2.3
Food and Kindred Products	2.7	2.7	2.7	2.7
Textile and Wood Products	4.5	3.3	4.4	2.6
Lumber and Wood Products	3.4	1.9	2.8	3.2
Paper and Allied Products	2.8	2.4	2.7	2.8
Printing and Publishing	2.3	0.4	1.9	0.5
Petroleum Products	5.2	0.9	4.1	1.8
Primary Metal Industries	2.0	0.4	1.6	0.9
Fabricated Metal Products	1.7	0.8	1.4	1.3
Transportation Equipment	2.8	0.7	2.4	0.9

(percentages computed at compound annual rate)

Source: U.S. Department of Labor, Bureau of Labor Statistics, Productivity Division

and reveals a post-1973 downturn, the fluctuations are not as large as for multifactor productivity and the shift is not as obvious; this highlights the role of inputs other than labor.

Also, note that while the productivity growth slowdown appears more dramatically in 1973-75 and post-1979 in the multifactor than labor productivity growth index, a subsequent upswing occurs, particularly for nondurables (textiles). Whether the productivity slowdown appears extreme, therefore, depends critically not only on the productivity growth measure used and the industry, but also on the time period specified. Studies that include only a short period after 1973 or 1979 thereby indicate a much worse slowdown than those considering the pattern over a longer time frame.

This has been taken by many researchers as an indication that something dramatic that happened in 1973 and 1979 may be the "culprit" – and the most obvious choice is the energy price increases experienced at those times. More generally, of course, the greater differences between years and industries in multifactor than labor productivity must be a result of interactions with other inputs. Investment, for

Table 8.3: U.S. Labor and Multifactor Productivity Growth Rates, percent

	Manufacturing		Textiles		Primary Metals	
	Labor	Multi	Labor	Multi	Labor	Multi
1950	1.9	5.2	1.1	-0.6	-2.2	6.8
1951	-0.9	0.3	4.2	-0.3	11.0	3.3
1952	4.2	1.4	7.8	4.2	0.4	-4.3
1953	3.5	1.8	3.5	0.6	9.6	2.5
1954	2.2	-0.4	3.5	3.8	-8.9	-7.1
1955	4.3	3.0	7.6	3.0	12.5	6.0
1956	-0.6	-1.4	2.5	1.6	-1.2	-3.0
1957	2.1	0.8	4.2	3.1	-3.5	-1.4
1958	1.4	-1.3	5.4	3.5	-1.9	-8.5
1959	3.1	5.0	2.3	0.8	3.8	4.0
1960	0.6	-0.2	4.0	1.5	-0.4	-2.3
1961	4.0	1.5	5.9	0.7	3.3	0.6
1962	2.3	2.5	5.1	3.3	4.4	0.3
1963	4.0	3.1	6.4	3.2	1.6	2.8
1964	4.3	3.1	6.4	3.2	1.6	2.8
1965	1.9	2.8	1.5	1.2	2.0	0.7
1966	0.9	0.7	3.7	1.8	4.8	1.3
1967	4.0	-1.1	6.1	0.9	-0.1	-3.1
1968	3.1	0.7	3.7	-1.1	2.6	-2.4
1969	0.8	0.7	5.5	1.6	-1.1	-1.2
1970	2.6	-1.9	7.2	4.2	-2.4	-2.6
1971	6.5	3.0	7.2	2.6	5.7	0.9
1972	4.0	4.1	5.0	2.3	8.4	2.2
1973	2.2	3.3	-1.9	-0.7	5.1	4.7
1974	0.7	-3.2	4.7	-4.2	0.5	-1.8
1975	2.3	-3.2	6.4	0.6	-4.4	-11.0
1976	4.4	3.1	0.3	5.2	0.5	0.1
1977	3.2	1.3	9.7	7.7	-0.5	-3.2
1978	1.2	0.2	-0.2	-1.8	3.2	1.6
1979	-0.4	0.0	3.3	2.7	-0.1	-1.2
1980	0.4	-0.7	0.4	2.0	1.1	0.4
1981	1.5	0.8	1.8	0.3	3.2	0.5
1982	3.2	0.4	5.0	2.1	-6.5	-5.3
1983	2.9	2.0	7.7	3.2	7.1	-1.5
1984	1.7	2.1	0.3	0.0	3.1	4.4
1985	1.0	2.9	-3.1	-7.3	-0.8	2.3
1986	1.6	2.4	6.5	10.5	1.2	2.0

Source: U.S. Department of Labor, Bureau of Labor Statistics, Productivity Division example, also declined during these periods, which could have had an important impact. Consideration of the energy price hypothesis therefore requires looking at both the direct impact of energy prices and the role of other inputs, particularly through their relationship with energy use. Analyses of these linkages and interactions provide additional insights into the determinants of productivity growth fluctuations, although these again also stimulate additional questions.

The pattern of productivity growth taking into account the impacts of different inputs is, of course, reflected in measures of multifactor productivity. The time pattern of these indexes for the U.S. manufacturing, textile and primary metals industries was seen in Table 8.2. The average annual growth rates for these indexes, and corresponding averages for some other major manufacturing industries, are given in Table 8.4. "Multifactor" here means the measure includes not only labor and capital but also energy, intermediate materials and purchased services.[7] These numbers suggest that in total – including all input use – more variation between years as well as differences across industries exists for MFP than appears in labor productivity indexes, but the productivity growth slowdown remains pervasive.

These measures can be broken down to assess the individual impacts of different inputs. The influence of capital productivity changes on multifactor productivity growth can be seen in Table 8.5. These changes were dramatic, particularly for durable goods. The petroleum industry, for example, experienced a drop from a pre-1973 1.4 % increase in capital productivity to a post-1973 average of -3.0 %.

This implies that the capital stock may have been larger than optimal in terms of economic performance in the later years, so investment would be relatively low. Since capital productivity growth was lower and more often negative than labor productivity, overall productivity growth fell increasingly short of labor productivity growth. Capital intensity may therefore be an important determinant of measured productivity growth, which suggests that the roles of investment, capital utilization, and other features of the capital stock and capital use are important to explore.

[7] These data were graciously provided by Mike Harper at the Bureau of Labor Statistics.

Table 8.4: U.S. Multifactor Productivity Growth Rates, percent

	1949-73	1973-86	1949-79	1979-86
Manufacturing	1.5	0.6	1.1	1.4
Food and Kindred Products	0.8	0.5	0.6	1.0
Textile Mill Products	1.8	1.5	1.7	1.4
Lumber and Wood Products	2.0	1.0	1.6	1.9
Paper and Allied Products	1.2	0.3	0.8	1.2
Printing and Publishing	0.7	-0.6	0.4	-0.6
Petroleum Products	0.9	-0.1	0.6	0.3
Primary Metal Industries	0.0	-1.1	-0.5	0.3
Fabricated Metal Products	0.6	0.2	0.4	0.7
Transportation Equipment	1.1	0.2	0.9	0.4

Source: U.S. Department of Labor, Bureau of Labor Statistics, Productivity Division.

Table 8.5: U.S. Capital Productivity Growth Rates, percent

	1949-73	1973-86	1949-79	1979-86
Manufacturing	0.3	-1.9	-0.2	-1.8
Food and Kindred Products	1.0	0.0	0.7	0.4
Textile Mill Products	3.0	0.6	2.6	0.5
Lumber and Wood Products	0.0	0.3	-0.7	3.7
Paper and Allied Products	0.9	-1.7	0.2	-0.7
Printing and Publishing	-0.4	-1.3	-0.5	-1.5
Petroleum Products	1.4	-3.0	0.8	-4.0
Primary Metal Industries	-0.9	-4.7	-1.4	-5.8
Fabricated Metal Products	-0.5	-3.0	-1.1	-2.5
Transportation Equipment	-0.5	-2.3	-0.8	-2.4

Source: U.S. Department of Labor, Bureau of Labor Statistics, Productivity Division.

Table 8.6: Multifactor Productivity Growth Rates, percent

	1965-73	1973-79	1979 – 82*	1973-82
Canada	3.1	1.0	-4.8	-1.0
Finland	3.5	1.1	2.4	1.5
France	4.1	2.6	0.1	2.0
Germany	3.4	2.2	-0.9	1.2
Italy	4.6	1.6	4.7	2.1
Norway	3.3	-0.3	-1.4	-0.7
Sweden	4.0	0.1	-1.0	-0.3
U.K.	2.2	-1.2	-2.6	-1.6
U.S.	2.2	0.6	-0.6	0.2

* For Italy the terminal years is 1980, for France, 1981

Source: Berndt and Hesse [1986], Table 5.

The general patterns of productivity trends found for the U.S. also are evident for other countries. Thus, the resulting questions about the causes of these patterns parallel those outlined here. As an indication of this similarity, multifactor productivity growth rates were computed by Berndt and Hesse [1986] for the manufacturing industries of nine countries. These numbers, presented as Table 8.6, verify the existence of a productivity growth slowdown in the manufacturing sectors of industrial countries in general, although the severity and the timing of the slowdown differs somewhat across countries, and post-1979 improvement has been evident in most cases.

Although consideration of various industries and countries, yearly variations and alternative types of productivity growth indexes highlighting different inputs paints a more detailed picture of productivity patterns than the overall summary measures, evidence of a downturn in productivity growth persists in this more extended analysis. This is particularly true for durable goods industries, although 1973-75, when dramatic energy price changes were encountered, seems to be a turning point for both durable and nondurable industries. Many of these industries are also those in which investment rates have dropped during the post-1973 period, which supports the common conclusion that strong investment drives strong productivity growth. A "snap-back", however, appears to have occured to some degree in most manufacturing sectors since 1979, indicating the importance of relationships among inputs and flexibility of firms' responses. Again, therefore, although confirmation of productivity growth problems and some insights about important considerations to take into account are provided by this more complete analysis, additional questions also arise.

Some researchers have argued that these patterns could simply be generated by cyclical factors; it is well-established that traditionally measured multifactor and labor productivity growth are both procyclical, and therefore when the economy is moving toward recession (which may arise from a number of things including energy price increases), productivity growth may be expected to decline.

Our overview above, however, has suggested that a number of individual determinants might be identified and their impacts assessed to provide greater interpretation of productivity fluctuations. A large and increasing body of research has concentrated on pursuing these possibilities further to find "explanations" of *why* these time trends have been observed – to isolate what has *caused* the productivity growth slowdown and its time- and industry- pattern.

For example, we have identified a possible role for energy price changes. Substantial research has been devoted to trying to determine whether energy could be the primary culprit since the productivity declines appear to occur simultaneously with energy price increases, and energy and capital-intensive industries had the worst productivity (and investment) records. However, since energy is such a small component of total costs for firms, it would seem unlikely for the direct effect of energy price changes to have been as large as the productivity growth declines suggest. This will be elaborated in the next section.[8]

Related studies have suggested that indirect effects such as obsolescence of capital could augment the direct impact of energy price changes. However, the magnitude of the productivity growth effect appears very large for even a combination of direct and indirect impacts to have been the primary determinant. Along similar lines, some researchers have recognized the increase in environmental concerns during this time period and have suggested that additional expenses to clean up the environment might be identified as a contributing problem. These costs again, however, do not appear large enough to have caused the considerable impact on productivity growth that has been observed.[9]

One approach toward incorporating these and other different possible explanations of the slowdown, as reflected in the discussion above of research comparing U.S. and Japan productivity growth patterns, has been to construct empirically implementable models of production processes. These can then be used to assess deviations among industries in levels of investment and input use. This has often provided the basis for evaluation of biases, as discussed later in this chapter. It is important, however, to recognize that *why* these different patterns might have occured is perhaps the most critical question. Although studies of biases often do not focus on this aspect of the problem, the production theory structure often allows assessment of this general issue.

This type of framework has also allowed researchers to identify other restrictions of traditional accounting methods for productivity growth measurement that are unlikely to be satisfied, and see whether these errors have caused significant biases in productivity growth measures

[8]It is worth noting that many explanations that have been proferred, like sensitivity to energy prices and problems with aggregate demand (possibly stimulating low research and development (R&D) rates) suggest that productivity growth might be expected to recover with relaxations in these constraints facing firms. This will be an important topic to address in future research, for example, in the context of the declining (relative) energy prices experienced in the late 1980s. However, due to lack of sufficient data, little work has yet been done to evaluate this.

[9]These adaptations will be considered in more detail in the next chapter.

over time that would result in evidence of a slowdown. In particular, it has provided a vehicle in which to consider not only substitution among inputs, but also such characteristics of the production process as capacity utilization and returns to scale.[10] Essentially, this involves trying to identify technical change independently from other components of the productivity residual that has been called the "measure of our ignorance" – "decomposing" the residual. Accomplishing this requires incorporating capacity utilization and returns to scale in the model used to represent production, and including measures of these characteristics into the mechanism used for constructing productivity growth measures.

In the next sections we will explore some of these routes taken to provide explanations of the productivity growth slowdown.

8.2 A Focus on Energy

Energy became an important focus of research into explanations of the productivity growth slowdown because the dramatic price increases of 1973-74 and 1979-80 due to OPEC seemed to coincide with productivity downturns. The hypothesis that energy was the "villain" is analyzed in more detail in Berndt and Wood [1987]; many of their points are summarized only briefly here.

Perhaps a useful way to initiate a discussion of the effects of energy price changes is by considering energy productivity growth rates. These are summarized for a number of U.S. manufacturing industries in Table 8.7.

These average growth rates highlight the impact of energy prices on energy conservation. According to these figures, most industries tended to "use" energy to fuel productivity growth in the earlier period, but reduced energy use dramatically to generate positive and large energy productivity growth after 1973. The ability to conserve energy, however, seemed to differ across industries; durable goods in-

[10] Other possible "villains" that could be taken into account in this way include markups, and other components of costs that we will discuss further in the next two chapters.

Table 8.7: U.S. Energy Productivity Growth Rates, percent, by industry

	1949-73	1973-86	1949-79	1979-86
Manufacturing	-0.9	2.8	-0.3	3.2
Food and Kindred Products	-1.3	2.7	-0.4	2.1
Textile Mill Products	0.9	2.7	1.5	1.3
Lumber and Wood Products	-2.2	3.3	-1.1	3.0
Paper and Allied Products	0.1	3.0	0.1	5.6
Printing and Publishing	-3.1	1.1	-1.6	-1.9
Petroleum Products	1.1	2.4	1.5	1.9
Primary Metal Industries	-0.1	0.2	-0.4	1.6
Fabricated Metal Products	-2.1	0.7	-1.2	-0.9
Transportation Equipment	-0.4	1.5	0.1	1.1

Source: U.S. Department of Labor, Bureau of Labor Statistics, Productivity Division.

dustries which generally tend to be more energy and capital intensive did not seem to have as much scope for substitution as did industries for more nondurable goods.[11]

This brief analysis of the energy productivity growth numbers provides the foundation to elaborate some arguments presented by researchers to demonstrate the importance of the "energy crisis" to the productivity growth slowdown. The basis of most "energy is the villain" explanations is that attempts by firms to conserve energy caused serious obstacles for efficient production. Varying assumptions about characteristics of the production process may, however, be critically important for evaluating the determinants and effects of energy conservation. Whether the share of energy in costs is large enough to stimulate significant adaptations to production processes, and whether existing complementary and substitutable relationships among inputs are consistent with those required for "energy crisis" hypotheses to work, have been two primary questions raised.[12]

[11] For obvious reasons, this is not the case as strongly for the petroleum industry. Analysis of energy in this industry is complicated by the fact that energy is here both an input and output.

[12] For more details about these arguments, see Berndt and Wood [1987].

For example, Rasche and Tatom [1977] founded their argument about the impacts of energy prices on the assertions that energy is very substitutable in the long run with both capital and labor, but that both these inputs are fixed in the short run. In this case, energy price increases will stimulate attempts to conserve energy, but with a limited amount of other inputs available this will cause a decline in output produced and a resulting reduction in productivity growth. Once labor and capital are able to increase to substitute for energy, output will again increase but the reduced productivity of these inputs will cause lower overall productivity growth than before.

These conclusions resulting from their scenario depend on the assumption that the impact of energy adjustments is large, which suggests considerable responsiveness of firms to energy price changes, and that energy should be a large proportion of costs. In addition, long run substitutability of other inputs for energy is required to drive their results. These assumptions may, however, be erroneous. The extensive conservation necessary to drive the Rasche and Tatom results did not materialize, even though a significant amount did occur. Further, the cost share of energy is too small directly to affect productivity substantially. In addition, responses of other inputs varied from those required for the Rasche-Tatom hypothesis to hold.

A number of researchers have pointed out the problems arising from such underlying assumptions, which are common in the literature on energy price impacts. For example, on the basis of the assumption that energy and labor were perfect substitutes (which would cause the most extreme substitution possible for energy and thus the greatest drop in labor productivity), Okun [1974] showed that the maximum possible increase in employment from observed energy price increases would be on the order of 0.2 of one percent. This suggests a negligible, rather than dramatic, effect on labor productivity, even with the most favorable assumptions for the Rasche-Tatom arguments. It is possible, however, for other direct and indirect relationships with inputs in the short and long run to lead to a contradiction of Okun's reasoning.

The capital-energy relationship postulated in the Rasche-Tatom model also seems to be inconsistent with currently available evidence; a consensus appears to be emerging that although energy and labor are substitutes, energy-capital complementarity predominates.[13] In this case, for increasing energy prices to have a depressing effect on productivity growth due to its relationship with capital, it may be that attempts to conserve energy coincide with a lower desired capital stock and therefore lower capital investment levels. Then, if investment fuels productivity growth as is generally found, growth rates will be smaller than would otherwise be the case. This will be a long run process if capital is quasi-fixed in the short run, which will cause capacity utilization to be affected. This utilization issue is important, not only because capacity utilization adjustments must be made for productivity growth measures to be correct (as we have seen), but also because obsolescence issues arise (as discussed further in the next chapter).

Given the importance of the energy-capital relationship on productivity growth, a number of researchers attempted early in the productivity slowdown debate to determine whether energy prices seemed to have the depressing impact on investment suggested by complementarity. Denison [1980],[14] for example considered changes over time in the growth rate of net and gross capital stock and found higher growth rates after 1973 than before. Studies based on capital-output ratios, such as Jorgenson [1984], supported this finding for a number of individual industries as well as for the aggregates. If, however, capital-labor ratios are used instead, the data reveal that growth in these measures declined for the private business sector even though not for manufacturing alone.

The required decrease in capital formation was found only by researchers who based their analysis on the idea of utilized capital rather than direct investment rates. For example, Kopcke [1980] mul-

[13] See, for example, Berndt and Wood [1975, 1979] and Hudson-Jorgenson [1974]. For an alternative view, see Griffin and Gregory [1976] and Pindyck [1979].

[14] See also the other papers in this volume, particularly the one by Ernst R. Berndt [1980].

tiplied capital stock measures by the Federal Reserve Board (FRB) capacity utilization measure. Since capacity utilization as measured by the FRB dropped substantially in most industries post-1973, this adjustment resulted in a net decline in the growth rate of investment, as required by the theory. As we have seen, use of a mechanical capacity utilization measure to carry out this adjustment has very little theoretical justification. The results still suggest, however, that developing a valid treatment of capacity utilization fluctuations in the wake of energy price changes might be both theoretically and intuitively important for evaluating the impact of energy price changes on productivity growth.[15]

Overall, as elaborated further by Berndt and Wood [1987], the impact of energy prices on productivity growth is as yet unclear, but appears to be somewhat small due to the small cost share of energy. Indirect impacts, however, particularly those associated with capital, may ultimately prove energy impacts to be more important.

A comprehensive assessment of the relationship between energy prices and economic growth requires consideration of the direct and indirect relationships among inputs in the short and long run, and of how investment and utilization will be influenced by price changes. These interactions are obviously complex to model and measure. One implication of this is that a more complete framework for analysis and construction of capacity utilization measures – and subsequent adjustment of productivity growth indexes – is necessary, since traditional accounting productivity growth measures are not capable of distinguishing these effects. As we will see in the following sections and Chapter 9, recent research indicates structural production theory models provide important steps in this direction, and thus insights about the productivity growth slowdown.

[15] This reasoning is supported by evidence that, although levels of the FRB as compared to economic CU measures differ, rates of change are quite similar (as noted in Chapter 3).

8.3 The Impact of Capacity Utilization and Scale Adjustments

The impact of capacity utilization adjustments on productivity growth measurement has been considered by, among others, Berndt and Fuss [1986] and Hulten [1986]. Separate and combined utilization and scale effects have been identified in Morrison [1986a, 1989b]. As discussed in Chapter 4, the methods used by these researchers for capacity utilization adjustments differ, but all find the influence of capacity utilization adjustments to be relatively small. Due to the small impact of the adjustments, Hulten, in fact, does not provide estimates in his analysis, but focuses on the theoretical specification. This section will therefore examine only the published numbers presented by Berndt-Fuss and Morrison, which provide some evidence of the impact of utilization flucutations on productivity growth and the slowdown.

As we saw before, the Berndt and Fuss study uses an *ex-post* as compared to *ex-ante* valuation of the firm to impute a (shadow) value to the capital stock for utilization adjustments. The *ex-post* measurement can be carried out in a number of ways; Berndt-Fuss explore both a Tobin's q measure and a residual measure based on the returns or revenue per year.

The Tobin's q measure approximates the shadow value of capital Z_K as $Z_K(t) = q(t)p_K(t)$ where $q(t)$ is a measure of manufacturing Tobin's q based on securities' market data and $p_K(t)$ is the traditional Hall-Jorgenson *ex-ante* rental price of capital including tax variables and the Moody Baa corporate bond yield as the interest rate. The Tobin's q measure in effect takes the ratio of the entire market valuation of the firm to the book value of the capital stock, to generate a measure of the returns to the existing plant and equipment. The residual method computes Z_K as $Z_K = p_Y \cdot Y - VC$, where $VC = \Sigma_j p_j v_j$ is variable costs. This value was adjusted as in Gollop and Jorgenson [1980] for tax and inventory revaluation effects. Both these measures adapt the valuation of the capital stock to reflect differences between *ex-post* and *ex-ante* returns, but they also include returns to any factor not recognized in the analysis.

Table 8.8: Traditional and temporary equilibrium measures of TFP average annual growth rates, U.S. manufacturing

Time Period	Traditional Measure		Adjusted (residual method)		Adjusted (q method)	
	(VA)	(GO)	(VA)	(GO)	(VA)	(GO)
1948-81	1.54	0.54	1.57	0.57	1.67	0.60
1948-65	2.06	0.67	2.02	0.68	2.23	0.76
1965-73	1.64	0.59	1.63	0.58	1.45	0.50
1973-81	0.32	0.22	0.55	0.31	0.73	0.37

Source: Berndt and Fuss [1986], Table 1.

Berndt and Fuss carry out two adjustments of traditional productivity growth measures based on these two kinds of shadow value computations, and report the standard and adjusted measures as in Table 8.8, where VA indicates a value added measure and GO a gross output measure.

A quick glance at these numbers confirms how little the adjustment for capacity utilization affects the traditional measures, although the bias for ignoring capacity utilization does increase during the slowdown, and the q method adjustments alter the estimates more than using the traditional residual method. For example, for the residual method, the numbers for 1948-65 and 1965-73 change almost imperceptively for both measures; from .67 to .68 and .59 to .58 on average for the GO measures. However, the adjustment does have a larger impact between 1973 and 1981 – the .22 % measured increase per year rises to .31 %. The increment is even larger for the q method; .22 % becomes .37 %. These numbers thereby suggest a partial "explanation" for the slowdown, but are not convincing evidence that capacity utilization significantly affected productivity growth measurements.

The Morrison [1986a] study also establishes only a small influence of capacity utilization adjustments.[16] In this study a number of adjustments are taken into account to include not only capacity utilization

[16] For a similar type of adjustment procedure for OECD countries based on econometrically measured capacity utilization rates, see Berndt and Hesse [1986].

Table 8.9: Average TFP Growth Rates, Observed and Adjusted, U.S. manufacturing

Time Period	Traditional Measure	CU Adjusted	EXP Adjusted	ADJC Adjusted	RTS Adjusted
Capital only quasi-fixed					
1949-79	0.835	0.813	0.833	0.873	0.811
1949-65	1.094	1.058	1.071	1.107	1.015
1965-73	0.708	0.696	0.715	0.760	0.706
1973-79	0.391	0.388	0.423	0.469	0.464
Capital and Labor quasi-fixed					
1949-79	0.900	0.909	0.923	0.943	0.895
1949-65	1.297	1.282	1.316	1.342	1.253
1965-73	0.651	0.686	0.659	0.682	0.629
1973-79	0.280	0.313	0.331	0.335	0.385

Source: Morrison [1986a], Table 2.

but the impacts of nonstatic expectations (EXP), explicit costs of adjustment (ADJC), and returns to scale (RTS), which are all measured within a production theory-based parametric model such as that outlined in the preceding chapters. The results of adapting traditional measures for these characteristics of the technology are presented in Table 8.9 for both a capital-only-quasi-fixed model and one with labor also quasi-fixed.

The most relevant comparison for our current discussion is between the first and second columns, which shows the capacity utilization adjustments. The scale adjustment reflected in the last column, however (motivated also in Chapter 4) seems to have a slightly greater impact, although neither is large. The utilization adjustment reduces the growth rate for all periods negligibly when only capital is considered quasi-fixed, and decreases the largest growth rate (for 1949-65) relative to the others when labor fixity is recognized. There is therefore a slight smoothing of the numbers, implying a somewhat smaller impact of the slowdown, when labor fixity is taken into account.

A reasonable question is why this impact appears so slight, since one would think *a-priori* that with large fluctuations in the economy like those in the 1970s subequilibrium would have an important role in cost changes. One reason the Morrison study seems to show even less impact than found by Berndt-Fuss may be that the nonparametric framework independently identifies the shadow value of capital separately from returns to other factors, resulting in less deviation than for nonparametric methods which generate residual measures. However, there may also be conceptual problems with the adjustments outlined here which diminish the impacts.

In particular, the Morrison framework really only isolates the difference between the primal and dual measure with the adjustment carried out, in a sense identifying the two components of the full primal measure, assuming the measures were computed correctly originally. Therefore the error bias from incorrect assumptions discussed in Chapter 4, which may augment the difference between the dual and primal measures, is not taken into account.

A more complete decomposition of productivity growth measures including not only the deviation between primal and dual measures from erroneous assumptions, is provided in Morrison [1989b]. A summary table with the biases from the cost-side computations for the U.S., Japanese and Canadian manufacturing sectors is provided below as Table 8.10, where "Trad" indicates traditionally measured cost-side growth and "Corrected" means the error bias has been taken into account. In addition, "R" denotes the returns to scale adjustment, "F" the fixity adjustment, "A" incorporates adjustment costs and "T" refers to the total adjustment allowing for all of these characteristics, similarly to the (less comprehensive) development of these error biases in Chapter 4.

Only technical change is measured in these indexes since they are based on the cost derivative; the adjustment to the primal measure based on output price is not carried out. However, since returns to scale and markup behavior appear nearly to counteract each other in these data,[17] the cost and primal side measures are very close in value

[17]The equality between revenues ($p_Y Y$) and costs (C) is closely approximated.

Table 8.10: U.S. Multifactor Productivity Growth, Average Annual Growth (percent)

Year	Trad $-\epsilon_{Ct}$	Corrected $-\epsilon_{Ct}^{R}$	Bias	$-\epsilon_{Ct}^{F}$	Bias	$-\epsilon_{Ct}^{A}$	Bias	$-\epsilon_{Ct}^{T}$	Bias
U.S.									
1960-81	.807	.446	-.361	.735	-.072	.723	-.084	.359	-.448
1960-73	.976	.476	-.500	.874	-.102	.870	-.106	.359	-.619
1973-81	.512	.393	-.119	.492	-.021	.466	-.046	.358	-.154
Japan									
1960-81	1.223	.592	-.631	1.608	.385	1.611	.388	.987	-.236
1960-73	1.659	.872	-.787	2.131	.472	2.120	.461	1.315	-.344
1973-81	.459	.102	-.356	.694	.235	.719	.260	.414	-.045
Canada									
1960-82	.580	.153	-.427	.485	-.095	.511	-.069	.062	-.518
1960-73	1.025	.395	-.629	1.021	-.004	1.034	.010	.371	-.654
1973-81	.103	-.249	-.352	-.038	-.140	-.053	-.156	-.429	-.533
1973-82	-.113	-.224	-.111	-.348	-.235	-.302	-.189	-.419	.307

Source: Morrison [1989b], Table 2.

once the errors in traditional measurement techniques are taken into account.

In this table, the productivity slowdown reflected in the first column for all three countries is at least partially "explained". When the effects of subequilibrium and scale economies are removed from the measure for the U.S., for example, the remaining technical change component of productivity growth appears virtually constant across all years in terms of annual averages. This smoothing is not nearly as evident in Japan and Canada, where productivity slowdowns are still observed, but the gaps between pre- and post-1973 are lower because much of the pre-1973 strong productivity growth appears to have been due to scale economies and utilization.

In sum, a substantial portion of observed historical cost fluctuations appears to have been erroneously attributed to technical change when it instead is due to these other production characteristics, particularly in years of substantial output growth. The adjustments therefore tend to smooth both cyclical and secular productivity growth fluctuations, although the impact of utilization seems minor compared to that of scale economies.[18] This sugggests further research on the existence and impact of scale economies and utilization fluctuations may be informative about the determinants of productivity growth patterns.

8.4 Biases and Their Contribution

If technical change biases are to be implicated in the productivity growth slowdown debate, it must be the case that some input which has an input-using bias has experienced relatively reduced demand (less intensive use of this factor in production), or an input which has an input-saving bias has experienced relatively increased demand. This results because, as we saw in Chapter 4, if technical change is input j-using, then technical progress implies that this input is used in ever greater proportion. If instead the proportion of this input's costs in total cost declines due to substitution, then technical change will tend to be stifled.

Two major questions therefore arise when considering the impacts of biases; what are the biases and what causes them? In other words, if, for example, technical change is energy-using and demand for energy declines due to increasing energy prices, this will depress the rate of technical change. Therefore it is important to ascertain whether technical change is energy- using or -saving. In addition, however, this bias could change over time if the pattern of biases is not inherent in the process of technical change but induced by other factors. In this case, a likely reason an energy-using bias is found in early data is that declining relative prices induced technical change which was relatively energy intensive. This suggests that post-1973 there might be potential to observe energy-saving technical change.[19]

[18] See Morrison [1989b] for further elaboration of the model, numbers, and analysis.

[19] Note that this implies the bias must depend on the data, whereas for some functional forms, as noted for the translog in Chapter 4, it is just a parameter and therefore the determinants of the bias are ignored by construction.

Although we will not pursue this induced technical change argument here, clearly this has importance for long run trends, and consideration of its potential must be carried out in a structure in which the entire pattern of production decisions may be characterized. In particular, the production theory-based models outlined in this text may be used to discover the determinants of biases, since in most cases the resulting bias measure is a function of the exogenous variables which appear as arguments of the cost function.

In terms of assessing short run impacts on productivity growth, however, it is simply necessary to determine the sign and size of the biases with respect to technical change. This has been the focus of a number of studies about technical change biases,[20] which have highlighted the response of productivity growth to energy prices, and thus concentrated on determining whether technical change is energy-using or -saving.

An often-cited study by Jorgenson and Fraumeni [1981], for example, concludes that overall the most frequent pattern of productivity growth is capital, labor and energy using, and materials saving.[21] This has important implications for whether energy price increases will slow down or quicken productivity growth, although the determinants of the biases cannot be ascertained due to the translog framework. Specifically, Jorgenson and Fraumeni [1981] find that in almost all of the 36 sectors of the U.S. economy, technical progress is energy-using. This implies that at the sectoral level productivity growth is reduced when energy prices increase, although one would not think productivity growth would change very substantially since the cost share of energy is generally small. Moreover, if this is accompanied by capital-using technical change and energy-capital complementarity, this could have a much larger impact than the small energy cost share would indicate.

[20]See Jorgenson and Fraumeni [1981], Norsworthy, Harper and Kunze [1979], Berndt and Wood [1982], Morrison [1988b] and Jorgenson [1988] and the references cited for example.

[21]Note from section 8.1 above that Jorgenson et al find materials using and labor saving is more common for both the U.S. and Japan. The energy and capital biases, however, remain the same and they appear to have had a less dramatic effect in Japan.

It is important, however, to consider whether these results on the biases of technical change are convincing. For instance, as Berndt and Wood [1982] point out, the Jorgenson framework is not only an instantaneous adjustment framework but also imposes substantial curvature restrictions and therefore does not allow for full substitution among inputs. These biases are therefore difficult to interpret if substitution and fixity in the short run do occur. Once a more complete production process is specified, as we have discussed, the distinction between short and long run may be made, which may change the bias results.

Morrison [1988b], for example, finds for the U.S. and Canadian steel industries that technical change appears to be capital- and labor-intensive or -using both in the short and long run; it is relatively energy and materials- saving. The capital result is, however, somewhat different from that found by Jorgenson for this industry. The measure indicates that the shadow value for productive capital increases relative to the market value with an increase in the state of technology. This in turn implies that investment in capital tends to coincide with an increase in productivity growth, where capital investment is measured using standard practices.

This result is consistent with the Jorgenson *et al* capital-using bias for most industries, but not with that for the primary metals industry. This difference between the short and long run framework may occur because the more complete structure identifies extra factors, such as dynamic adjustment, fluctuations in capital utilization and obsolescence, that are important for correctly assessing the role of capital. Since little use has been made of these more detailed structural models in the literature on biases, however, more study is required to obtain some basis for consensus.

Another problem with using the standard bias measures to assess the impact of changes in, say, energy prices on technical change, is that these bias measures are based on the assumption of disembodied technical change (as mentioned in Chapter 4). To take into account the possibility of embodied technical change it may, for example, be useful to identify the effects of technical change on the vintage composition of the capital stock. Since energy use may depend critically on this composition, an important part of the story may otherwise be ignored. This issue will be further considered in Chapter 9.

This is closely related to the utilization question which was dealt with in our development by constructing a short run model. If utilization is changed, as discussed above, the usual procedures for measuring capital may not be valid, and therefore the measured biases will be erroneous. The impacts on the shadow value of capital, captured in a short run model such as that implemented in Morrison [1988b], will reflect this more correctly than standard measures. Moreover, additional information may be obtainable from utilization biases.

Morrison considered utilization biases and found that investment in capital is (relatively) materials-saving and energy- and labor-using. This suggests that overutilization of capital in the short run is supported only from extraordinary application of materials inputs to meet the required production level. In reverse, for energy and labor, shortages of capital result in input-saving relative to an optimum long run production point. In terms of our analysis, this indicates that when attempts are made to save energy, this will cause lower utilization and therefore a lower "effective" capital stock or service flow. This has important implications for adjustments to the analysis of standard productivity growth measures, and for the magnitude of the productivity growth slowdown.[22]

Scale biases might also be important. The availability of scale economies to exploit, for example, suggests that growth over time will cause input and cost changes distinct from those generated by technical change. If scale biases exist, therefore, input mixes will change independently of technical change. Unless productivity growth is defined as including both technical change and scale effects, these changes should not be attributed to productivity growth, or should at least be separately analyzed.

[22]To see this, recall from Chapter 4 that if investment is input j-using, increasing capital implies S_j increases since $\partial S_j/\partial \ln K > 0$. Therefore, is demand is too high relative to capital, overutilization results; $\partial \epsilon_{CK}/\partial \ln p_j > 0$. Therefore, $CU_c = 1 - \epsilon_{CK}$ declines with an increase in p_j. This interpretation is not obvious; to motivate it further, refer to the discussion of interpretation of utilization (and scale) biases in Chapter 4.

Morrison [1988b] found that output increases are relatively labor and energy saving in the short run, but materials using. This is consistent with the biases with respect to capital; if output demand increases, capital is utilized more intensively, stimulating extra use of those inputs which are saved by additional capital stock (M), and less use of those which are used by capital expansion (L, E). If, in response, the firm invests in additional capital, this in turn saves on materials and uses labor and energy.

* * * * *

Although there are numerous different factors that might partially "explain" productivity growth fluctuations, many of them can be assessed within an econometric model which allows identification of their effects, similarly to the analysis of substitution among inputs, capacity utilization and scale effects, and the contributions of biases outlined in this chapter. These characteristics include monopoly power, regulations, obsolescence of capital, inventory holding, additional inputs and outputs, selling costs and many other factors affecting firm behavior. Most of these may be incorporated and therefore considered in the framework developed in preceding chapters.

These types of extensions to the analysis, many of which are outlined in Diewert and Morrison [1990], are the subject of further scrutiny in the next two chapters. As we shall see, recognizing these characteristics of production provides a richer structure for analysis, resulting in adjustments to productivity growth measures that further facilitate analysis of productivity growth fluctuations and the productivity growth slowdown.

Chapter 9

Other Factors Affecting Productivity Growth: Some Recent Developments

A number of different determinants of costs and therefore production may be important for representing firm behavior, depending on the focus of the analysis and the industry or firm under consideration. Some representative factors affecting firm behavior mentioned in previous chapters include capital obsolescence, the regulatory environment, and imperfect competition. These constraints, "goods" or choices for the firm have very diverse characteristics, but all affect costs and therefore measured productivity growth in important ways.

Adaptations to take these and other factors into account in measurement of economic performance often take the form of changing the measure of an input or output price to more closely approximate the true marginal (shadow) value of the output or input. For example, the value of output on the margin may not be correctly measured. This problem could originate from different technological and market attributes. We have already seen how measures must be adapted when scale economies exist; this adaptation requires recognizing that the relevant valuation of output is not at average but at marginal cost. Market power, however, can also cause the value of output to differ from cost. This must again be accommodated by measuring the value of output at marginal cost, which differs in this case from the observed output price. Similarly, government regulations might affect the value of output or rate of return to capital, which requires altering the weight applied to the measure of changes in output or capital for productivity growth computations.

Conversely, taking these characteristics into account may often be accomplished by adjusting the measured quantities of output and inputs. To accommodate the existence of regulation, for example, it might be recognized that the amount of capital that is in use for purposes other than production (such as facilitating safety or protecting the environment) is different than that measured using standard assumptions and techniques. This interpretation implies that the quantity measure of capital rather than its value might be altered. Obsolescence might also cause the measured level of the capital stock (and thus of the growth rate of capital) to be incorrect; it implies that some of the "observed" capital stock should not be considered an effective input because obsolescence has rendered it virtually useless for production.

Formally, in most cases these and other extensions of productivity growth analysis involve considering what measures are relevant to use for the derivatives, elasticities and growth rates of output and inputs that appear in the cost-oriented productivity growth expression (2.12). This expression may be reproduced here (without the $\epsilon_{CY} = 1$ restriction) as:

$$\frac{\partial \ln C}{\partial t} = -\epsilon_{CY}\frac{dY/dt}{Y} + \sum_j \epsilon_{Cj}\frac{dv_j/dt}{v_j} = \epsilon_{Ct} \tag{9.1}$$

where $\epsilon_{CY} = \partial \ln C/\partial \ln Y$ (= 1 with constant returns to scale and instantaneous adjustment) and $\epsilon_{Cj} = \partial \ln C/\partial \ln p_j$ ($= p_j v_j/C = S_j$ when Shephard's lemma is valid, i.e., for inputs not subject to fixity or monopsony).

In previous chapters the possibilities were considered that $\epsilon_{CY} \neq 1$ from scale economies or $v_j \neq \partial C/\partial p_j$ due to subequilibrium, and corresponding adjustments were proposed. Similar adjustments based on invalid assumptions about market power, obsolescence and regulations will be developed in this chapter.

In particular, if the measure of capital services is endogenous (depending on factors such as the price of energy or the vintage structure) the adjustment of productivity growth takes the form of adapting the quantity measure (the time derivative with respect to K) to be measured at its "effective" value. This allows obsolescence to be taken into account as in Section 9.1. If imperfect competition exists, as noted above, the valuation of output should be at marginal cost rather than price (discussed in Section 9.2). If pollution abatement capital is legislated marginal cost must be adapted for the cost of such capital, or the capital stock actually used for production should be identified as the relevant capital input (as in Section 9.3). Similarly, fixity of capital implies that capital should be evaluated at its shadow value rather than rental price, as we have seen, or at its adapted shadow value if rate of return regulation prevails (Section 9.3).

Our production theory structural approach to modeling and measuring firm behavior and economic performance permits these types of extensions to be made. This is accomplished, as motivated in previous chapters, within an integrated model of firm decisions which captures true shadow or marginal values and dependencies of "effective" quantity levels on exogenous factors within the model. The resulting possible valuation and quantity adjustments are wide-ranging, and exemplify a major focus of current methodological developments for productivity measurement.

9.1 The Impact of Obsolescence on the Measurement of Capital Input

A number of researchers interested in the impact of energy prices on the measurement of capital services have suggested that incorrect representation of capital obselescence might have an important impact on productivity growth measures. For example, Baily [1981],

Berndt [1983], Berndt and Wood [1984] and Hulten, Robertson and Wykoff [1989] have focused on how increasing energy prices in the 1970s might have caused less energy efficient capital equipment to become obsolete, so that standard measures of capital services became increasingly overstated. Similarly, Morrison and Nelson [1989] examined not only the impacts of energy price changes on capital, but also those from vintage effects and embodied technical change, to obtain a quality-adjusted measure of the capital stock. Attempts to take such characteristics of capital into account can be thought of as special cases of the more general efforts of researchers to measure capital inputs appropriately.

Baily suggests that the capital obsolescence issue arises because of a lack of evidence on scrapping of old capital or on technological changes embodied in the capital stock, which should be incorporated in the capital measure. He argues that standard capital data may have understated growth of the effective capital stock in the 1950s and 1960s, and overstated growth from the late-1960s on, due to investment patterns after World War II and changes in the production structure in the 1970s and 1980s.

In particular, he believes that in the 1950s and 1960s substantial investment was for capital that "supplemented and modified the capital already in place", whereas technological advances of the late 1960s and 1970s, some of which might have been stimulated by high energy prices, made much of this capital obsolete. This therefore caused scrapping and low economic value of the remaining capital stock, which was not reflected in the standard measures. In this scenario, much of the observed investment during the 1970s and 1980s was required simply to replace this capital, as well as to respond to changing energy prices and satisfy environmental regulations, so net investment was significantly overstated.

Baily supports his argument that capital growth has been exaggerated largely on the basis of analysis of Tobin's q measures. Recall that, as outlined in Chapters 3 and 4, these measures are designed to reflect the market value of capital as compared to the replacement cost. Baily contends that q has been below unity since 1968 and has declined steadily since the late 1960s. Thus, if capital is evaluated at the implied shadow price, the total value of the capital stock is much lower than that reflected in standard measures. Although this is similar to the adjustments by q to deal with fixity discussed in Chapter 4, Baily interprets this in terms of obsolescence instead of fixity or utilization. The distinction between the two is not straightforward, particularly with an all-encompassing measure of firm value such as Tobin's q.

The obsolescence adjustment can be given a stronger theoretical basis by employing an hedonic function that either specifies the effective (shadow) price as a function of both the measured price and exogenous changes that will affect obsolescence, or identifies the effective quantity as a function of the measured quantity and these changes. These are dual notions, as was discussed in the context of factor augmentation (as it pertains to technical change) in Chapter 5. Since the shadow value of capital will likely vary for a number of reasons other than obsolescence, and since the concept of obsolescence seems more sensibly expressed in terms of a quality-adjustment to the quantity of capital, studies focusing on these issues tend to be formulated as an adjustment to the measured level rather than valuation of capital.

Once these quality-adjustments to obtain the effective service flow of the stock of capital have been carried out, modeling and measuring the resulting impacts on production processes may be accomplished using a synthesis of hedonic and production theory modeling approaches. One basis for this synthesis has been provided by the theoretical development of Lau [1982], which was further pursued by Berndt [1983] and Berndt and Wood [1984].[1]

This approach is based on incorporating a scalar index of quality in the production function for each quality-adjusted input. If, for example, capital is the only input for which the effective and measured units differ, the production function $Y = f(K, v)$ (where v is again a vector of J variable inputs), can instead become $Y = f(K, b_K, v) = f(K', v)$, where K' is the quality-adjusted or effective stock of capital and b_K is an index of capital quality. The production function therefore explicitly depends on b_K, which can be a function of what-

[1] A similar approach was used by Hulten, Robertson and Wykoff [1989] to adjust for obsolescence for a number of specific types of machines.

ever exogenous variables are thought to affect quality; $b_K = h_K(z_K)$ where z_K is the vector of these characteristics.[2]

This quality adjustment can take various forms. Berndt and Wood [1984], for example, explicitly incorporated the dependence of overall capital quality on fuel efficiency by recognizing the dependence of the desired fuel efficiency of new investment goods in each period on the expected price of energy perceived during that period, (p_{Et}). This results in a distributed lag specification of capital expressed in energy-efficiency or quality units which depends on the price of fuel prevailing in all previous periods when currently used capital equipment was initially purchased. The Berndt-Wood [1984] version of this function is expressed as

$$K_t' = K_t + \sum_{\tau=0}^{t-1} (p^*_{EK,t-\tau}/p^*_{EK,t})^{\sigma} K_{t,t-\tau}, \tag{9.2}$$

where p^*_{EK} is the value of the expected life cycle relative fuel-capital equipment services price function, $K_{t,t-\tau}$ is the amount of vintage $t-\tau$ investment surviving to time t, and σ is the substitution parameter of a CES sub-production function between fuel and capital equipment.

Since the production function depends on K', the dual restricted cost function will also depend on this effective capital service flow. Thus, to implement this model using a restricted cost function framework, the cost function $G(p, K)$ is adapted to $G(p, K') = G(p, b_K, K)$. This function can then be used as the basis for estimation and analysis, to establish the effects of quality-adjusting capital on indicators of firm behavior and productivity growth.[3]

The effect on productivity growth measurement of quality-adjusting the capital stock can be expressed quite simply in terms of accounting methods if no fixity, scale economies or markups are assumed to exist.

[2] This quality adjustment is more rigorously and completely developed in Berndt and Wood [1984].

[3] For estimation the hedonic function may be estimated in the system of equations, as in Morrison and Nelson [1989]. However, due to the complicated nature of the Berndt-Wood hedonic expression, different assumptions about the parameters were made and a grid search was made to find the highest likelihood, rather than using standard systems estimating procedures.

In this case K' must simply be substituted for K in the computation of costs, shares and changes in the capital stock. This results in an error bias term in the productivity growth computations which depends on the ratio of K' to $K, \beta_K = K'/K$, where β_K is called the quality-conversion ratio for capital.[4]

This occurs because if $K' = \beta_K K$, $d\ln K'/dt = d\ln K/dt + d\ln \beta_K/dt$. Thus, if the correct measure of productivity growth based on the effective capital stock is

$$\epsilon'_{Yt} = d\ln Y/dt - \sum_j S_j d\ln v_j/dt - S_K d\ln K'/dt,$$

and the standard measure is

$$\epsilon_{Yt} = d\ln Y/dt - \sum_j S_j d\ln v_j/dt - S_K d\ln K/dt,$$

the relationship between ϵ_{Yt} and ϵ'_{Yt} becomes $\epsilon'_{Yt} = \epsilon_{Yt} - S_K d\ln \beta_K/dt$, where the last term is the error bias. In terms of the energy price adjustment of Berndt and Wood, if obsolescence rates rose after energy prices increased in 1973, then the $d\ln \beta_K/dt$ term is negative and productivity growth will be understated using standard measures of capital services.

In the Berndt-Wood study quality-adjusting the capital stock in this way to take fuel-efficiency-induced obsolescence into account had a large impact on productivity growth indexes for U.S. manufacturing. This was increasingly true in the late 1970s as the effect of inflated energy prices in the earlier part of the decade became compounded. They found that for most years before 1971 the existing capital could be exploited more heavily than originally planned because relative energy prices were actually decreasing. Thus costs of utilizing the capital stock were less than expected. However, after 1971, and especially post-1973 and -1978, effective capital services taking obsolescence into account eventually became only about 80 % as large as those measured without the obsolescence adjustment. This implies

[4] β_K clearly is related to the index of capital quality b_K, although they only coincide if the production function can be written in the form $Y = f(K, b_K, v) = f(b_K K, v) = f(\beta_K K, v) = f(K', v)$.

growth rates of real capital input were generally overstated and the productivity downturn exaggerated over this time period.

In particular, Berndt and Wood show that using the standard multifactor productivity growth measure a slowdown of 0.39 percent was found, but for the adjusted measure this became 0.30 percent. The traditional measure therefore overstates the slowdown by approximately 25 percent, but the slowdown still remains after obsolescence is accounted for. A significant amount of "smoothing" of the productivity growth measure also occurs within the 1973-81 period. As Berndt and Wood [1987] state for the 1973-75, 1975-78, and 1978-81 periods: "the traditional measure first understates productivity growth by .52 percent (.16-.68 percent), then overstates growth during the recovery by .25 percent (1.18-.93 percent) and finally understates growth in the second OPEC price shock by .19 percent (.96-.77 percent)".[5]

Direct adjustment of economic performance indicators for obsolescence becomes more complicated, however, when it is recognized that the adapted value of $K(K')$ also figures importantly in estimation of the production structure by parametric methods. It thus is inherently connected with the representation of capacity utilization and scale economies. When capacity utilization and scale adjustments are incorporated in the estimated model, therefore, a complex pattern of dependence on factors determining obsolescence results.

This is even more evident when other characteristics of production affecting capital quality are taken into account. Morrison and Nelson [1989], for example, attempted also to include vintage and embodied technical change effects explicitly as determinants of effective capital services. A somewhat different methodology was used, however, than that developed by Berndt and Wood, since the Berndt-Wood model is difficult to implement empirically for even one quality-adjustment factor, and is infeasible analytically to implement with more factors.

Morrison and Nelson specified a more standard hedonic expression for K' where the dependence of the obsolescence level on fuel efficiency

[5]For more details about the model and results see Berndt and Wood [1984, 1987].

(measured by current values of p_E), vintage or embodied technical change (reflected in the purchase year or vintage of the capital stock, v), and the passage of time or disembodied technical change impacts (incorporating by a standard time counter, t), is represented by $K' = g(b_K, K) = g(b_K(p_E, t, v, K), K)$ at any time t.

Various assumptions about the functional form of this relationship can be made. Morrison-Nelson worked initially with a linear function but found the interactions between the different arguments of the K' function were important to incorporate. Therefore, a functional form along the lines of the Generalized Leontief was proposed and used. Although their study is still ongoing, preliminary results for 22 coal-fired generating plants in the electric utilities industry suggest that productivity growth declines in the 1970s were not as severe as those measured using standard methods, because obsolescence caused the productive capital stock to grow less slowly than implied by the traditional measures.

9.2 Markups and Their Contribution to the Analysis

In the implementable production theory framework developed in previous chapters perfect competition was generally assumed. Except for a few preliminary comments in Chapter 5, in these models either the assumption that output is given (no optimization behavior with respect to price), or the assumption that $p_Y = MC$ (where p_Y is output price and MC is marginal cost) was maintained. This only holds, of course, when firms have no market power in the output market. If imperfect competition exists and thus firms have some "monopoly" power, this effect may be measured as a markup representing the ratio of price over marginal cost, p_Y/MC. An important adaptation to the usual analysis of the production structure, and therefore the measurement of productivity growth, must be carried out when this ratio differs from one.

In particular, cost-side productivity growth measures remain valid when market power exists, because the perfect competition assumption is not invoked for construction of these measures. Cost rather than price data is contained in the dual. The duality of output- and cost-side productivity measures, however, no longer exists when imperfect competition prevails. This is because, as with scale and fixity, the primal-side measurement procedure incorporates an additional component in the productivity residual. In this case the productivity residual reflects returns to monopoly power as well as to technical change. This demand-determined element of the measure must be identified independently from the part attributable to technical change in order to decompose and interpret composite output-oriented productivity growth indexes.

This idea has recently provided the focal point of a number of studies of economic performance, although Robert Hall [1988a] is generally thought to have initiated interest in this area. The process for adapting productivity growth measures used by these researchers tends to be quite similar, primarily since the Solow residual expression (the expression defining ϵ_{Yt}) provides the basis for measuring the markup in a number of these studies. However, other methods for measuring the markup, which concentrate on the production theory structure, have also been proposed.[6]

Hall's approach to measuring marginal costs and therefore markups was discussed in detail in Chapter 5.[7] He used Solow's [1958] contribution toward measuring productivity growth in the context of technical change to highlight the importance of evaluating output growth appropriately at its marginal value. This is, of course, reflected if market power exists by marginal cost (MC) rather than output price (p_Y). Hall's implementation of the model was carried out for aggregate data, and was based on the assumption of a constant markup over time. His measurement procedures require some estimation, but can be accomplished using single equation methods.

---

[6]Note that there are also more ad-hoc ways to measure markups. As Fisher and McGowan [1983] have elaborated, accounting rates of return are often used (erroneously) as indicators of economic profit, although the theoretical basis for this is virtually nonexistent.

[7]See Section 5.1 for more details.

Little scope for analysis of the interactions between different components of the production structure exists, however, in this framework. In addition, interpretation of the measured numbers is limited because of the simplicity of the model. Both the markup and returns to scale measures generated by this framework are extremely large and implausible for some industries, and the reasons for this are not readily evident.[8]

Domowitz, Hubbard and Petersion [1987, 1988] used the same structure, but included other variables, permitted the markup to vary, and based their analysis on an industrial organization perspective that suggested markups would vary in response to variables like concentration ratios. This somewhat more complete framework allows consideration of the impact of adding materials inputs, and also demand determinants like unemployment to the analysis. Including variations in the markup also facilitates assessment of the cyclical nature of markups, which in their study was accomplished by comparing markup and capacity utilization fluctuations.

Morrison [1988c, d] used a production theory approach like the one we have been developing. This approach allows a more complete analysis of the patterns and determinants of the markup, since the estimated markup is explicitly dependent on arguments of both the cost and demand functions, so elasticities can be computed with respect to these exogenous supply (cost) and demand variables. Developing this type of production theory parametric model requires adapting the cost function framework to include a price determination equation based on the $MR = MC$ (where MR is marginal revenue) condition for the profit maximizing firm. Since this extension was already outlined in Section 5.3, here I provide only a brief outline of the model and its implications for productivity growth analysis.

As mentioned in Chapter 5, incorporating market power within the usual structure is accomplished by adding an inverse demand equation $p_Y = D^{-1}(Y, \rho)$ to the optimization process, where ρ is a vector of shift variables for the demand function. This results in the maxi-

[8]See Hall [1988a, b] for these measures.

mization problem

$$\mathrm{Max}_{v,\Delta x,Y} R(0) = \int_0^\infty e^{-rt} \left(p_{Y\,t} Y_t - \sum_j p_{jt} v_{jt} - \sum_k a_{kt} z_{kt} \right) dt, \tag{9.3}$$

subject to the constraints represented by the demand function $Y = D(p_Y, \rho)$, the restricted cost function $G = G(Y, \gamma) = \Sigma_j p_j v_j$ (where γ denotes all arguments of $G(\cdot)$ other than Y), the definition of gross investment $z_k = \Delta x_k + \delta_k x_k$, the vector of depreciation rates δ, and the asset purchase prices of x, a.

This optimization specification adds profit maximization to the firm's optimization problem. Shephard's lemma and the Euler equations represent optimal variable input demand and investment levels as before, but now these levels depend on the profit maximizing level of output. This output level is defined by maximizing the (instantaneous) variable profit obtainable at time t, subject to the variable cost function obtained in the first stage and conditional on the levels of x and Δx, resulting in

$$\begin{aligned} MR &= \frac{\partial p_Y(Y,\rho)}{\partial Y} Y + p_Y = MC, \qquad \text{so} \\ p_Y &= -\frac{\partial p_Y(Y,\rho)}{\partial Y} Y - \frac{\partial G(Y,\gamma)}{\partial Y}, \end{aligned} \tag{9.4}$$

where $MC = \partial C / \partial Y = \partial G / \partial Y$ (marginal cost) can be computed directly from the cost function $G(Y, \gamma)$, and $\partial p_Y / \partial Y$ from the inverse demand function $p_Y = D^{-1}(Y, \rho)$.

Expression (9.4) can be included in the system of estimating equations, and the resulting parameter estimates can be employed to compute the optimal price $p_Y(Y, \rho)$ and associated marginal cost $\partial G(Y, \gamma)/\partial Y$. These expressions are in turn used to construct the markup ratio $p_Y(Y, \rho)/MC(Y, \gamma)$. This measure provides the basis for adaptation of productivity indexes for the existence of market power. The index also depends in an explicit manner on the exogenous cost and demand determinants. This dependence permits measurement of the responsiveness of the markup, and therefore also its impact on productivity growth, to different factors affecting the inverse demand and cost functions.

This kind of model was specified and developed in Morrison [1988c] and applied to analyze the impact of market power on productivity growth measures by Morrison [1989b] for the U.S., Canadian and Japanese manufacturing sectors.[9] In the latter study the adjustment of standard productivity growth computations is handled similarly to those for utilization and scale in Chapter 4. The markup adjustment differs conceptually somewhat, however, because the market power adjustment can be thought of as a demand side adjustment, whereas those for scale and utilization are supply (cost) side adjustments.

To motivate the adaptation of productivity growth measures for market power, it is useful to note that the markup ratio p_Y/MC is analogous to the standard Lerner measure of market power, which is based on the inverse demand elasticity facing the firm.[10] In particular, it is easy to show that $p_Y/MC = 1/(1+\epsilon_{PY})$ where ϵ_{PY} measures the inverse demand elasticity facing the firm, $\epsilon_{PY} = \partial \ln p_Y(Y,\rho)/\partial \ln Y$.[11] The size of the markup is therefore completely determined by the demand elasticity; the level of marginal costs simply identifies the output level chosen for evaluation of the markup. The importance of this development is that the markup index, like the measures of capacity utilization and scale economies relied on before for adjustment of productivity growth measures, depends only on an elasticity. In this case the index relies on the inverse demand elasticity ϵ_{PY}, whereas the cost elasticity ϵ_{CY} was the basis for the other adjustments.

This can be used to formalize the difference between cost and revenue shares, and thus primal- and cost- side productivity growth measures, that results with market power because $p_Y Y \neq C$. Specifically, the relationship between revenue and costs in this case becomes $p_Y Y = C(p_Y/MC) = C/(1+\epsilon_{PY})$[12] As the measure of revenues

[9] A similar model was also constructed for estimation in Diewert and Morrison [1987], and discussed in Diewert and Morrison [1990].

[10] This relationship and many related issues are discussed in Bresnahan [1989].

[11] $MC = MR$ in short run equilibrium for the profit maximizing firm, where MR is marginal revenue, so the expression for p_Y/MC becomes $p_Y/(p_Y + Y \cdot \partial p_Y/\partial Y) = p_Y/[p_Y \cdot (1+\partial \ln p_Y/\partial \ln Y)] = 1/(1+\epsilon_{PY})$.

[12] Using reasoning analogous to that developed in Chapter 4, it can be shown easily that this adapts to $p_Y Y = C(p_Y/MC)CU_c\epsilon_{CY}^L = \epsilon_{CY}C/(1+\epsilon_{PY}) \neq MC \cdot Y \neq C^* \neq C$ if nonconstant returns and subequilibrium also exist.

$(p_Y Y)$ captures returns to all characteristics of the production process that cause $p_Y Y \neq C$, whereas C includes only *ex-ante* returns to inputs, primal productivity growth measures based on revenue shares include not only technical change (and scale and utilization effects) but also the impact of market power.

Since returns to this market characteristic are not interpretable as a valid part of productivity change, this impact should be isolated independently from the technical change measure on the primal side. This implies a correction to distinguish cost (production structure) from market structure impacts, similar to the error bias corrections for the utilization and scale adjustments outlined in Chapter 8.

The error bias correction has a somewhat different form here, however. The cost-side measure of productivity growth ϵ_{Ct} is not based on assuming the equality $p_Y Y = C$ is true; it depends only on cost elasticities so no error bias exists in the cost measure.[13] Instead the primal measure ϵ_{Yt} must be adapted, since strictly speaking the shares of inputs used to generate an aggregate input growth measure should be in terms of costs instead of revenue. This removes the impact of the return to market power commonly included in the denominator of the output shares, an effect which should not be attributed to increased efficiency.

More specifically, since imperfect competition implies $(1 + \epsilon_{PY}) \neq 1$ and thus $(1 + \epsilon_{PY}) = MC/p_Y = C/p_Y Y$, the share adjustment becomes $S_j = M_j(1 + \epsilon_{PY})$ where S_j is the revenue share $(p_j v_j / p_Y Y)$ and M_j is the cost share $(p_j v_j / C)$. Therefore, the primal measure ϵ_{Yt} can be written as $\epsilon_{Yt} = -\epsilon_{Ct} + \epsilon_{PY} \cdot \Sigma_j M_j(\dot{v}_j / v_j)$, which appropriately measures the input shares in terms of costs rather than revenue. This means that correcting the ϵ_{Yt} computation for markups requires computing

$$\epsilon_{Yt}^{M} = -\epsilon_{Ct} = \epsilon_{Yt} - \epsilon_{PY} \cdot \sum_j Mj(\dot{x}_j / x_j),$$

[13]This also implies that markups do not affect the cost elasticities determining capacity utilization and scale economies.

where

$$\epsilon_{PY} \cdot \sum_j M_j(\dot{x}_j/x_j)$$

may be considered the "error bias" in the usual primal measurement of productivity growth, and M stands for the "Markup correction". The bias thus depends on the cost shares, the inverse demand elasticity (or markup), and the growth rates of the inputs. This is, of course, analogous to the Hall [1988a] adjustment for market power, since his treatment simply evaluates the shares in terms of $MC \cdot Y$ instead of $p_Y Y$.

The result of the adjustment for markups found by Morrison [1989b] is a smoothing of productivity growth fluctuations and a counterbalancing of the productivity growth slowdown. The smoothing effect stems primarily from the time trend in the markup; the markup ratio has been increasing, so traditional measures increasingly underestimate productivity growth. However, interactions among markups, subequilibrium and scale economies provide very interesting additional implications. When the full series of corrections are made to accommodate low marginal (as compared to average) costs of production and capacity utilization fluctuations as well as markup behavior, the smoothing result is at least partially offset. This occurs because the cost characteristics imply minimal profitability, even with markup behavior, consistent with Hall [1989].

9.3 Some Views of the Impact of Regulation

For firms in certain industries regulation may be a very important determinant of costs, and therefore it may be important to include measures of the regulatory environment in models of the production process and productivity. In some industries the most consequential regulatory constraints may be those for safety of employees or for consumers of products. In others, requirements to constrain pollution by purchasing pollution abatement capital may significantly affect costs of producing a given output level. In certain cases, primarily those where a natural monopoly might be thought to exist, regulation may take the form of government control of output levels or even of the accepted rate of return.

These and other types of regulatory constraints suggest an increasing role of government in the economy, which has often been cited as a contributing factor to lower traditionally measured productivity growth. This can arise, for example, if regulations increasingly cause inputs to be purchased to produce something other than measured output. Presumably the result of this production would take the form of some perceived benefit gained from the regulation, such as safety.

Incorporating regulations into the analysis of firm production and productivity requires determining how they will change the assumptions on which the model is based. In some cases regulations may be defined directly in terms of a level of costs the firm must incur in order to satisfy the regulations. In such a case, nonparametric methods may sometimes be used to adapt productivity growth measures, since the costs attributed to production of unmeasured output may simply be identified and eliminated. In other situations specific constraints must directly be imposed on the optimization model to specify their impact on production processes. Thus, since adaptation of the cost function framework is implied, parametric estimates are generally necessary.

Government regulations on safety and environmental pollution provide one example where the impact of regulation is manifested in a particular level of costs that must be incurred for production to take place. In this instance the contention underlying adjustment of productivity measures is that expenses incurred to satisfy safety or environmental regulations, such as investment in pollution abatement capital, are unproductive in terms of measured output. Investments are foregone because resources that otherwise would be productive must be used to satisfy the regulations, and the goal of the regulations – pollution abatement or safety – has no marketable and therefore quantifiable effect in terms of productivity. Thus conventional productivity growth measures will be biased downward as the impact of such regulations increases.

This hypothesis has been explored by researchers such as Denison

[1979]. He attempted to determine the effects of environmental regulation by first estimating the incremental costs of production due to environmental regulations, and then using these estimates to impute the percentage reduction in output per unit of input attributable to regulation. Related nonparametric approaches to modeling the impacts of the costs of such regulations have been pursued by, among others, Gray [1984] and Conrad and Morrison [1989].[14] Gray [1984] considered the impacts of OSHA (The Occupational Safety and Health Administration in the U.S.) and the EPA (Environmental Protection Agency) in an accounting framework.

Gray's approach depends on whether compliance costs may be attributed to a particular input. For example, if only capital costs are affected, which might be thought to occur when pollution abatement capital is required, Gray states that capital input is generally measured as $K = K' + R$ where R is the amount of regulatory capital. Although measures of K are generally used for construction of productivity growth indexes, since the R component of K is not "productive" capital it should not be included; K' should be used rather than K.

If the fraction of K used for regulation is δ, so $\delta = R/K$, true productivity growth may be expressed (using our notation) as $\epsilon'_{Ct} = \epsilon_{Ct} - S_K\delta$, where S_K is the cost share of K and ϵ'_{Ct} is the (negative) cost-side productivity growth measure based on the productive capital stock measure K'. When compliance costs cannot be divided across inputs, but other measures of regulation applied to different industries such as enforcement effort (M) can be found, Gray incorporates this by computing $\epsilon'_{Ct} = \epsilon_{Ct} - M$.

These simple measures of δ and M, adapted to sum across different industries as outlined by Gray, can be used to adjust standard productivity growth measures as long as δ can be measured for any input affected by compliance. Applying this approach to a rich data set including a number of industries, Gray finds that introducing additional safety and environmental regulations does have a large depressing effect on productivity growth, at least in the short run.

---

[14] Also see Crandall [1981].

Conrad and Morrison [1989] also consider pollution abatement capitall regulations in a nonparametric framework, but the theoretical structure is developed more extensively, and the resulting implementation thus differs somewhat from Gray's treatment. The firm's production decision is assumed to be based on the maximization of profits, depending on investment in both productive capital (K) and pollution abatement (regulatory) capital (R). This optimization decision can be written as:

$$\max_{x,IK_t,IR_t,Y} \sum e^{-rt}\{p_{Yt}Y_t - G(Y_t,K_t,p_t) - PI(IK_t + IR_t)\}, \quad (9.5)$$

subject to $IK_t = K_{t+1} - K_t + \delta_t K_t$ and $IR_t = R_{t+1} - R_t + \delta_t R_t$, where IK_t and IR_t are gross investment in K and R, respectively, and PI is the common asset price of investment goods so $PI(IK_t + IR_t)$ is the expenditure on investment in both types of capital.

In addition, this maximization problem is constrained by two less standard conditions: $TE_t = \xi \cdot Y_t$, and $\overline{NE} - f_t(R) \cdot \underline{TE} \geq 0$, where TE is total emissions; NE is non-abated emissions; $\overline{NE}$ is the standard set for allowable emissions; ξ is an emission to output parameter representing the constant proportional relationship between pollutant discharge and production when no standards and therefore no pollution abatement capital exist; and $f(R)$ is the reduction of emissions, reflecting the dependence on the level of pollution abatement capital. The first of these conditions therefore represents the flow of pollution from the production process without regulation, and the second characterizes the resulting level of emissions.

The variable cost function is assumed to depend on K but not R, since R is not productive; R is not in the production function for output and thus not in the dual cost function. R is, however, included in total costs as a fixed cost, because if output changes, even if this causes greater fixed costs from greater required R, these costs are not in the form of greater variable input use but instead are "rental" costs. This is similar to the distinction between adjustment costs that are external rather than internal to the production process.

The first order conditions for this model are adapted only slightly from those for the general production-theory model we have been developing. Output is determined by the equality $p_Y - \tau f(R)\xi =$

$\partial G/\partial Y = MC$ (assuming perfect competition), where $\tau = \tau(1+r)^t$ is the current (undiscounted) shadow value of non-abated emissions. This reflects the fact that additional revenue with a change in output must cover both the increase in production costs and the extra required costs of abatement on the margin. Optimal K is determined as the capital stock satisfying the equality $-\partial G/\partial K = Z_K = p_K$, as before. The condition for optimal R is also represented by a shadow value-type equation, but in this case $p_R = p_K = -\tau f'(R)\xi x$ (where the rental price of all capital goods is assumed the same).

Some further manipulations of these optimization conditions and interpretation of the shadow value condition on R results in an adjusted productivity growth equation:

$$\epsilon'_{Ct} = \frac{\partial \ln C}{\partial t} = \left(-p_Y Y + q_K \frac{R}{C}\right)\frac{\dot{Y}}{Y} + \sum_j \frac{q_j v_j}{C}\frac{\dot{v}_j}{v_j} + \frac{q_K K}{C}\frac{\dot{K}}{K}. \quad (9.6)$$

The final adjustment of ϵ_{Ct}, even with this more complex theoretical framework, is thus very simple. It is based on purging the influence of pollution abatement capital from the output value measure to capture marginal costs correctly, and removing the R component from the total capital stock. An important insight stemming from this development, therefore, is that the value of output as well as the input value or quantity should be adapted. This adjustment can be written in terms of an error bias as

$$\epsilon'_{Ct} = \epsilon_{Ct} - q_K \frac{R}{C}\left(\frac{\dot{R}}{R} - \frac{\dot{Y}}{Y}\right) \quad (9.7)$$

where the second term reflects the error in traditional computations from assuming R is used to produce output instead of a cleaner environment.

Using this framework, Conrad and Morrison compute nonparametric measures of productivity growth and biases for U.S., Canadian and German manufacturing that suggest treating R incorrectly in productivity computations has biased productivity measures downward, particularly for the late 1970s, and for poor productivity growth years in general. Some evidence is also found that investment in pollution abatement capital depresses productivity growth for these countries on average, with the greatest (but still quite small) impact in the North American countries.

Although the more complete theoretical framework underlying the Conrad-Morrison regulation model provides a somewhat richer basis for interpretation of the adjustments and results than a simple accounting approach, a more detailed consideration of the impact of regulation requires an even more complex model. One way of accomplishing this is to consider the associated adaptation of our parametric production theory-based model. This may be dealt with, for example, as a variant of the general extension incorporated in Chapter 5 where the r_n variables were added as arguments of the cost function. As discussed there, these arguments can include various determinants of costs, including regulatory variables. An illustration of this is provided in Morrison [1987a, 1988b].[15]

In these studies the regulatory variable incorporated in the function once again is specified as pollution abatement or regulatory capital, R. In this case, however, R is included directly in the cost function as one of McFadden's "z-variables", where increases in R cause costs of producing a given output level to rise. This necessitates including R in the capacity utilization expression ($CU_c = 1 - \epsilon_{CK} - \epsilon_{CR}$) and in the productivity computations.

This directly implies an adaptation to productivity growth indexes similar to those we have been discussing. Due to the production theory structure, however, in this case a more in-depth analysis is possible; the focus of the analysis in these studies is on the bias of technical change that stems from regulation. In this context, a short run Hicksian regulatory bias was developed as:

$$B_{jn} = \frac{\partial S_j}{\partial \ln r_n} = \frac{p_j v_j}{C}\left(\frac{\partial v_j/\partial r_n}{v_j/r_n} - \frac{\partial C/\partial r_n}{C/r_n}\right) = S_j(\epsilon_{jn} - \epsilon_{Cn}), \quad (9.8)$$

where $\epsilon_{jn} = \partial \ln v_j/\partial \ln r_n$ and $r_n = R$, analogous to the scale and utilization biases outlined in Chapter 4. This bias reflects a regulatory distortion.

[15]This was also the focus of Norsworthy *et al* [1979].

If, for example, $B_{jn} < 0$, additional regulation (increased amount of required pollution abatement capital) will cause the firm to use input j proportionately less; regulation increases are relatively input j saving. The symmetry condition of biases, $B_{jn} = B_{nj}$, is also useful for analysis of the impact of regulation; the interpretation of $B_{nj} < 0$ is that an increase in p_j reduces the existing cost impact of regulation. In reverse, if regulatory changes are input j-using (say energy-using), increases in p_j (p_E) will cause regulatory measures to cost more, and therefore be more disruptive, than would be the case if they were input j-saving (energy-saving).

Assessment of these regulation biases therefore provides significant interpretive power concerning the impacts of regulation on the production process. For example, the bias measures presented in Morrison [1988b] show that regulation tends to be relatively labor and materials saving and energy using for the primary metals industry. Recall, however, that this does not imply an absolute decrease in labor and materials use, or increase in energy use, with additional regulation. In particular, consideration of the components of the bias measure for labor presented by Morrison implies that regulation causes increased employment, given output production ($\epsilon_{LR} > 0$). The small positive value of ϵ_{LR} is, however, swamped by a larger increase in overall costs with a regulatory change, primarily driven by increased energy requirements, resulting in a negative relative bias.

The impacts of regulation on technical change, capacity utilization, and valuation of capital are also possible to determine from the bias measures, if the bias is defined in terms of the cost elasticities with respect to these variables rather than with respect to p_j (as discussed in Chapter 4). The B_{tR} bias ($\partial \epsilon_{Ct} / \partial \ln R$), for example, represents the change in productivity growth when pollution abatement capital increases. The converse bias interpretation is that B_{Rt} reflects a change in the costs of regulation relative to other inputs due to technical progress. Similarly, B_{YR} reflects a change in capacity utilization due to changes in required pollution abatement capital. It is clear, therefore, that including regulation in a parametric production theory framework leaves significant scope for assessing the impacts of regulation on the production structure.

A final extension of this type of model to consider briefly is one which explicitly recognizes the impact of some types of regulation on the rate of return and output price. W.E. Diewert [1981b] has provided a useful framework for evaluation of the impact of rate of return legislation, and of regulations that impose average cost pricing.[16] This provides a context for assessing the impact of these regulations on the deviation of price (or marginal revenue) from marginal (or average) cost, and of the shadow value and market price of capital. This framework, based on the Averch-Johnson [1962] model of the regulated firm, has the potential to be adapted to allow consideration of a number of different possible types of pricing policies, such as Ramsey strategies on the shadow value of capital to the firm.

The main extension of this model is to impose on the problem of the profit-maximizing firm with some market power (outlined in Chapter 5 and the previous section) the requirement that profits cannot exceed a certain rate of return. This results in an additional constraint, along with production being technologically feasible (the production function) and output supply being consistent with demand (the output demand function), that the optimization process must satisfy.

Formally, the model in (9.6), subject to the demand function $D(p_Y, \rho)$, and the restricted cost function $G = G(Y, \gamma)$ (representing the production function) must now also be subject to the condition:

$$p_Y Y - \sum_j p_j v_j - \sum_k p_k x_k \leq e_k x_k, \tag{9.9}$$

where e_k are the K "excess profit" rates that the regulated firm is allowed to earn on its use of each of K stocks of capital, x_k. This is based on the assumption that rate of return regulation allows expensing of the kth type of capital services at a rental price $r_k + e_k \equiv s_k$, where s_k is the "fair rate of return" set by the regulators.

This condition adds a third type of first-order condition to the Shephard's lemma conditions $v_j = \partial G/\partial p_j$, and $p_Y + Y \cdot \partial p_Y/\partial Y = \partial G/\partial Y$, which motivate substitution for $\partial G/\partial p_j$ and $\partial G/\partial Y$ in the expression used for measurement of productivity growth. The third

[16] See also the other papers in this volume for additional contributions on the impact of regulation on economic performance.

condition becomes $p_k = -\partial G/\partial x_k + \beta_t e_k$ rather than $p_K = -\partial G/\partial x_k = Z_k$ as for the subequilibrium model we encountered earlier, where β_t is a function of the Lagrange multiplier from the optimization problem (which may be estimated for each period t). Only if capital is being used efficiently so $\beta_t = 0$ will the usual shadow value equation be valid.

This implies that for the parametric model an appropriately adapted shadow value expression must be appended to the system of estimating equations of the model. In addition, the adapted valuation of x_k must be substituted in the productivity growth measurement expression (9.1) (as in equation (4.3) of Chapter 4). This requires, of course, a measure of the allowed "excess profit rates" e_k set by the regulator.

This is a straightforward adaptation of the shadow value of fixed inputs to represent correctly the impact of these inputs on productivity growth. Since this extension is based on a structure consistent with the adaptations already accomplished, it has considerable appeal for application to productivity growth in industries where rate of return regulation is found. It implies further indirect adaptations, however, since adjustments to productivity growth to accommodate capacity utilization and scale will also be affected; they depend on the elasticity of costs with respect to the quasi-fixed inputs. In addition, although the markup will not change for any particular value of output since it depends directly on the elasticity of demand, the adaptation of the first order conditions for fixed inputs will affect marginal costs and thus the level of output at which the markup is evaluated.

* * * * *

This overview of extensions to the theory and measures of productivity growth is designed to be representative of a number of issues that have generated interest in this area. It is by no means a comprehensive list; numerous other issues might be important for different applications. Instead, the topics dealt with in this chapter encompass some of the more common problems encountered when modeling firm behavior. In addition, the methodologies outlined provide insights into how further adaptations might be accomplished. Thus, although the focus of these few extensions may appear rather narrow, the implications are much wider.

For exampe, issues of measurement errors due to quality changes in output may be conceptualized similarly to those about the correct measurement of the "effective" capital stock in the first section of this chapter. If monopsony is important to incorporate for a particular industry, an input expenditure curve for the relevant input could be appended to the model in a manner comparable to that for the output demand curve in the second section. Similarly, if research and development (R&D) is a significant component of costs for a firm, the treatment of pollution abatement capital as an additional capital input (outlined in the final section) could be used as a guide for including R&D. The topics dealt with in this chapter are therefore simply suggestive of the different extensions that are possible.

In the next, and final, chapter, we follow up this initial sketch of possible extensions by outlining some ongoing work extending these models further, selected related studies focusing on different aspects of the productivity puzzle, and specific problems of interpreting empirical results from production theory-based models.

Chapter 10

Pulling it Together

The measurement of economic performance is a wide ranging topic that can be approached from various angles and perspectives. In this text we have focused primarily on the measurement of productivity growth and its determinants. This has led us to consider in detail indicators of production structure and performance such as utilization and investment levels for inputs, profitability and scale economies, as well as technical change.

It has also provided motivation for the development of a production theory model allowing measurement of these characteristics. This type of model permits many characteristics of the production process to be identified. Thus, working within such a framework has permitted us to refine and extend our interpretation and understanding of productivity growth, both theoretically and in terms of empirical results. In this final chapter we tie together some loose ends left hanging as we explored this approach, and indicate some omissions.

Section 10.1 first summarizes very briefly the performance indicators which can be measured, and their interactions assessed, within our empirically implementable production theory model. The next section overviews some interpretation problems with econometric estimates arising from the typical necessity of using aggregate data. In Section 10.3 two recent extensions to the production theory model which are currently being pursued, and have important implications for modeling firm behavior and thus productivity growth, are presented. Section 10.4 then outlines a number of crucial contributions to the literature on productivity measurement that have been ignored or just touched on briefly in this text. These omissions are due only to limits on the scope of analysis possible in this study, and not to the importance of the material. Finally, some concluding remark are presented in Section 10.5.

10.1 A Summary of Economic Performance Indicators and Their Interactions

We have seen in this text that productivity growth and capacity utilization are closely linked, and that a number of factors can have important impacts on their measurement. Some of these factors are also used as independent indicators, for example profits, labor demand (employment and unemployment) and investment levels. However, our analysis has emphasized the interrelationships among all these aspects of economic performance.

The relationship that has provided the primary focus of this text has been that between productivity growth and capacity utilization. We have concentrated on determining to what extent capacity utilization adjustments are erroneously attributed to productivity growth fluctuations using standard measurement techniques. However, we have also explored how changes in other factors such as scale economies might also cause trends in cost patterns and thus also be embodied in productivity growth indexes. If they are, the interpretation and application of the indexes become problematic unless these interrelationships are isolated and assessed within an integrated structure.

In sum, due to their substantial interaction effects, we have seen that economic indicators cannot be evaluated independently. However, since we have been able to identify what their interactions should be in a model of firm behavior, we can also potentially measure the extent of their impact on one another.

Providing a sufficiently comprehensive theoretical structure for determining these interactions, however, requires a multi-dimensional analysis. The framework we have outlined in this text is capable of incorporating many facets of firm behavior that might have important effects on economic performance, including capacity utilization and investment in capital and other stocks. It also allows consideration of demand and supply responses to regulation, demand shifts, changes in potential scale economies, and obsolescence from fluctuations in exogenous factors. In addition, inventory holding and advertising or other selling decisions are possible to incorporate, as we will see below. Since this wide range of firm behavior can be analyzed explicitly in our framework, the specification of theoretically consistent indicators is possible for technical change, employment, investment and capacity utilization, profits and markups, scale economies, inventory/sales ratios and many other interrelated performance determinants.

This integrated structure also permits us to trace the direct and indirect impacts of a change in an exogenous variable such as the price of energy, and establish its effects on the different performance indicators. In addition, we can explicitly determine the impacts of changes in one indicator on the measured value of another – say, the impact of changes in capacity utilization on traditionally measured productivity growth rates. These patterns are reflected in a set of elasticities of the indicators (of technical change or capacity utilization for example) with respect to exogenous changes (which are expressed as biases) and elasticities of demand and supply.

Since this production-theory based model facilitates specification of the full pattern of demand and supply responses of firms, it provides a rich framework for analysis of most issues about the economic performance of firms and industries.

10.2 Interpretation Problems with the Parametric Measures

Although this structure provides important insights to facilitate analysis, some remaining problems should be kept in mind when using these models. One important and difficult problem to deal with, as discussed in Chapter 6, is data construction. If the data are not relevant for application to the model, it is tricky to interpret the findings.[1] A related issue identified in that context involves aggregation. Aggregation questions abound whenever doing empirical work, especially when implementing microeconomic models using data that are aggregated across firms. Data aggregation was discussed at some length in Chapter 6, but the aggregation issue is even broader. Serious interpretation difficulties arise when applying the essentially micro framework we have developed to aggregate data.

The theoretical issues that arise revolve to a large extent around whether production structure characteristics are internal or external to firms. Evaluating the shapes of individual firm cost and demand curves, which affect utilization, scale economies and markups for a firm, would seem to require data at the firm level. In fact, no aggregation theory exists that justifies aggregation across firms and assessment of overall markups and returns to scale unless perfect competition and constant returns to scale exist. Therefore, when using industry data it is tricky to interpret evidence of markups and returns to scale.

This is also true for other production characteristics that have different implications for the firm and the industry. For instance, advertising may be justified at the firm but not (or at least not as much) at the industry level because of redundancy. Another example is monopsonsy or external adjustment costs that suggest upward sloping expenditure curves for inputs to firms. These characteristics again manifest internal effects that should be distinguished independently from the overall industry impact.

These issues ultimately must be dealt with in detail using aggregation theory. However, some rationales do exist to facilitate and support interpretation of the results from these models as has been suggested in this text. These solutions and justifications have long been used by the numerous researchers who apply models of the firm to industry data.

One remedy, of course, would be to rely on disaggregated data.

[1]See Griliches [1989b] for a useful discussion of data issues.

There is a marked movement in this direction in the current literature on application of production theory models. Although many researchers are attempting to use more disaggregated data, however, little "clean" data at the firm level exists. This is due to a number of obstacles.

A major issue stems from problems of confidentiality. Most firm managers are not amenable to economists analyzing their data for research purposes, and government agencies are subject to stringent confidentiality laws that do not allow public access to individual firm data. In addition, difficulties arise because firm level data may not be carefully collected and documented, so errors often occur,[2] resulting in large deviations over time which cause severe complications for empirical implementation.[3] By contrast, these errors and volatility tend to "wash-out" in aggregate data because the data represents, in a sense, the average firm. This is the basis for the standard rationale of working with aggregate data; it can be thought of as measuring the responses of a "representative" firm.

Another way to deal with the aggregation issue is to regard evidence of the existence of, say, markups and scale economies, primarily as a confirmation that perfect competition and constant returns do not exist, while acknowledging difficulties interpretating the measured levels. This is valid because if these restrictions were defensible at the firm level, aggregation theory indicates they would also be acceptable at the more aggregated industry level (price would equal measured marginal cost and long run marginal and average cost would coincide).[4] In this sense the importance of these characteristics can be assessed even if direct interpretation of the evidence in the context of a firm demand or cost curve is difficult to justify. This provides a

[2]The data necessary for adapting standard accounting measures to their relevant economic counterparts may be particularly sparse and error-prone.

[3]These problems have arisen, for example, with the U.S. Bureau of the Census LRD and LED data sets which a number of researchers (including Lichtenberg and Siegel [1987, 1989a,b] and McGuckin and Andrews [1988]) have tried to work with since they are a rich source of disaggregated data.

[4]This is the one case in which aggregation theory provides a definitive conclusion about the relationship between disaggregated and aggregated data. Appelbaum [1979] has emphasized this for a model of imperfect competition. See that study for an elaboration of this justification.

rationale for incorporating demand and scale effects in the analysis simply to pick up whatever internal or external effects are embodied in the data.

Such a rationale is further supported by consideration of the empirical results generated by empirical implementation of production-theory models including these characteristics. Berndt and Khaled [1979], for example, carried out a number of tests of different scale assumptions using U.S. manufacturing data, and found that the more restrictive specifications could be soundly rejected. They alse found that allowing for scale economies increased the plausibility of other empirical results generated by the model. Similarly, Morrison [1988c] found that imposing perfect competition on a model caused empirical results to be more volatile and not as sensible compared to the more general imperfect competition model.

This reasoning is further supported by comparison of results based on alternative types of specifications. For example, Hall [1988a,b] and Morrison [1989a] both measured scale economies and markups using two-digit manufacturing industry data, and found them to be very significant. The production theory model used by Morrison, however, allowed less restrictions to be imposed. The estimated scale economies and markups for most industries were also quite reasonable, and much more plausible than those found by Hall, even using the aggregated data. This implies that the estimates of these characteristics do reflect important features of production processes, even given the difficulties of direct interpretation.

Another possible way to mitigate aggregation problems is to attempt a direct interpretation in terms of external as compared to internal impacts. For example, in the context of returns to scale, "thick market" external benefits (mentioned in a number of recent macroeconomic studies including Hall [1989]) could cause scale economies to be evident. Another possibility, proposed by Romer [1986], is that if knowledge has an increasing marginal product external economies will result, which can be considered a scale effect even in the absence of technical change. Explicit consideration of the theoretical basis of the internal and external effects can facilitate interpretation. Again, however, often the critical consideration is whether scale appears to affect costs, not necessarily how it manages to accomplish this.

It might also be feasible to develop industrial organization models that determine what types of imperfect competition would result in similar firm and industry results. For example, it could be useful to pursue whether an assumption of Cournot oligopoly would generate any useful predictions about the relationship between firm and industry demand curves. Shapiro's [1987] result about the relationship between industry and firm demand elasticities seems to be a move in this direction.[5]

Another important line of research in this area initiated and implemented by Stoker [1986] and Jorgenson and Stoker [1984] explicitly recognizes the effects of the heterogeneous distribution of micro units on estimates generated using aggregate data. Stoker develops the idea that if economic agents do not make their decisions on the basis only of total variables in the economy, aggregate behavior will depend on what individual variables are also important. For example, investment by a firm may depend not only on the levels of their capital stock but also on its vintage. In this case the distribution of old as compared to new capital stock will be an important determinant of aggregate investment behavior; the percentage of firms with old capital may be a necessary "distribution variable" to take into account in the analysis. This type of approach appears quite promising to date, although it has not yet been used by many applied researchers.

An ideal solution to the aggregation problem, perhaps based on developing an integrated model of the interactions between firm and industry cost and demand functions, and using pooled cross-section time-series data on a number of firms in an industry, does not yet exist. This may not be too serious a problem in practice, however, since current research in this area has generated plausible and useful results about production and productivity in a number of industries. Therefore, although it will be desirable in future work to attempt to deal with these aggregation issues, the rich structure available from production theory for empirical work has broad scope and promise for analysis of production processes and productivity growth.

[5] As long as there is information on how many firms are included in the data, so significant disaggregation is necessary even in this case.

10.3 Some Current Work on Extensions to the Production Theory Framework

Many aspects of firm behavior confer benefits as well as costs and thus become decision variables for the firm. Some of these can be thought of as selling costs. Depending on the industry, different selling costs may be important and should be included in analyses of the behavior of the firms in the industry. One important cost for many industries that might be thought of as a selling cost because it is incurred in order to facilitate processing of orders, is the cost of inventory holding. Another is advertising. In this section I provide an overview of some ongoing work incorporating these costs into the types of models used in this monograph.

Inventory holding facilitates sales by allowing firms to be flexible in response to changing economic conditions; inventories provide a "buffer" to production that can smooth the impact of cyclical economic conditions faced by firms. Yet inventories impose substantial expenditures on firms for storage and planning. Since these are not allowed for in typical measurement procedures, this might cause a bias in estimates of productivity growth. Due to the substantial magnitude of such expenditures, the bias could be large (96.7, 240.3 and 856.3 billion (current) dollars were held in inventories in 1950, 1970 and 1986 respectively in the U.S.) and could vary over time (the inventory-to-sales ratio decreased from 4.44 to 3.32 and then 2.83 for these years, a significant drop).[6]

Incorporating inventory holding involves constructing a dynamic model that recognizes the stock and flow aspects of inventory holding.[7] The short run models developed in this text therefore provide a useful basis for analysis, because if instantaneous adjustment could take place inventory holding would be unnecessary. If instead short run constraints on changing stock exist, like costs of adjustment, inventory holding provides an alternative route to deal with exogenous fluctuations such as demand changes.

---

[6] This information is available in the U.S. *Economic Report of the President.*

[7] This type of model is outlined further and references are provided in Morrison [1989d].

To adapt the standard models of production processes to take such inventory decisions into account, the potential benefits and costs of holding inventories must be identified.[8] Inventories impose holding costs on the firm. However, benefits are also provided because an increased demand for output may be accommodated using less inputs if adjustment of production is not immediately possible. This balancing of costs may be represented by introducing a holding cost function and specifying the benefits in terms of reduced short run costs.

Holding costs can be represented by a function $H(N)$, where N denotes the stock of inventories of finished goods and $\partial H/\partial N > 0$, $\partial^2 H/\partial N^2 > 0$. The benefits of inventory holding in terms of reduced input fluctuations can be captured by including inventory stocks in the restricted cost function as $G(x, \Delta x, p, t, Y, N)$ (where Δx, representing a vector of investment levels dx_k/dt, and N are considered components of the r vector introduced in Chapter 5). In addition, using the definition of inventory change $\Delta N = Y - S$, where S is sales, $G(\cdot)$ also becomes a function of $\Delta N; G(x, \Delta x, p, t, S - \Delta N, N) = G(x, \Delta x, p, t, S, \Delta N, N)$.

These is a similarity between the x_k variables and N. For example, a shadow value-type expression can be developed for N. Having inventories as a buffer allows less input use for a given amount of sales, so $\partial G/\partial N < 0$. The shadow value $-\partial G/\partial N = Z_N$ can therefore be envisaged as arising from a kind of "options value". Also analogously, Z_N in equilibrium should equal the marginal holding cost when inventory changes are not occurring; marginal costs and benefits are balanced.

Differences between the treatment of x_k and N also exist, however, because ΔN is a component of output rather than an input. The dependence of G on ΔN is equivalent to that for S since they are simply additive; $\partial G/\partial S = \partial G/\partial N = \partial G/\partial Y = MC$. An additional slight adaptation of the standard treatment is necessary if price setting is to be taken into account; the revenue function is respecified as $R = p_S(S, \rho) \cdot S$, where R is total revenue and $p_S(S)$ is the inverse demand curve for the sales of the firm.

[8]See Morrison [1989d] for further elaboration of this model.

The full profit maximization problem facing the inventory-holding firm, analogous to (5.4) in Chapter 5, is therefore,

$$\begin{aligned}\mathrm{Max}\overline{V}(0) &= \int_0^\infty e^{-rt}\Big[p_S(S,\rho)\cdot S - G(p,x,\Delta x,N,\Delta N,S,t) \\ &\quad - \sum_k p_k x_k - H(N)\Big]\,dt, \end{aligned} \tag{10.1}$$

where $V(0) = V(0) - q_K K(0)$. This maximization process is carried out in steps to determine optimal choices of variable input demands, sales, and inventory and capital levels and accumulation. This is accomplished as in the models already outlined, where optimal variable input demand is based on Shaphard's lemma, the profit maximizing level of sales is represented by $MR = p_S + [\partial p_S(\cdot)/\partial S]\cdot S = \partial G/\partial S = MC$, and the chosen paths of x_k and N are determined according to the Euler necessary conditions as in (5.5) of Chapter 5. The only major difference in the equations of the model, therefore, is the dependence of all equations on ΔN and the addition of an Euler equation for N.

The equilibrium condition for inventory accumulation implied by this Euler equation is only slightly different than for the x_k variables. In equilibrium where $\Delta N = 0$, the Euler expression for inventories becomes $-\partial G/\partial N = \partial H/\partial N + r\partial G/\partial\Delta N = \partial H/\partial N + rMC$, where $-\partial G/\partial N = Z_N$ as above, $\partial H/\partial N = H_N$ is the marginal holding cost, and rMC is the interest cost of producing the last unit (at marginal cost) for storage and holding it in inventory rather than selling it. Since this last cost disappears if $\partial G/\partial\Delta N$ is evaluated at $\Delta N = 0$, in a steady state $-\partial G/\partial N = \partial H/\partial N$; marginal benefits and marginal costs of holding inventories are equated.

Adapting the model to include inventories has a number of possible implications for the measurement of elasticities. In general, all elasticities are likely to be affected since they depend on the "new" arguments of the cost function. For example, Blinder [1982] has suggested that higher levels of inventories cause firms to produce less, charge a lower price, expect to sell more, and reduce their planned inventory investment. Constructing the elasticities of Y, p_S, S and ΔN with respect to N identifies these responses explicitly.

Including inventory behavior also has implications for economic performance indicators, although they are not as decisive as some other adjustments we have encountered. For the output side of standard accounting productivity growth measures, inventories are implicitly already taken into account by adjusting sales to reflect production only; $Y = S - \Delta N$ for the productivity computations. However, inventories are often treated erroneously on the input side, depending on how they are valued and where they appear; this framework allows an explicit specification of the role of N and its marginal valuation. In addition, with an econometric framework used for adjustment of productivity indexes, inventory behavior will affect measures of capacity utilization, scale economies and markups and therefore the decomposition of overall productivity growth measures.

In terms of including inventories as inputs, thought must be given to where inventories appear in the data. It would seem that once inventory changes were purged from the sales data to obtain production, inventories should not be included as an input for productivity computations. In essense the costs of inventory holding therefore reflect a "nonproductive" output similar to pollution abatement capital; inventory holding costs result from fluctuating demand rather than the production technology. Therefore, for accounting measures of productivity growth the impact of inventories should, like "R" in Chapter 9, be removed from both the output and input measures. This again can be accomplished directly by making sure measured input as well as output levels do not include N (as in the treatment by Gray), or by using the marginal valuation of inventories to adjust the marginal value of output and to weight inventory changes (as in Conrad and Morrison). Like R, however, it is often the case that inventories are included as part of the capital stock.[9] This is, of course, necessarily also the case when capital is measured as a residual.

In spite of the fact that including inventories in a justifiable manner might affect productivity growth measures and their decomposition,

[9]This is true, for example, of the capital data produced by the Bureau of Labor Statistics.

no empirical evidence about this is yet available. Some insight about the impact can, however, be obtained. Although inventory levels are often high, inventory changes tend to be quite small, so this extension is unlikely directly to affect productivity growth measures significantly. Indirect impacts might, however, be more substantial. These would arise, for example, due to the effect of inventory holding on capacity utilization; demand for inputs such as capital, and thus investment, might be affected if it becomes more cost-effective to reduce inventory holdings. In addition, technical change could change the nature of the inventory process by, for example, stimulating practices such as the "just-in-time" inventory methods begining to be adopted by many companies, due to computerization and imitation of Japanese business practices. The resulting adapted relationships among technical change, inventory holdings and use of other inputs will be reflected in measured productivity growth.

Another type of selling cost that has been ignored in the literature is advertising. The magnitude of expenditures on advertising in the U.S. again, however, suggest that advertising has very important costs and benefits that should be taken into account in the analysis of firm behavior.

In particular, the benefits from advertising stem from affecting demand and thereby increasing or at least maintaining market shares in a rivalrous industry. Firms must perceive these benefits to be substantial, because advertising is also very costly; advertising expenditures in 1940, 1970 and 1987 were 2.11, 19.55 and 109.86 billion dollars in the U.S. (in current values), respectively – equivalent to 40 % of U.S. national defense outlays in 1987.[10] These expenditures have not only significantly increased over time, but they have increased relative to overall spending in the economy (advertising as a percentage of gross national product (GNP) grew from 1.93 % to 2.45 % from 1970 to 1987, a 25 % increase). The bias in measures of productivity growth ignoring this component of costs could therefore be large and might be increasing over time.

Advertising costs have not yet been incorporated in any production

[10]See Berndt [1990] Ch. 8, and the U.S. Economic Report of the President for these values.

theory-based study that I am aware of, although preliminary work on analysis of their impact on productivity is in progress, as in Morrison [1989e].[11] One potential way to include advertising in the production theory structure is to incorporate the dependence of both the demand and cost functions on advertising by including it as an argument. This captures the benefits from market expansion, and the large impact on costs that stem from advertising.

This suggests a profit maximization problem of the form:

$$\mathrm{Max}_{v,\Delta x,Y,A} R(0) = \int_0^\infty e^{-rt} \left(p_Y(Y, A, \rho) \cdot Y - G(Y, A, \gamma) - \sum_k a_k z_k \right) dt, \quad (10.2)$$

where A is Advertising, and the remaining notation is analogous to that in the standard monopoly model from Section 9.2.[12]

One might think productivity growth would be affected heavily by advertising because of the magnitude of advertising expenditures. Although output increases caused by advertising are by default included in the measure of output changes for productivity growth measurement, the costs are ignored when only "standard" inputs are measured. Therefore, increases in output due to increased advertising expenditures are attributed incorrectly to augmented efficiency. Since advertising expenses have increased over time, this might imply that changes that have been perceived as technical advances are actually due to these selling costs; in this case the productivity slowdown might be worse than usually measured. The importance of this remains to be evaluated.

[11]Note that advertising may be included in material or purchased services inputs, although the demand-changing characteristics of this type of input are ignored when it is dealt with in this fashion.

[12]This simple formulation is based on the assumption that advertising has only a current effect, which is supported by some marketing literature indicating that advertising's effect likely lasts no more than one year. However, one might think that some stock measure of advertising (analogously to capital, which was cumulated over time based on an assumed depreciation rate) might be more valid. In this case A should be treated more explicitly like other stocks, such as capital, in the optimization process.

A number of problems exist, however, in terms of implementing the advertising model to assess this impact. One possible difficulty is identifying the differential impacts of output changes (movements along the demand and cost curves) and advertising (shifts in the curves), since advertising affects both functions. In addition, data is an issue, both for theoretical and practical reasons.

An important theoretical problem is that the analysis of monopolistic competition (which Hall suggests is consistent with the data) implies that advertising effects, even if important at an individual firm level to maintain market share, may be "washed out" at the industry level because of redundant expenditures. If any one firm does not advertise it loses, but as a whole advertising may not affect the industry unless it actually changes demand for the product. At a practical level, this suggests that analysis of different firms in any given industry should be undertaken to untangle these different impacts. However, advertising expenditure data at any defensible level of disaggregation is not readily available. Therefore, although incorporating advertising may be useful for productivity growth analysis, the development and implementation of such models is still preliminary.

10.4 Other Important Contributions to the Literature on Economic Performance

Most of the topics considered in this text are related directly to my work in the area of productivity growth and capacity utilization measurement. Our overview of these issues has included reference to other production and performance indicators such as measures of scale economies, investment, profits and inventory/sales ratios. There are many contributions to research on economic performance, however, that have been either partially or totally neglected in this text. Some of these address the same issues in different ways, and some consider the impact of economic behavior that we have ignored. This section elaborates selected contributions in this literature, with emphasis on the microeconomic perspective.

In particular, the literature on productivity measurement includes important contributions dealing with:

(i) output and capital measurement issues;

(ii) the effect of R&D, patents and innovations;

(iii) the increasing importance of the service sectors, and poor productivity performance of the non-manufacturing sectors;

(iv) the impact of the tax system and the changing role of government on economic growth;

(v) labor and/or management failures; and

(vi) changes in infrastructure or public capital available to firms.

Pursuing ways to deal with measurement problems has perhaps the greatest potential for providing insights into the productivity productivity growth puzzle. A number of measurement issues emergy when considering productivity growth indexes. The fundamental problem is that when measuring output, the value of output must be divided into its price and quantity components. If quality is altered and/or new products are introduced, relative prices vary or any other changes occur which are difficult to quantify, these may show up as a mismeasurement of the price of a unit of output and therefore also of the quantity. An overstatement of price growth, for example, due to quality increases, will manifest itself as an understatement of output increases, and therefore of productivity growth.[13]

Anomalies in the data suggest the possible importance of this type of mismeasurement. Baily and Chakrabarti [1988] point out that measured productivity in the construction industry collapsed in 1968, stimulating at least some of the perceived slowdown in aggregate productivity growth. However, it is hard to believe that construction workers suddenly metamorphasized into less efficient beings. Although there could be some truth to this, it is more likely that the observed change is at least in part a measurement issue. Since

[13]The impacts of falling relative prices are elaborated in more detail in Baily and Chakrabarti [1988, p.26]. A detailed analysis of different industrial sectors and their measurement issues is available in Baily and Gordon [1988].

each construction project is unique and thus measurement of a valid price for construction projects is very difficult, output may well be mismeasured.[14] Griliches [1988] pursues this further to identify problems with the plausibility of not only the construction, but also the mining and various service sector data, which imply that one must "doubt some of the other numbers that are not obviously strange at first glance".

Another more direct and dramatic example cited by a number of researchers including Triplett [1989][15] is the index used for the price of output in the computer industry. Even with the formidable increase in quality that has occurred in this industry in the past two decades, until very recently the producer price index constructed by the Bureau of Labor statistics has not included a price index for computers; this is equivalent to assuming the deflator index was equal to one over this entire period.[16] This implies, of course, that growth in the quantity of computers produced, measured in any plausible manner in terms of computer power, is enormously underestimated. The Triplett survey of hedonic studies of computer prices finds startling confirmation of this; he finds that "by 1984, computer processor prices had fallen to *one-tenth of one percent* of their introductory level in 1963...".

Finally and more generally, Lichtenberg and Grilliches [1989] have considered other issues related to the measurement of the producer price index and determined that less than half of true quality change is adjusted for in the published index.

Although the premise of output measurement errors might have some potential as an explanation of productivity growth patterns, it cannot legitimately be offered as a reason for a large slowdown in growth rates unless the mismeasurement of quality or other changes became worse in the late 1970s. Rees [1980] in fact argues that in the U.S. the Bureau of Labor Statistics has been doing increasingly better in

---

[14] For further details of this and a slightly different viewpoint, see Pieper [1989].

[15] See also Baily and Gordon [1988], Dulberger [1989] and Gordon [1989].

[16] Since 1986, however, the Bureau of Economic Analysis has published a computer price index. See Berndt [1990] Chapter 4 for more information on this issue.

its measurement procedures for quality adjustment. It is even less likely that all industrial countries at once became worse at measurement, although the slowdown appears pervasive. Therefore, although refinements in measurement practices are likely to have an impact on productivity growth measures, one might expect the magnitude of the effect to be small, as has been found by researchers such as Baily [1982].

Other researchers such as Dean, Darrough and Neef [1985] cite problems resulting from the mismeasurement of capital. Their study of the U.S. and Japan considers statistical procedures and definitions of capital carefully in terms of comparisons between the countries. The points made in this study parallel much of the treatment of capital in this text. For example, a number of these issues were addressed in Chapter 6 in the context of capital measurement procedures, and many of the points about adjusting, say, for quality and aggregation, are similar to those mentioned in Chapter 9 for refinement of capital measures. It is worth noting, however, that these measurement issues, as well as those for output, have been receiving substantial attention in the recent literature on measurement errors.

Most of the measurement problems cited here are specific cases of the general problem of constructing valid index numbers. Caves, Christensen and Diewert [1982] and Diewert [1989a,b], for example, discuss these and other problems of index number construction in a general theoretical index number framework. In addition to the problems noted here, Diewert considers different assumptions about functional forms underlying index numbers construction that can generate biases in the resulting numbers.

In a somewhat different context, Diewert and Morrison [1986] and Morrison and Diewert [1989] provide another type of refinement of index numbers and output measurement, which focuses on more careful consideration of the treatment of imports and exports.[17] Traded goods are generally absorbed into the output vector, where net output is taken to be domestic plus exported output less imports. However, these diverse components could have very different characteristics,

[17] Also see Cas, Diewert and Ostensoe [1986].

and also dissimilar degrees of imperfection, in their markets. Therefore, it would seem reasonable to disaggregate this vector to take the components separately into account. In addition, changes in the terms of trade can be thought of as a determinant of "welfare", in addition to technical change. An improvement in the terms of trade indicates that more output is available (consumption or production goods) for a given amount domestic expenditure (quantity of scarce inputs), and therefore welfare has increased. Including the "terms of trade effect", therefore, augments productivity growth or technical change indexes to generate a more overall "welfare" indicator of economic performance.

The second important strand of thought in the productivity growth literature mentioned above involves the impact of research and development (R&D) on productivity growth. This can be more generally phrased in the context of "the possible exhaustion of the wellsprings of technological progress" (Griliches [1988]). As shown by Griliches,[18] similarly to energy price increases and imposition of environmental and safety regulation, the onset of a decline in R&D coincides quite well with the beginning of the productivity slowdown. To take this into account, R&D is generally considered an input into the production process as an alternative form of capital.

Some problems arise in implementing this framework due to data difficulties specifying R&D expenses in a relevant manner. The valuation of R&D, for example, is usually dealt with by assuming the Gross Domestic Product deflator is appropriate to use, although it too includes many diverse components. It is also difficult to impute current benefits to earlier R&D, or to determine a valid level of depreciation; it is generally assumed that R&D does not depreciate, although it could well experience obsolescence.

These difficulties may not be serious, however, since R&D appears to have a small impact. In particular, it turns out that the elasticity of

[18]This is also documented and analyzed in a number of other papers, including Griliches and Lichtenberg [1984] (and others in the same volume), Griliches [1980, 1986a, 1988, 1989], Nadiri and Bitros [1980], Schankerman and Nadiri [1986], Bernstein and Nadiri [1988a], Scherer [1984] and Lichtenberg and Siegel [1989a]. For an international perspective, see Piekarz, Thomas and Jennings [1984].

output with respect to R&D and the return to R&D are not large, at least in the aggregate. Therefore, although R&D appears to have a statistically significant role in productivity growth, using R&D as an "explanation" of the productivity slowdown seems dubious.

Extensions to the basic framework including R&D provide little additional insight into the role of R&D. For example, even when indirect effects ("spillovers") are taken into account,[19] it appears R&D has a small effect on productivity growth. In addition, as Griliches [1988] notes, the R&D slowdown was less pronounced in countries other than the U.S., even though productivity growth declined significantly in these countries; and most of the decline was from government-supported research, which appears to have an even smaller role in determining productivity than privately financed R&D. Other hypotheses, such as a change in the linkage between R&D and productivity growth or a decline in "inventiveness" or R&D opportunities also do not appear to carry much weight.[20] A final suggestion, that similarly to capital plant and equipment the energy price increases of the 1970s stimulated obsolescence of the stock of R&D "capital" or knowledge, has been offered by some researchers. Griliches [1988] argues, however, that although this is conceivable, the magnitude of the effect is unlikely to have been large.

The association between R&D and productivity growth therefore appears quite weak, even though conceptually it would appear to be important. Future research refining measurement techniques for R&D and more completely determining the effect of spillovers, however, may provide more support for the notion that R&D is an important contributing factor to productivity fluctuations.

Thirdly, some productivity growth researchers have focused on the shift toward service industries. This could "explain" the slowdown in three ways; productivity growth in these industries could be lower

---

[19]See, for example, Jaffe [1986].

[20]This is mentioned in Griliches [1988]. However, based on analysis of a number of individual industries, Baily and Chakrabarti [1988] conclude that "... explanations of the slowdown leave a large puzzle that strongly suggests productivity growth was pulled down by slow innovation". This suggests that one of the main causes may be R&D-related issues, if they are analyzed correctly and completely.

Table 10.1: Average Annual Multifactor Productivity Growth Rates in the U.S. (by sectors and periods)

	1949-66	1967-73	1974-85
Total Private Industry	1.3	0.4	0.1
Agriculture, Forestry & Fisheries	-1.8	0.1	1.4
Mining	0.5	1.9	-4.3
Construction	1.7	-5.1	-1.1
Manufacturing	2.0	1.8	1.4
Transportation	1.0	1.6	0.1
Communication	2.7	3.0	2.3
Utilities	3.7	2.4	1.2
Wholesale Trade	0.8	0.8	-0.5
Retail Trade	0.6	0.0	-0.4
Finance, Insurance, etc.	-0.3	-0.9	-0.6
Services	-0.6	-0.2	0.1

Source: Shapiro [1987]

because they tend to rely less on processes which could be augmented by technology,[21] there may be a shift to have a larger share of GNP provided by the service sector (often proposed as a "composition of output" argument), and output for these industries could be mismeasured, which would bias estimates.[22]

Documentation of the importance of shifts to service industries from other sectors is available from Shapiro [1987], who presents a table on relative productivity growth declines for different sectors of the economy, reproduced here as Table 10.1.

This table highlights the lower overall productivity growth of the ser-

[21]This is consistent with the Baumol and Wolff [1979] thesis that differences in the potential of growth in an industry rather than differences in the levels of productivity are the crux of the issue, and the potential for automation in the service sector as a whole is limited.

[22]This is a special case of the measurement issues discussed separately above, although discussions of the two problems are often combined.

vice sectors; as the composition of output moves toward the industries listed at the bottom of Table 10.1 it seems evident that this will have a depressing effect on aggregate productivity growth. This conclusion assumes, however, as noted by Baily and Chakrabarti, that moving a worker between sectors will in some important sense change his/her marginal product, which seems to have little validity even if markets are not full efficient, implying measurement errors. In addition, using this argument implies that the magnitude of the shift to services has been dramatic enough to have a recognizable effect, although the changes in fact have not been very large.[23] Finally, not all service industries have had a history of low and decreasing productivity; as can be seen from Table 10.1, for example, communication services have fared quite admirably.

Although research in this area is still being pursued,[24] therefore, it has not generated very much support as an "explanation" for the slowdown due to the limited effect of corrections. The most promising line of research on service sector impacts appears to be addressing problems in the measurement of service sector output, as outlined in a more general fashion in the context of measurement issues above.[25]

The impact of tax and other government policy on economic growth is the fourth important focus of productivity growth analysis. As Boskin [1988] points out, since output growth appears to arise primarily from technical change and investment the effects of tax policy on both of these factors should be considered to analyze how tax policy might have affected productivity. Policies that will stimulate economic growth, therefore, are those enhancing technological change, labor force quality and growth in the capital-labor ratio. These often take the form of policies affecting the costs of spending on capital and R&D compared to other spending, such as investment tax credits

---

[23]See Baily and Chakrabarti for further discussion.

[24]Important references include Kendrick [1985] and Baily and Chakrabarti [1988].

[25]For further discussion of measurement issues focusing on the service sector, see Kendrick [1985] and Englander [1989]. Additional work is currently being carried out by Elizabeth Kremp and Jacques Mairesse at the National Bureau of Economic Research using French data. See, for example, Kremp and Mairesse [1990].

(particularly for high productivity industries) and financial support for research (which implies an overlap with the R&D literature mentioned above).

Boskin argues on this basis that two major recent U.S. tax reforms (in 1981 and 1986) could have helped stimulate the surge in productivity growth seen in the 1980s compared to the 1970s. These initiatives counteracted policy in the 1970s that raised real effective tax rates on capital income, contributing to low investment and therefore economic growth. Although he maintains that this may have had a recognizable effect on productivity growth rates in the 1970s, this effect is difficult to quantify, and thus is uncertain. In addition, other mechanisms for tax policy to affect growth, such as those which affect the rate of human investment, R&D, resource allocation and saving, may be important. These again, however, are often difficult to identify and quantify, and the effect seems likely to be small. Although these results do not provide strong evidence linking tax policy with productivity growth, they are suggestive and provide some potential direction for future work in this area.[26]

Potential labor and management failures were alluded to as a fifth reason for productivity growth declines. Potential failures include a possible decrease in the skill and experience or simply motivation of the workforce, and the proliferation of financial manipulation at the expense of productive investment, development of technology and true output production. These are considered as two separate hypotheses in Baily and Chakrabarti [1988], who assess a number of studies on these topics and conclude that neither of the hypotheses is completely born out by the data.[27]

Further, Denison [1985], considers the effects of education on worker's income and the distribution of educational attainment and constructs a measure of human capital in the workforce. These numbers, far from confirming the hypothesis of a decline in worker's skills, show a

---

[26]See also Diewert [1981a] for a theoretical treatment of tax issues, Tolley and Shear [1984] for an international comparison of tax rates and their effects on growth, and Hall [1981] for consideration of tax treatment of capital and its effect on the measurement of capital income.

[27]See this study for more details about the assertions presented below.

slight post-1973 acceleration in the contribution of education. Even adjusted for a possible decline in educational quality, as measured by SAT scores or worker effort, the conclusion of little if any impact is maintained.

Taking demographic changes into account, by contrast, does have some effect. However, this does not contribute much to an explanation of the pattern in the 1970s, or convey why the shift in the demographic pattern in the 19880s has not been reflected in the productivity growth indexes. In addition, due to measurement procedures, this effect largely arises from an increase in lower paying jobs, most of which are likely service industry jobs. Therefore, care must be taken not to double-count this effect or mistakenly attribute it to demographics, when it is in large part a compositional shift.

The proposition that management problems have caused productivity declines was presented by Hayes and Abernathy [1980]. Their arguments are motivated by the belief that managers in the U.S. have begun to focus on short run profits at the expense of long run development. To at least some extent this can be attributed to management practices that emphasize financial manipulation, such as takeovers, to achieve quick results. Baily and Chakrabarti, however, note that "the idea of managers in New York, London, Bonn and Paris simultaneously and abruptly becoming incompetent after 1973 seems pretty farfetched". Overall, there are limited possibilities to quantify this effect, little concrete evidence in support of this hypothesis and a negligible amount of current research being done on this hypothesis.

A related focus of researchers, however, on the effect of mergers on productivity growth seems to have somewhat greater promise. The overall issue is whether changes over time in management behavior with respect to mergers has affected productivity growth. Although results presented as yet appear somewhat trivial and intuitive (e.g., firms with low productivity and thus value relative to the overall industry are likely to be bought out and improve performance), Lichtenberg and Siegel [1987, 1989a,b], Dunne, Roberts and Samuelson [1987], McGuckin and Andrews [1988] and others have found some interesting patterns of mergers and technical change. Much of this work has been carried out at the Bureau of the Census Center for Economic Studies using the LED-LRD database referred to earlier.

Finally, in terms of infrastructure services, Diewert [1986] provided a theoretical basis for studies of the benefits of infrastructure services to firms. Empirical work linking these services to productivity growth include Aschauer [1988] and Ram [1986]. Although little literature exists on this topic as yet, the results by these authors appear to point to an important direction for future studies on causes of the productivity decline.

10.5 Final Remarks

Many important lines of research are currently being pursued in an attempt to identify the determinants of productivity growth fluctuations. Most of these involve developing more applicable and interpretable measures of economic performance. Since these types of measures are often used as a basis for evaluation of a firm, industry or economy, this research has very important implications. As we have been emphasizing since Chapter 1, however, many of these measures are somewhat ambiguous or at least the diverse components embodied in the generated indexes are not well understood. To avoid using measures that are by nature uninterpretable or erroneous, it is important to work through what they really reflect. Only if we can effectively determine how performance and welfare are changing, and what causes these changes, can appropriate policies to accomplish goals be formulated.

In this text we have found that simple measures of economic performance include so much disparate information that it is difficulmt if not impossible to use them as the basis for appropriate policy responses. As we have seen, productivity growth indicated by such a measure could arise due to increasing use of scarce and therefore expensive resources which are not counted in the measure. This effect is not an increase in welfare in general, and must therefore be separately identified for useful policy decisions to be formulated. In addition, other technical and market characteristics such as changes in capacity utilization, scale economies and markups may have impacts on productivity growth which should be isolated to allow interpretation of the measures in terms of technical change, efficiency and welfare.

Although the need to untangle this combination of productivity determinants is great, this is difficult to accomplish because the number of pieces to the productivity growth puzzle is very large. We have considered a number of the different factors that might be important for modeling production processes, and interpreting the resulting information on economic performance. These include not only those factors directly embodied in productivity growth and capacity utilization indexes, but also those reflecting other aspects of the production structure, such as investment and profitability; the latter are often measured independently in the form of economic performance indicators. However, the impacts of most of these characteristics are also implicitly incorporated in standard measures of productivity growth. Thus, for valid interpretation of productivity growth indexes, measures of these diverse impacts must be used to separately identify them from true productivity growth or technical change.

Our analysis of productivity growth indexes has pursued this in an attempt to facilitate interpretation of productivity growth measures and to heighten our understanding of productivity growth fluctuations. This theoretical and empirical analysis has been based primarily on considering methodological advances (to relax assumptions inherent in traditional measures), and data issues (to construct more appropriate measures of the quantities and values of outputs and inputs) for productivity growth measurement. The development and implementation of the resulting framework has in turn been based on an exploration of how production theory-oriented structural models may be used to motivate such analyses, and to provide a foundation for the measurement and interpretation of economic performance.

Much work remains to be done in the area of economic performance and productivity growth analysis. There are serious problems conceptually and in terms of implementation that have yet to be dealt with effectively. Also, no studies have yet provided a very complete "explanation" of the productivity growth patterns experienced by industrial countries in the past two decades. One quite clear indication from the current body of literature, however, is that econometric modeling is necessary to untangle the different factors affecting production processes and economic performance in a consistent manner. The conceptual, theoretical and empirical framework developed in this text provides a basis to move in this direction, and to facilitate greater understanding of these issues.

References

- Appelbaum, Eli [1979], "Testing Price Taking Behavior", *Journal of Econometrics*, Vol.9, No.3, February, pp.283-294.
- Aschauer, David A. [1988], "Government Spending and the 'Falling Rate of Profit'", *Economic Perspectives*, Vol.12, pp.11-17.
- Auerbach, Alan J. [1983], "Taxation, Corporate Financial Policy and the Cost of Capital", *Journal of Economic Literature*, Vol.21, No.3, September, pp.905-940.
- Averch, H., and L. Johnson [1962], "Behavior of the Firm under Regulatory Constraint", *American Economic Review*, Vol.52, December, pp.1053-1069.
- Baily, Martin N. [1981], "The Productivity Growth Slowdown and Capital Accumulation", *American Economic Review*, Papers and Proceedings, Vol.71, No.2, May, pp.326-331.
- Baily, Martin N. [1982], "The Productivity Growth Slowdown by Industry", *Brookings Papers on Economic Activity*, No.2, pp.423-454.
- Baily, Martin N. and Alok K. Chakrabarti [1988], *Innovation and the Productivity Crisis*, Washington, D.C.: The Brookings Institution.
- Baily, Martin N. and Robert J. Gordon [1988], "The Productivity Slowdown, Measurement Issues, and the Explosion of Computer Power", *Brookings Papers on Economic Activity*, No.2, pp.347-420.
- Baumol, William J. and Edward Wolff [1979], "On the Theory of Productivity and Unbalanced Growth", manuscript, New York University, November.

- Berndt, Ernst R. [1978], "Aggregate Energy Efficiency, and Productivity Measurement", *Annual Review of Energy*, Vol.3, Palo Alto, California: Annual Reviews Inc., pp.225-274.

- Berndt, Ernst R. [1980], "Energy Price Increases and the Productivity Slowdown in United States Manufacturing", *The Decline in Productivity Growth*, Proceedings of a Conference held in June 1980, Boston: Federal Reserve Board of Boston, pp.60-89.

- Berndt, Ernst R. [1983], "Quality Adjustment, Hedonics and Modern Empirical Demand Analysis", in W. Erwin Diewert and Claude Montmarquette (eds.) *Price Level Measurement*, Proceedings from a Conference Sponsored by Statistics Canada, Ottawa: Minister of Supply and Services Canada, October, pp.817-863.

- Berndt, Ernst R. [1985], "From Technocracy to Net Energy Analysis: Engineers, Economists and Recurring Energy Theories of Value", Ch. 12 in Anthony Scott (ed.), *Progress in Natural Resource Economics*, Oxford: Clarendon Press, pp.337-367.

- Berndt, Ernst R. [1990], *The Practice of Econometrics; Classic and Contemporary*, Boston: Addison-Wesley Publishers.

- Berndt, Ernst R., and Laurits R. Christensen [1973], "The Translog Function and the Substitution of Equipment, Structures, and Labor in U.S. Manufacturing 1929-68", *Journal of Econometrics*, Vol.1, No.1, pp.81-114.

- Berndt, Ernst R., Melvyn Fuss and Leonard Waverman [1980], *Empirical Analysis of Dynamic Adjustment Models of the Demand for Energy in U.S. Manufacturing Industries 1947-74*, Final Research Report, Palo Alto, California, Electric Power Research Institute, November.

- Berndt, Ernst R., and Melvyn Fuss [1986], "Productivity Measurement Using Capital Asset Valuation to Adjust for Variations in Utilization", *Journal of Econometrics*, Vol.33, No.1/2, Oct./Nov., pp.7-30.

- Berndt, Ernst R., and Melvyn Fuss [1989], "Economic Capacity Utilization and Productivity Measurement for Multiproduct Firms with Multiple Quasi-Fixed Inputs", National Bureau of Economic Research Working Paper #2932, April.
- Berndt, Ernst R., and Dieter Hesse [1986], "Measuring and Assessing Capacity Utilization in the Manufacturing Sectors of Nine OECD Countries", *European Economic Review*, Vol.30, pp.961-989.
- Berndt, Ernst R., and Mohammed S. Khaled [1979], "Parametric Productivity Measurement and Choice Among Flexible Functional Forms", *Journal of Political Economy*, Vol.87, No.6, pp.1220-1245.
- Berndt, Ernst R. and Charles Kolstad [1987], "The Nature of Productivity Growth and Technical Change in Manufacturing: An International Comparative Analysis", manuscript, August.
- Berndt, Ernst R., Catherine J. Morrison and David O. Wood [1983], "The Modeling, Interpretation and Measurement of Capacity Utilization", Bureau of the Census Technical Note, May.
- Berndt, Ernst R. and N. Eugene Savin [1975], "Estimation and Hypothesis Testing in Singular Equation Systems with Autoregressive Disturbances" *Econometrica*, Vol.43, No.5/6, September/November, pp.937-957.
- Berndt, Ernst R. and David O. Wood [1975], "Technology, Prices and the Derived Demand for Energy", *Review of Economics and Statistics*, Vol.56, No.3, August, pp.259-268.
- Berndt, Ernst R., and David O. Wood [1979], "Engineering and Econometric Interpretations of Energy-Capital Complementarity", *American Economic Review*, Vol.69, No.3, September, pp.342-354.
- Berndt, Ernst R., and David O. Wood [1982], "The Specification and Measurement of Technical Change in U.S. Manufacturing", in John R. Moroney (ed.), *Advances in the Economics of Energy and Resources*, Vol.4, Greenwich, CT: JAI Press, pp.199-221.

- Berndt, Ernst R., and David O. Wood [1984], "Energy Price Changes and the Induced Revaluation of Durable Capital in U.S. Manufacturing During the OPEC Decade", M.I.T. Energy Laboratory Report No. 84-003, March.

- Berndt, Ernst R., and David O. Wood [1987], "Energy Price Shocks and Productivity Growth: A Survey", in Richard L. Gordon, Henry D. Jacoby and Martin B. Zimmerman (eds.), *Energy: Markets and Regulation*, Cambridge: MIT Press.

- Bernstein, Jeffrey I., and M. Ishaq Nadiri [1988a], "Rates of Return on Physical and R&D Capital and Structure of Production Process: Cross Section and Time Series Evidence", in B. Raj (ed.), *Advances in Econometrics and Modeling*, Kluwer Academic Publishers.

- Bernstein, Jeffrey I., and M. Ishaq Nadiri [1988b], "Investment, Depreciation and Capital Utilization", National Bureau of Economic Research Working Paper No. 2571, April.

- Betancourt, Roger R., and Christopher K. Clague [1981], *Capital Utilization: A Theoretical and Empirical Analysis*, Cambridge University Press, Cambridge.

- Binswanger, H. [1974], "The Measurement of Technical Change Biases with Many Factors of Production", *American Economic Review*, Vol.64, December, pp.964-76.

- Blackorby, C., D. Primont and R.R. Russell [1978], *Duality, Separability and Functional Structure: Theory and Economic Applications*, North Holland: Elsevier Press.

- Blades, Derek [1983], "Service Lives of Fixed Assets", OECD Working Paper No.4, Paris: OECD, March.

- Blinder, Alan S. [1982], "Inventories and Sticky Prices: More on the Microfoundations of Macroeconomics", *American Economic Review*, 72, June, pp.334-48.

- Boskin, Michael J. [1988], "Tax Policy and Economic Growth: Lessons from the 1980's", *The Journal of Economic Perspectives*, Vol.2, No.4, Fall, pp.71-98.

- Bresnahan, Timothy [1989], "Empirical Studies of Industries with Market Power", Chapter 17 in Richard Schmalensee and Robert Willig (eds.), *Handbook of Industrial Organization*, Amsterdam: North Holland, pp.1011-1057.
- Brown, Randall S., and Laurits R. Christensen [1981], "Estimating Elasticities of Substitution in a Model of Partial Static Equilibrium: An Application to U.S. Agriculture 1947 to 1974", in E.R. Berndt and B.C. Fields, eds., *Modeling and Measuring Natural Resource Substitution*, Cambridge, Massachusetts: M.I.T. Press, pp.209-229.
- Cas, A., W.E. Diewert, and L. Ostensoe [1986], "Productivity Growth and Changes in the Terms of Trade in Canada", Discussion Paper No.86-11, Department of Economics, University of British Columbia, Vancouver, Canada, March.
- Cassels, J.M. [1937], "Excess Capacity and Monopolistic Competition", *Quarterly Journal of Economics*, May, Vol.51, pp.426-43.
- Caves, D.W., L.R. Christensen and W.E. Diewert [1982], "The Economic Theory of Index Numbers and the Measurement of Input, Output, and Productivity", *Econometrica*, Vol.50, pp.1393-1414.
- Christensen, Laurits, R., Dianne Cummings and Dale W. Jorgenson [1980], "Economic Growth 1947-73: An International Comparison", in John W. Kendrick and Beatrice N. Vaccara (eds.), *New Developments in Productivity Measurement and Analysis*, Studies in Income and Wealth Vol.44, Chicago: The University of Chicago Press, pp.595-698.
- Christensen, Laurits R., and William H. Greene [1976], "Economies of Scale in U.S. Electric Power Generation", *Journal of Political Economy*, Vol.84, No.4, Part 1, August, pp.655-676.
- Christensen, Laurits R., Dale W. Jorgenson and Lawrence J. Lau [1973], "Transcendental Logarithmic Production Frontiers", *Review of Economics and Statistics*, Vol.55, No.1, February, pp.28-45.

- Christensen, Laurits R., and Dale W. Jorgenson [1969], "The Measurement of U.S. Real Capital Input, 1919-67", *Review of Income and Wealth*, Series 15, No.4, December, pp.293-320.

- Conrad, Klaus, and D.W. Jorgenson [1985], "Sectoral Productivity Gaps Between the United States, Japan and Germany, 1960-79", in H. Giersch (ed.) *Probleme und Perkpektiven der weltwirtschaftliches Entwicklung*, Berlin: Duncker & Humblot Press.

- Conrad, Klaus, and Catherine J. Morrison [1989], "The Impact of Pollution Abatement Investment on Productivity Change: An Empirical Comparison of the U.S., Germany and Canada", *Southern Economic Journal*, Vol.55, No.3, January, pp.684-698.

- Conrad, Klaus, and Ralph Unger [1989], "Productivity Gaps and Capacity Utilization in the Manufacturing Sectors of Five OECD-Countries, 1963-1982", *The Journal of Productivity Analysis*, Vol.1, No.2, June, pp.101-122.

- Crandall, Robert W., [1981], "Pollution Controls and Productivity Growth in Basic Industries", in Thomas G. Cowing and Rodney E. Stevenson (eds.), *Productivity Measurement in Regulated Industries*, Academic Press, pp.347-368.

- David, Paul A., and Theodore van de Klundert [1965], "Biased Efficiency Growth and Capital-Labor Substitution in the U.S., 1899-1960", *American Economic Review*, Vol. 55, No.3, pp.357-395.

- de Leeuw, Frank [1962], "The Concept of Capacity", *Journal of the American Statistical Association*, September, pp.826-840.

- Dean, Edwin, Masako Darrough, and Arthur Neef [1985], "Alternative Measures of Capital Inputs for Computation of Multifactor Productivity Growth in Japanese Manufacturing", presented at the U.S.-Japan Productivity Conference on Research in Income and Wealth, National Bureau of Economic Research, August.

- Denison, Edward F. [1979], *Accounting for Slower Economic Growth*, Washington D.C., The Brookings Institution.

- Denison, Edward F. [1980], "Comment on Kopcke", *The Decline in Productivity Growth*, Boston: Federal Reserve Board of Boston Conference Series No.22, pp.54-59.

- Denison, Edward F. [1985], *Trends in American Economic Growth, 1929-1982*, Washington, D.C., Brookings Institution.

- Denny, Michael [1980], "Comment" on Diewert's "Aggregation Problems in the Measurement of Capital", in Dan-Usher (ed.), *The Measurement of Capital*, Chicago: University of Chicago Press, pp.529-534.

- Diewert, W.E. [1974], "Applications of Duality Theory", in M.D. Intriligator and D.A. Kendrick (eds.) *Frontiers of Quantative Economics*, Vol.II, Amsterdam: North-Holland, pp.106-170.

- Diewert, W.E. [1976], "Exact and Superlattive Index Numbers", *Journal of Econometrics*, Vol.4, pp.115-145.

- Diewert, W.E. [1980], "Aggregation Problems in the Measurement of Capital", in Dan Usher (ed.), *The Measurement of Capital*, Chicago: University of Chicago Press, pp.433-528.

- Diewert, W.E. [1981a] "On Measuring the Loss of Output Due to Nonneutral Business Taxation", in Charles R. Hulten (ed.), *Depreciation, Inflation and the Taxation of Income from Capital*, Washington, D.C.: The Urban Institute, pp.57-80.

- Diewert, W.E. [1981b], "The Theory of Total Factor Productivity Measurement in Regulated Industries", in Thomas G. Cowing and Rodney E. Stevenson (eds.) *Productivity Measurement in Regulated Industries*, New York: Academic Press.

- Diewert, W.E. [1984], "Duality Approaches to Microeconomic Theory", in K.J. Arrow and M.D. Intriligator (eds.), *Handbook of Mathematical Economics*, Vol.2, North-Holland Press.

- Diewert, W.E. [1986], *The Measurement of the Economic Benefits of Infrastructure Services*, Vol.#278 in the series "Lecture Notes in Economics and Mathematical Systems", Berlin: Springer Verlag Press.

- Diewert, W.E. [1989a], "The Measurement of Productivity", Discussion Paper No.89-04, University of British Columbia, January.

- Diewert, W.E. [1989b], "Fisher Ideal Output, Input and Productivity Indexes Revisited", Discussion Paper No. 89-07, University of British Columbia, February.

- Diewert, W. Erwin, and Catherine J. Morrison [1986], "Adjusted Output and Productivity Indexes for Changes in the Terms of Trade", *Economic Journal*, Vol.96, September, pp.659-679.

- Diewert, W. Erwin and Catherine J. Morrison [1987], "The Impact of Imperfect Competition in Net Output Markets on Productivity Fluctuations: An Econometric Investigation of the U.S., Canada and Japan", manuscript, February.

- Diewert, W. Erwin and Catherine J. Morrison [1990], "New Techniques for Multifactor Productivity Measurement", *Journal of Productivity Analysis*, Vol.1, No.4, pp.267-285.

- Diewert, W. Erwin and T.J. Wales [1987], "Flexible Functional Forms and Global Curvature Conditions", *Econometrica*, Vol.5, No.1, January, pp.43-68.

- Domowitz, Ian, R. Glenn Hubbard, and Bruce C. Petersen [1987], "Market Structure, Durable Goods, and Cyclical Fluctuations in Markups", manuscript, Northwestern University, June 1987.

- Domowitz, Ian. R. Glenn Hubbart, and Bruce C. Petersen [1988]. "Market Structure and Cyclical Fluctuations in U.S. Manufacturing", *The Review of Economics and Statistics*, Vol.70, No.1, February.

- Dulberger, Ellen R. [1989], "The Application of a Hedonic Model to a Quality Adjusted Price Index for Computer Processors, in Dale W. Jorgenson and Ralph Landau (eds.), *Technology and Capital Formation*, Cambridge: The MIT Press, pp.37-76.

- Dunne, Timothy, Mark Roberts and Larry Samuelson [1987], "The Impact of Plant Failure on Employment Growth in the U.S. Manufacturing Sector", mimeo, Pennsylvania State University.

- Englander, A.S. [1989], "Tests for Measurement of Service Sector Productivity", presented at the International Seminar on Science, Technology and Economic Growth, OECD, June; Federal Reserve Bank of New York manuscript, April.

- Fischer Stanley [1988], Symposium on the Slowdown in Productivity Growth", *The Journal of Economic Perspectives*, Vol.2, No.4, Fall, pp.3-8.

- Fisher, Franklin M., and John J. McGowan [1983], "On the Misuse of Accounting Rates of Return to Infer Monopoly Profits", *The American Economic Review*, Vol.73, No.1, March.

- Foss, Murray F. [1963], "The Utilization of Capital Equipment: Postwar Compared with Pre-war", *Survey of Current Business*, June, Vol.43, pp.8-16.

- Fromm, G., L.R. Klein, F.C. Ripley, and D. Crawford [1979], "Production Function Estimation of Capacity Utilization", presented at the Econometric Society Meetings, Atlanta, December.

- Fuss, Melvyn and Leonard Waverman [1986], "The Extent and Sources of Cost and Efficiency Differences Between U.S. and Japanese Automobile Producers", N.B.E.R. Working Paper #1849, March.

- Gollop, Frank M. and Dale W. Jorgenson [1980], "U.S. Productivity Growth by Industry, 1947-73", in John W. Kendrick and Beatrice N. Vaccara (eds.), *New Developments in Productivity Measurement and Analysis*, National Bureau of Economic

Research Studies in Income and Wealth, Vol.44, Chicago: University of Chicago Press, pp.117-124.

- Gordon, Robert J. [1989], "The Postwar Evolution of Computer Prices, in Dale W. Jorgenson and Ralph Landau (eds.), *Technology and Capital Formation*, Cambridge: MIT Press, pp.77-126.

- Gray, Wayne B. [1984], "The Impact of OSHA and EPA Regulation of Productivity", National Bureau of Economic Research Working Paper #1405, July.

- Green, H.A.J. [1964], *Aggregation in Economic Analysis: An Introductory Survey*, Princeton, N.J.: Princeton University Press.

- Griffin, James M. and Paul R. Gregory [1976], "An Intercountry Translog Model of Energy Substitution Responses", *American Economic Review*, Vol.66, No.5, December, pp.845-857.

- Griliches, Zvi [1980], "R&D and the Productivity Slowdown", *American Economic Review*, 70, No.2, May, pp.343-48.

- Griliches, Zvi [1986a], "Productivity, R&D and Basic Research at the Firm Level in the 1970s", *American Economic Review*, Vol.76, No.1, pp.141-154.

- Griliches, Zvi [1986b], "Economic Data Issues", in Zvi Griliches and Michael D. Intriligator (eds.), *Handbook of Econometrics*, Vol.3, Amsterdam: North Holland Publishing Co., pp.1465-1514.

- Griliches, Zvi [1988], "Productivity Puzzles and R&D: Another Nonexplanation", *The Journal of Economic Perspectives*, Vol.2, No.4, Fall, pp.9-22.

- Griliches, Zvi [1989], "Patents: Recent Trends and Puzzles", National Bureau of Economics Working Paper #2922, April.

- Griliches, Zvi, and Frank Lichtenberg [1984], "R&D and Productivity Growth at the Industry Level: Is There Still a Relationship?", in Zvi Griliches (ed.), *R&D, Patents and Productivity*, Chicago: University of Chicago Press, pp.465-496.

- Guilkey, David, C.A. Knox Lovell, and Robin C. Sickles [1983], "A Comparison of the Performance of Three Flexible Functional Forms", *International Economic Review*, Vol.24, No.3, October, pp.591-616.

- Hall, R.H., and D.W. Jorgenson [1967], "Tax Policy and Investment Behavior", *The American Economic Review*, Vol.LVII, No.3, June.

- Hall, Robert H. [1981], "Tax Treatment of Depreciation, Capital Gains and Interest in an Inflationary Economy", in Charles R. Hulten (ed.), *Depreciation, Inflation and the Taxation of Income from Capital*, Washington, D.C.: The Urban Institute, pp.149-170.

- Hall, Robert H. [1986], "Market Structure and Macroeconomic Fluctuations", *Brookings Papers on Economic Activity*, No.2, pp.285-338.

- Hall, Robert H. [1988a], "The Relation Between Price and Marginal Cost in U.S. Industry", *Journal of Political Economy*, Vol.96, No.5, October, pp.921-947.

- Hall, Robert E. [1988b], "Increasing Returns; Theory and Measurement with Industry Data", manuscript, presented at the N.B.E.R. Conference on Economic Fluctuations, Cambridge, Massachusetts, October.

- Hall, Robert E. [1989], "Invariance Properties of Solow's Productivity Residual", National Bureau of Economic Research Working Paper #3034, July.

- Hansen, Lars Peter and Kenneth Singleton [1982], "Generalized Instrumental Variables Estimation of Nonlinear Rational Expectations Models", *Econometrica*, September, Vol.50, pp.1269-1286.

- Hansson, Bengt [1988], "Productivity Measurement Under Imperfect Competition", manuscript, Uppsala University Department of Economics, Sweden, June.

- Harper, Michael, J., Ernst R. Berndt and David O. Wood [1989], "Rates of Return and Capital Aggregation Using Alternative Rental Prices", in Dale W. Jorgenson and Ralph Landau (eds.), *Technology and Capital Formation*, Cambridge, MA: MIT Press, pp.331-372.

- Harper, Michael J. and William Gullickson [1989], "Cost Function Models and Accounting for Growth in U.S. Manufacturing, 1949-86", paper presented at the Workshop on Price and Output Measurement, National Bureau of Economic Research, July.

- Hausman, Jerry A. [1975], "An Instrumental Variable Approach to Full Information Estimates for Linear and Certain Nonlinear Econometric Models", *Econometrica*, Vol.43, No.4, July, pp.727-738.

- Hayashi, Fumio [1982], "Tobin's Marginal q and Average q: A Neoclassical Interpretation", *Econometrica*, Vol.50, No.1, January, pp.213-224.

- Hayes, Robert H. and William J. Abernathy [1980], "Managing Our Way to Economic Decline", *Harvard Business Review*, Vol.58, July-August, pp.67-77.

- Hickman [1964], "On a New Method of Capacity Estimation", *Journal of the American Statistical Association*, Vol.59, No.306, June, pp.529-549.

- Hicks, J.R. [1946], *Value and Capital*, 2nd ed., Oxford: Clarendon Press.

- Hirschleifer, Jack [1980], *Price Theory and Applications*, Englewood Cliffs, New Jersey: Prentice Hall.

- Hudson, Edward A. and Dale W. Jorgenson [1974], "U.S. Energy Policy and Economic Growth, 1975-2000", *Bell Journal of Economics and Management Science*, Vol.5, Autumn, p.461.

- Hulten, Charles [1986], "Short Run and Long Run Cost Functions and the Measurement of Efficiency Change", *Journal of Econometrics*, Vol.33, No.1/2, Oct/Nov., pp.31-50.

- Hulten, Charles R. and Frank C. Wykoff [1980], "Economic Depreciation and the Taxation of Structures in U.S. Manufacturing Industries: An Empirical Analysis", Ch.2 in Dan Usher (ed.), *The Measurement of Capital*, Chicago: University of Chicago Press for the National Bureau of Economic Research, pp.83-109.

- Hulten, Charles R. and Frank C. Wykoff [1981a], "The Estimation of Economic Depreciation Using Vintage Asset Prices: An Application of the Box-Cox Power Transformation", *Journal of Econometrics*, Vol.15, No.3, August.

- Hulten, Charles R. and Frank C. Wykoff [1981b], "The Measurement of Economic Depreciation", in Charles R. Hulten (ed.), *Depreciation, Inflation and the Taxation of Income from Capital*, Washington, D.C.: The Urban Institute, pp.81-125.

- Hulten, Charles R., James W. Robertson, and Frank C. Wykoff [1989], "Energy, Obsolescence, and the Productivity Slowdown", in Dale W. Jorgenson and Ralph Landau (eds.), *Technology and Capital Formation*, Cambridge: MIT Press, pp.225-258.

- Jaffe, Adam [1986], "Technological Opportunity and Spillovers of R&D", *American Economic Review*, Vol.76, No.5, pp.984-1000.

- Jorgenson, Dale W. [1984], "The Role of Energy in Productivity Growth", *Energy Journal*, Vol.5, No.3, July, pp.11-26.

- Jorgenson, Dale W. [1988], "Productivity and the Postwar U.S. Economic Growth", *Journal of Economic Perspectives*, Vol.2, No.4, Fall, pp.23-42.

- Jorgenson, Dale W. and Barbara Fraumeni [1981], "Substitution and Technical Change in Production", in Ernst R. Berndt and Barry C. Field (eds.), *Modeling and Measuring Natural Resource Substitution*, Cambridge, MA: M.I.T. Press, pp.17-47.

- Jorgenson, Dale W., Frank Gollop and Barbara Fraumeni [1987], *Productivity and U.S. Economic Growth*, Cambridge, Massachusetts: Harvard University Press.

- Jorgenson, Dale W., and Zvi Griliches [1967], "The Explanation of Productivity Change", *Review of Economic Studies*, Vol.34 (3), No.99, July, pp.249-282.

- Jorgenson, Dale W., Hikaru Sakuramoto, Kanji Yoshioka, and Masahiro Kuroda [1989], "Bilateral Models of Production for Japanese and U.S. Industries", forthcoming in C. Hulten (ed.), *Productivity Growth in Japan and the United States*, Chicago: University of Chicago Press.

- Jorgenson, Dale W., and Thomas M. Stoker [1984], "Aggregate Consumer Expenditures on Energy", in John R. Moroney (ed.), *Advances in the Economics of Energy and Resources*, Vol.5, Greenwich: JAI Press, pp.1-32.

- Kendrick, John W. [1979], "Productivity Trends and the Recent Slowdown", in William Fellner (ed.), *Contemporary Economic Problems*, American Enterprise Institute, Washington, D.C., pp.17-69.

- Kendrick, John W. [1985], "Measurement of Output and Productivity in the Service Sector" in Robert P. Inman (ed.), *Managing the Service Economy: Prospects and Problems*, Cambridge: Cambridge University Press.

- Kendrick, J.W. and E. Grossman [1980], *Trends and Cycles in Productivity in the United States*, Baltimore: Johns Hopkins University Press.

- Klein, L.R. [1960], "Some Theoretical Issues in the Measurement of Capacity", *Econometrica*, April, Vol.28, pp.272-86.

- Koopmans, Tjalling [1947], "Measurement Without Theory", *Review of Economics and Statistics*, Vol.29, pp.161-72.

- Kopcke, Richard W. [1980], "Capital Accumulation and Potential Growth", in *The Decline in U.S. Productivity Growth*, Boston: Federal Reserve Board of Boston, Conference Series No.22, pp.26-53.

- Kremp, Elizabeth and Jacques Mairesse [1990], "A Look at Productivity at the Firm Level in Nine French Service Industries", presented at the Conference on Output Measurement in the Services Sector, National Bureau of Economic Research, Charleston, South Carolina, May 4-5.

- Kulatilaka, Nalin [1985], "Tests on the Validity of Static Equilibrium Models", *Journal of Econometrics*, Vol.28, No.2, May, pp.253-268.

- Lau, Lawrence J. [1978], "Applications of Profit Functions", in M. Fuss and D. McFadden (eds.), *Production Economics: A Dual Approach to Theory and Applications*, Amsterdam: North Holland Publishing Co.

- Lau, Lawrence J. [1982], "The Measurement of Raw Material Inputs", Ch.6 in V. Kerry Smith and John V. Krutilla (eds.), *Explorations in Natural Resource Economics*, Baltimore: Johns Hopkins Press for Resources for the Future, pp.167-200.

- Lau, Lawrence J. [1986], "Functional Forms in Econometric Model Building", in Zvi Griliches and Michael D. Intriligator (eds.), *Handbook of Econometrics*, Vol.3, Amsterdam: North Holland, pp.1515-1566.

- Lichtenberg, Frank R. and Zvi Griliches [1989], "Errors of Measurement in Output Deflators", *Journal of Business and Economic Statistics*, Vol.7, No.1, January.

- Lichtenberg, Frank R. and Donald Siegel [1987], "Productivity and Changes in Ownership of Manufacturing Plants", *Brookings Papers on Economic Activity*, No.3, pp.643-673.

- Lichtenberg, Frank R. and Donald Siegel [1989a], "The Impact of R&D Investment on Productivity – New Evidence Using Linked R&D-LRB Data", National Bureau of Economic Research Working Paper #2901, March.

- Lichtenberg, Frank R. and Donald Siegel [1989b], "The Effects of Leveraged Buyouts on Productivity and Related Aspects of

Firm Behavior", U.S. Bureau of the Census Center for Economic Studies, Discussion Paper #CES-89, January.

- McElroy, Marjorie B. [1987], "Additive General Error Models for Production, Cost, and Derived Demand or Share Equations", *Journal of Political Economy*, Vol.95, No.4, August 1987, pp.737-757.

- McFadden, D. [1978], "Costs, Revenue and Profit Functions", in M. Fuss and D. McFadden (eds.), *Production Economics: A Dual Approach to Theory and Applications*, Vol.1, Amsterdam.

- McGuckin, Robert H., and Stephen H. Andrews [1988], "The Performance of Lines of Business Purchased in Conglomerate Acquisitions", presented at the American Economic Association meetings, Chicago, Dec. 25-30.

- Moore, Geoffrey H. [1980], *Business Cycles, Inflation, and Forecosting*, National Bureau of Economic Research, Studies in Business Cycles No.24, Cambridge, Massachusetts: Ballinger Publishing Co.

- Moore, Geoffrey H. and John P. Cullity [1984], "Trends and Cycles in Productivity, Unit Costs and Prices: An International Perspective", in John W. Kendrick (ed.), *International Comparisons of Productivity and Causes of the Slowdown*, Cambridge: Ballinger Publishing Company and the American Enterprise Institute, pp.157-190.

- Mork, Knut A. [1978], "The Aggregate Demand for Primary Energy in the Short and Long Run for the U.S., 1949-75", M.I.T. Energy Laboratory Report # MIT-EL 7809-007WP, May.

- Morrison, Catherine J. [1982], "Three Essays on the Dynamic Analysis of Demand for Factors of Production", Ph.D. Dissertation, University of British Columbia, Department of Economics, Vancouver, British Columbia, December.

- Morrison, Catherine J. [1985a], "Primal and Dual Capacity Utilization: An Application to Productivity Measurement in the

U.S. Automobile Industry", *Journal of Business and Economic Statistics*, Vol.3, No.4, October, pp.312-324.

- Morrison, Catherine J. [1985b], "On the Economic Interpretation and Measurement of Optimal Capacity Utilization with Anticipatory Expectations", *Review of Economic Studies*, Vol.52, pp.295-310.

- Morrison, Catherine J. [1986a], "Productivity Measurement with Nonstatic Expectations and Varying Capacity Utilization: An Integrated Approach", *Journal of Econometrics*, Vol.33, No.1/2, Oct./Nov., pp.51-74.

- Morrison, Catherine J. [1986b], "A Structural Model of Dynamic Factor Demands with Nonstatic Expectations: An Empirical Assessment of Alternative Expectations Specifications", *International Economic Review*, Vol.27, No.2, June, pp.365-386.

- Morrison, Catherine J. [1987a], "Capacity Utilization and the Impacts of Pollution Abatement Capital Regulation and Energy Prices: A Comparison of the U.S. and Canadian Manufacturing Industries", in John R. Moroney (ed.), *Advances in Natural Resource Economics*, Vol.6, Greenwich, Connecticut: JAI Press.

- Morrison, Catherine J. [1987b], "Capacity Utilization Under Mobilization Condition", presented at the ICAF/FEMA conference on The Application of Economic Models for Mobilization Planning, January 17.

- Morrison, Catherine J. [1988a], "Quasi-Fixed Inputs in U.S. and Japanese Manufacturing: A Generalized Leontief Restricted Cost Function Approach", *Review of Economics and Statistics*, Vol.70, No.2, May, pp.275-287.

- Morrison, Catherine J. [1988b], "Subequilibrium in the North American Steel Industries: A Study of Short Run Biases from Regulation and Utilization Fluctuations", *Economic Journal*, Vol.98, No.391, June, pp.390-411.

- Morrison, Catherine J. [1988c], "Markups in U.S. and Japanese Manufacturing: A Short Run Econometric Analysis", National Bureau of Economic Research Working Paper #2799, December.

- Morrison, Catherine J. [1988d], "Capacity Utilization and Productivity Measurement: An Application to the U.S. Automobile Industry", in A. Doğramacı (ed.) *Studies in Productivity Analysis*, Boston: Kluwer Nijhoff Press, pp.163-194.

- Morrison, Catherine J. [1989a], "Markup Behavior in Durable and Nondurable Manufacturing: An Applied Production Theory Approach", National Bureau of Economic Research Working Paper #2941, April.

- Morrison, Catherine J. [1989b], "Unraveling the Productivity Growth Slowdown in the U.S., Canada and Japan: The Effects of Subequilibrium, Scale Economies and Markups", National Bureau of Economic Research Working Paper #2993, June.

- Morrison, Catherine J. [1989c], "The Impacts of Fixed Inputs on Firm Behavior and Productivity: An Empirical Comparison of the U.S. and Japanese Manufacturing Industries", forthcoming in C. Hulten (ed.), *Productivity Growth in Japan and the United States*, Chicago: U. of Chicago Press.

- Morrison, Catherine J. [1989d], "Inventory Behavior and the Profit-Maximizing Firm: The Relationships Between Inventory Holding, Markups and Capacity Utilization", manuscript, June.

- Morrison, Catherine J. [1989e], "Selling Costs for Manufacturing Firms: Are They Important?", outline, June.

- Morrison, Catherine J. and Ernst R. Berndt [1981], "Capacity Utilization: Underlying Economic Theory and an Alternative Approach", *American Economic Review*, Vol.7, No.2, May 1981, pp.48-52.

- Morrison, Catherine J. and W. Erwin Diewert [1989], "Productivity Growth and Changes in the Terms of Trade in Japan and the U.S.", forthcoming in C. Hulten (ed.), *Productivity Growth in Japan and the United States*, Chicago: University of Chicago Press.

- Morrison, Catherine J., and Randy Nelson [1989], "The Impacts of Obsolescence, Technical Change, and Vintage on Capacity Utilization and Productivity Growth: 1952-83", manuscript, September.

- Nadiri, M. Ishaq, and George C. Bitros [1980], "Research and Development Expenditures and Labor Productivity at the Firm Level: A Dynamic Model", in John W. Kendrick and Beatrice N. Vaccara (eds.), *New Developments in Productivity Measurement and Analysis*, Studies in Income and Wealth Vol.44, Chicago: The University of Chicago Press, pp.387-418.

- Nadiri, M. Ishaq, and Ingmar R. Prucha [1989], "Dynamic Factor Demand Models, Productivity Measurement, and Rates of Return: Theory and an Empirical Application to the U.S. Bell System", National Bureau of Economic Research Working Paper No.3041, July.

- Nelson, Charles R. [1973], *Applied Time Series Analysis*, Oakland, California: Holden-Day, Inc.

- Nerlove, Marc [1963], "Returns to Scale in Electricity Supply", Chapter 7 in Carl F. Christ (ed.), *Measurement in Economics: Studies in Honor of Yehuda Grunfeld*, Stanford, CA: Stanford University Press, pp.167-198.

- Nerlove, Marc [1972], "Lags in Economic Behavior", *Econometrica*, Vol.40, No.2, March, pp.221-251.

- Norsworthy, J. Randolph [1984], "Growth Accounting and Productivity Measurement", *Review of Income and Wealth*, Vol.30, No.3, September.

- Norsworthy, J. Randolph, Michael J. Harper, and Kent Kunze [1979], "The Slowdown in Productivity Growth: Analysis of Some Contributing Factors", *Brookings Papers on Economic Activity*, 2:1979, pp.387-421.

- Norsworthy, J. Randolph, and David H. Malmquist [1983], "Input Measurement and Productivity Growth in Japanese and U.S. Manufacturing", *American Economic Review*, Vol.73, No.5, December, pp.947-967.

- Ohta, M. [1975], "A Note on the Duality Between Production and Cost Functions: Rate of Returns to Scale and Rate of Technical Progress", *Economic Studies Quarterly*, 25, pp.63-65.

- Okun, Arthur M. [1962], "Potential GNP: Its Measurement and Significance", *Proceedings of the Business and Economics Section of the American Statistical Association*, Washington, D.C.: American Statistical Association, pp.98-104.

- Okun, Arthur M. [19794], "Unemployment and Output in 1974", *Brookings Papers on Economic Activity*, Number 2, pp.495-504.

- Olson, Mancur [1988], "The Productivity Slowdown, the Oil Shocks, and the Real Cycle", *Journal of Economic Perspectives*, Vol.2, No.4, Fall, pp.43-70.

- Parks, Richard W. [1971], "Price Responsiveness of Factor Utilization in Swedish Manufacturing, 1870-1950", *Review of Economics and Statistics*, Vol.53, No.2, May, pp.129-139.

- Perloff, Jeffrey M. and Michael L. Wachter [1979], "A Production Function Nonaccelerating Inflation Approach to Potential Output: Is Measured Potential Output Too High?", in Karl Brunner and Allan H. Meltzer (eds.), *Three Aspects of Policy and Policymaking: Knowledge, Data and Institutions*, Supplementary Series to the *Journal of Monetary Economics*, Vol.10, pp.113-164.

- Piekarz, Rolf, Eleanor Thomas and Donna Jennings [1984], "International Comparisons of Research and Development Outlays and Indicators of Technological Progress", in John W. Kendrick (ed.), *International Comparisons of Productivity and Causes of the Slowdown*, Cambridge: Ballinger Publishing Company and the American Enterprise Institute, pp.235-274.

- Pindyck, Robert S., [1979], "Interfuel Substitution and the Industrial Demand for Energy: An International Comparison", *Review of Economics and Statistics*, Vol.61, No.2, May, pp.169-179.

- Pindyck, Robert S., and Julio J. Rotemberg [1983], "Dynamic Factor Demands, Energy Use and the Effects of Energy Price Shocks", *American Economic Review*, Vol.73, No.5, December.

- Pindyck, Robert S., and Daniel L. Rubinfeld [1981], *Econometric Models and Economic Forecosts*, New York: McGraw-Hill Book Company, Second Edition.

- Pieper, Paul [1989], "Construction Price Statistics Revisited", in Dale W. Jorgenson and Ralph Landau (eds.), *Technology and Capital Formation*, Cambridge: MIT Press, pp.293-330.

- Ram, R. [1986], "Government Size and Economic Growth: A New Framework and Some Evidence from Cross-Section and Time-Series Data", *American Economic Review*, Vol.76, pp.191-203.

- Rasche, Robert H., and John A. Tatom [1977], "Energy Resources and Potential GNP", Federal Reserve Bank of St. Louis *Review*, Vol.59, No.6, June, pp.10-24.

- Rees, Albert [1980], "Improving Productivity Measurement", *American Economic Review*, Vol.70, No.2, May, pp.340-342.

- Romer, Paul M. [1986], "Increasing Returns and Long-Run Growth", *Journal of Political Economy*, 94, October, pp.1002-1037.

- Ruttan, V. [1954], "Technological Progress in the Meatpacking Industry, 1919-47", United States Department of Agriculture Marketing Research Report No.59, Washington, D.C., January.

- Ruttan, V. [1956], "The Contribution of Technological Progress to Farm Output: 1950-75", *Review of Economics and Statistics*, Vol.38, February, pp.61-69.

- Sato, R. [1970], "The Estimation of Biased Technical Progress and the Production Function", *International Economic Review*, Vol.II, June, pp.179-208.

- Schankerman, Mark and M. Ishaq Nadiri [1986], "A Test of Static Equilibrium Models and Rates of Return to Quasi-Fixed Factors, with an Application to the Bell system", *Journal of Econometrics*, Vol.33, No.1/2, October/November, pp.97-118.

- Scherer, F.M. [1984], "Using Linked Patent and R&D Data to Measure Interindustry Technology Flows", in Zvi Griliches (ed.), *R&D, Patents, and Productivity, Chicago: University of Chicago Press*, pp.417-461.

- Schnader, Marjorie H. [1984], "Capacity Utilization", *The Handbook of Economic and Financial Measures*, Homewood, Illinois: Dow Jones-Irwin.

- Shapiro, Matthew D. [1987], "Measuring Market Power in U.S. Industry", National Bureau of Economic Research Working Paper #2212, April.

- Shiskin, Julius [1977], "A New Role for Economic Indicators", *Monthly Labor Review*, Bureau of Labor Statistics, November, pp.3-18.

- Solow, Robert M. [1958], "Technical Change and the Aggregate Production Function", *Review of Economics and Statistics*, Vol.39, No.5, August, pp.312-320.

- Stoker, Thomas M. [1986], "Simple Tests of Distributional Effects on Macroeconomic Equations", *Journal of Political Economy*, Vol.94, No.4, August, pp.763-795.

- Tinbergen, Jan [1942], "Zur theorie der Iangfristigen wirtschaftsentwicklung" *Weltwirthschaftliches Archiv*, Band 55:1, pp.511-49. English translation, "On the Theory of Trend Movements", in Jan Tinbergen Selected Papers, L.H. Klassen, L.M. Koyck, H.J. Witteveen (eds.), Amsterdam: North Holland, 1959.

- Tolley, George S. and William B. Shear [1984], "International Comparison of Tax Rates and Their Effects on National Income", in John W. Kendrick (ed.), *International Comparisons of Productivity and Causes of the Slowdown*, Cambridge: Ballinger Publishing Company and the American Enterprise Institute, pp.197-226.

- Triplett, Jack [1989], "Price and Technological Change in a Capital Good: A Survey of Research on Computers", in Dale W. Jorgenson and Ralph Landau (eds.), *Technology and Capital Formation*, Cambridge: The MIT Press, pp.127-214.

- U.S. Department of Labor, Bureau of Labor Statistics [1983], *Trends in Multifactor Productivity, 1948-81*, Bulletin #2178, September.

- Usher, Dan [1975], Review of *Accounting for United States Economic Growth, 1939-1969* by Edward Denison, *Canadian Journal of Economics*, August 1975, pp.476-480.

- Winston, Gordon C. [1977], "Capacity: An Integrated Micro and Macro Analysis", *American Economic Review*, February, pp.418-422.

- Zellner, A., J. Kmenta and J. Dreze [1966], "Specification and Estimation of Cobb-Douglas Production Function Models", *Econometrica*, Vol.34, October, pp.784-795.

Author Index

Subject Index

GPSR Compliance

The European Union's (EU) General Product Safety Regulation (GPSR) is a set of rules that requires consumer products to be safe and our obligations to ensure this.

If you have any concerns about our products, you can contact us on ProductSafety@springernature.com

In case Publisher is established outside the EU, the EU authorized representative is:

Springer Nature Customer Service Center GmbH
Europaplatz 3
69115 Heidelberg, Germany

Batch number: 10844669

Printed by Printforce, the Netherlands